GOOD FAMILIES OF BARCELONA

GARY WRAY McDONOGH

GOOD FAMILIES OF BARCELONA

*A Social History of Power
in the Industrial Era*

PRINCETON UNIVERSITY PRESS

LIBRARY OF CONGRESS CATALOGING IN PUBLICATION DATA WILL BE
FOUND ON THE LAST PRINTED PAGE OF THIS BOOK

ISBN 0-691-09426-8

PUBLICATION OF THIS BOOK HAS BEEN AIDED BY GRANTS FROM THE
HAROLD W. MCGRAW, JR. FUND OF PRINCETON UNIVERSITY PRESS
AND THE PROGRAM FOR CULTURAL COOPERATION BETWEEN SPAIN'S
MINISTRY OF CULTURE AND NORTH AMERICAN UNIVERSITIES

THIS BOOK HAS BEEN COMPOSED IN LINOTRON SABON

CLOTHBOUND EDITIONS OF PRINCETON UNIVERSITY PRESS BOOKS
ARE PRINTED ON ACID-FREE PAPER, AND BINDING MATERIALS
ARE CHOSEN FOR STRENGTH AND DURABILITY. PAPERBACKS,
ALTHOUGH SATISFACTORY FOR PERSONAL COLLECTIONS,
ARE NOT USUALLY SUITABLE FOR LIBRARY REBINDING

PRINTED IN THE UNITED STATES OF AMERICA
BY PRINCETON UNIVERSITY PRESS
PRINCETON, NEW JERSEY

CONTENTS

LIST OF ILLUSTRATIONS

LIST OF TABLES

PREFACE

In 1893 a bomb tossed from the upper balcony of Barcelona's *Gran Teatre del Liceu* shattered the calm and sheltered world that the urban elite had created in their opera house. The bombing represented a response of the urban underclasses to the organizational and ideological claims of the elite and was met, in turn, with violent repression. This book ends with the complex tragedy of those events. Yet the classic stone facade of the Liceu with its great arched porticos still dominates a central section of the *Rambles*, downtown Barcelona's main promenade, which I traversed almost daily during my fieldwork. Inside, the triumphal marble staircase and plush red antechambers echo with the historical memories of the rise and fall of a power-holding group. The Liceu, however, not only epitomizes the nature of an elite and its relationship to urban society but also my relationship as an ethnographer to that urban power group. It is appropriate, then, to introduce this study via that same opera house and its changing meanings to me in the decade since I began my research in Barcelona.

In my preliminary summer field research in 1976 the Liceu was closed to me, both literally and figuratively. References to the theater appeared in novels, news reports, interviews, and wills. Yet, although I passed it frequently, there were no summer performances through which to observe the theater and its denizens; the Liceu remained dark.

When I returned for extended fieldwork in 1977, I eagerly awaited the opening of the opera season as a social historical event, even more than an aesthetic one. I spent the first night in the street outside to evaluate crowd reactions. The year before there had been reports of fur coats sprayed with paint and jeering at the opera goers by crowds standing on the street. Nonetheless, both elite display and popular response were modest.

Within a few weeks I went on my own to see *Fidelio* from the *galliner*, or fifth balcony. Although the ticket was inexpensive, the production was barely visible from my seat. The divisions of class that shaped the Liceu became painfully evident in my craning to catch the performance.

As the season progressed families invited me into another experience of the opera house in the aristocratic loges of the first balcony. The first performance that I saw from this vantage was Montserrat Caballé singing *L'Africaine* in her home theater. The magnificence of that performance highlighted the dualities of my role as participant observer—half-attentive to the stage and half-attentive to the dramas around me. More typical were later performances where, despite my interest in the music,

I might pass entire acts discussing family history in the Círculo del Liceo, the club attached to the opera.

The operas and ballets of subsequent years, as well as my discussion
of the Liceu with other Barcelonins, have developed this dialectic of analyst and participant. The theater became a place to meet those with
whom I worked, just as they have met each other in promenades or visits to boxes. My observations of behavior, clothes, and conversations
were tested by my own appearance and actions as a guest. And I con-
sciously studied the Liceu as a cultural landmark, a complex metaphor
for the class that built it.

Meanwhile, my sense of the wider urban meaning of the Liceu was
honed by the reactions of friends in other groups to my nights at the
opera. For some, such as those who lived and worked nearby in the impoverished port neighborhoods, the opera was a different world, of little interest in comparison with amusements like movies and television.
Academics and middle-class professionals tended to recall uncomfortable past visits and joke about the hazards of my work. Older people
reminisced about "the Liceu as it once was." Musicians, meanwhile,
criticized it for rushed rehearsals and slipshod performances. A critique
of the Good Families and their declining power was often part of these
conversations.

These reactions from other Barcelonins have reflected on changes in
the Liceu itself. On my final visit in January 1985 the opera had begun
to receive support from the revitalized Generalitat de Catalunya, with
concomitant changes. The program, for example, was printed in Catalan as well as Castilian. Members of the local and national political
structure mingled with the older aristocracy and bourgeoisie. The Liceu
is being redefined once again in terms of a vision of Catalonia and
power over Catalonia—and thus changing my appreciation of it anew.

Over a decade the Liceu has become much richer as both an experience and a metaphor for Barcelona. While its history involves a critical
analysis of the opera house as a social construction of power, it also
evokes the color and drama of elite life. The Liceu also summarizes, on
reflection, the methodological and analytic development underlying
the study that follows. The critique of the hierarchy of privilege that
made *Fidelio* difficult to see for those in the uppermost floors must be
linked to the sonorities of Caballé and to the hospitality of the individuals who graciously invited me to share in that experience as part of my
work. This book is critical of structures of social inequality and of the
processes of domination that have shaped Barcelona society in the past
150 years. It is also critical, at times, of actors within this pageant. Yet
it must be remembered that others, even from wealthy and powerful
families, have been entrapped and hurt by the demands of the coalescence and reproduction of power; such a realization must be linked to

critique and change. Like the Liceu, the lives of the people of Barcelona have many meanings and must ultimately be understood within the most general goals of anthropology as a field—an understanding of how human beings are constituted by and reconstitute their lives in society and of a human quest for comprehension, creation, freedom, and control.

Funding for this research has been provided by the Council for European Studies (1976), the Johns Hopkins University Program in Atlantic History and Culture (1976-1980), the Social Sciences Research Council (1977-1980), and the Generalitat de Catalunya, in conjunction with the Institut Català de Geografia, which in 1985 invited me for a series of lectures and discussion of the materials in this book.

In a project that has taken nearly a decade of my life it is difficult to acknowledge all who have helped through the years of planning, research, writing, and rewriting. The project emerged and was shaped in discussion with the faculty and students of the departments of anthropology and history at the Johns Hopkins University. Richard Price, Katherine Verdery, Richard Kagan, Beatriz Lavandera, Sir Edmund Leach, Jean Copans, Fredrik Barth, and Unni Wikan all provided important comments through the years, as have many fellow students.

Others in American academic circles have also been crucial. Edward Hansen suggested the project a decade ago and has provided some important comments thereafter. Kit Woolard, Susan DiGiacomo, Oriol Pi-Sunyer, and Flora Klein have all given both counsel and friendship. Above all, Jim Amelang has encouraged me, debated me, and shared the best and worst of the project with me. He has challenged me in this study as in others to go ever further in research, analysis, teaching, and human commitment. My debt to him is great and, fortunately, continues to grow.

Many people have worked with me in Barcelona as informants, academic colleagues, and friends. This encompasses members of the departments of anthropology, geography, sociology, and contemporary history at the Universitat de Barcelona and the Universitat Autònoma. In particular, I must acknowledge Josefina Roma, Carles Carreras Verdaguer, Mercedes Marín de Carreras, Ignasi Terradas, and Josep M. Fradera. Special thanks also go to Josep M. Sans and the staff of the Arxiu Notarial de Barcelona, to Joan Martorell, to Florentino and Cristina F. de Retana, to all the Roca family, and to the family García Alemán. All photographs, except for those of the cemetery in Chapter VIII, are from the collection of the Arxiu/Institut Municipal d'Història de Barcelona. Figures 27 and 30 were printed by Barbara Andrews. Others who gave generously of their time and history as informants and friends must remain anonymous; I hope that I have shown my gratitude through the years. Without their help this project could never have been done.

In the years of revision of the dissertation I have learned much more about the meaning of anthropology and history from working with students and faculty at New College. Tony Andrews, my colleague and *compadre*, has commented insightfully on all my work, while he, Barbara McClatchie Andrews, and Taco have provided a special home for me as well. In the final stages, Barbara Andrews has also managed illustrations for this text—photographic and genealogical—with both professional talent and loving care. Others who have read and commented on sections include Chuck Rutheiser, Mike Russell, Chris DeBodisco, Jean Schutt, and Melinda Anthes. And a very special debt of gratitude goes to Don Moore, Dale Nelson, Chris Pallm, and David Rogers, who have devoted considerable time to reading, commenting, and generally helping on the final manuscript, as well as immeasurably enriching my life as teacher and friend. And Mrs. Mildred Chisolm as well as the staff of the Georgia Historical Society, along with other friends in Savannah, have been warmly supportive as I worked on this text in the midst of another field project.

In this revision, too, my editors are also important. Four years ago Gail Ullman took an interest in a sprawling dissertation and has cajoled and supported me since. Cathy Thatcher has also been an exacting and valuable copyeditor, whose care has polished and improved the text. Thanks.

Finally, I wish to thank older friends and family who have done everything from proofreading to editing to supporting me mentally and spiritually over the past years. Karen O'Connor has always had time in her busy schedule to read, comment, scold, and generally push me to higher goals, she has been a friend, colleague, inspiration, and consoler. My brother Allen and my late aunt, Thelma Parsons, were also always there: it pains me that I cannot put a copy of the book in my aunt's hands to celebrate the love she gave me so generously after my parents' deaths. Ed, Gail, Lou, and Susan Henson, and the original Hensons of Star Hill Farm; Bob Cunningham, Bill Arnold, Tom Sydlowski, Didi Coyle (and Nicholas Brady Szydlowski), Tom O'Connor, and many others have been there, and cared.

It seems so little to dedicate this book to you all. But as a great Catalan author observed seven centuries ago:

Digues, foll: què són treballs, plants, suspirs, tribulacions, perills, en amich?—Respòs:—Plaer d'amat—. —Per què?—Per ço que.n sia més amat, e l'amich més guaardonat.

—Ramón Llull, *Llibre d'Amich e Amat*

A NOTE ON NAMES AND TRANSCRIPTIONS

The complexities of Catalan/Castilian bilingualism, as discussed in Chapter VI, preclude adoption of a single language for terminology, place names, personal names, etc. In order to avoid confusion I have used the following guidelines:

1. Where there exists established English form, I have used it—e.g., Catalonia rather than Catalunya or Cataluña. If not, I have used the Catalan form.

2. In terms referring to Catalan history or culture I have used the Catalan term with English translation, as in *hereu* (heir). If the Castilian term is widespread, both are given, with the Catalan term as the referent, e.g., *Caixa dels Marquesos* and *Caja de los Marqueses* (Treasury of the Marquesses—an old nickname for the Barcelona Savings and Loan). Some terms only appeared in Castilian in conversation, such as *señorito*, and are used that way. In all cases usage is consistent through the text.

3. Names pose a special problem. Surnames vary in pronunciation and even spelling: Rusiñol and Russinyol. I have always taken the most common form, especially that used by the family. In first names I have been guided by the language appropriate to the period, family, and situation, as well as the source of data used. In each case, though, an individual is always designated by the same name. The only variation is that occasioned by the use of patronym and matronym together as surnames. In general, I have been guided here by an individual's presentation in his or her own works or speech, as well as the atmosphere of the period and lineage.

All translations, unless otherwise noted, are my own.

GOOD FAMILIES OF BARCELONA

CHAPTER I

INTRODUCTION

Anthropology long has been concerned with social organization and change in preliterate societies as well as with disenfranchised groups in Western society. Today, anthropologists are beginning to realize the need to address the same questions to those who hold power in contemporary nation-states. The role of elites and the nature of their power over other groups and social processes is a central component of a holistic study of human society and culture. The absence of ethnographic investigation is all the more striking because of the potential contribution that anthropological theory and methods may make to research that has been dominated by historians, sociologists, and political scientists. The personal contact of fieldwork incorporates strategy, flexibility, and personality into abstract models of power. And from these studies of elites anthropologists can return to more "traditional" problems with a clearer sense of the framework within which peasants, workers, and tribesmen live.

An anthropological examination of elites, in fact, reveals processes of group formation strongly reminiscent of those that we have explored in so-called "traditional" societies. Above all, the role of the *family* as an economic, social, and cultural vehicle for elite solidarity is as widespread and pervasive in industrialized societies as in any classic case in anthropological literature—Trobriands, Nuer, or Zuñi. Indeed, social critics, novelists, and scions of ruling classes have made these observations before; ethnography is only slowly pursuing such insights and bringing field experience to reflect on models of power in complex human societies.

This study explores the meanings of family within one modern elite that has coalesced in Barcelona and the surrounding polity, Catalonia, since the Industrial Revolution of the nineteenth century. Through an examination of the family in multiple contexts, within the dynamics of elite formation, reproduction, and decay over time, this work incorporates power groups into the major theoretical and methodological concerns of modern anthropology.

The elite considered here, the Good Families of Barcelona, forms a small and relatively closed community of two thousand to three thousand men, women, and children. They constitute between one hundred and two hundred patrilineages in a city of approximately two million inhabitants amid over six million people in Catalonia. Despite the limited number of families involved, this tightly integrated social group has controlled economic power in Catalonia for much of the past 150 years. It also made a brief bid to dominate Catalonia as an autonomous political entity. In establishing their position the Good Families have synthesized a new capitalist bourgeoisie with a historic aristocracy. They thus include both old and new holders of power. Exchange and alliance have ennobled new wealth while reenriching and revalidating older nobility.

Family and kinship have played primary roles in the unity of this group. The household provided the framework for the consolidation of economic growth in the new leaders of the bourgeoisie. Social interconnection underlies a solidarity of power independent of formal political institutions. Yet, while family pervades the social history of power in Barcelona, it must also be examined as a continuous product—social and cultural—of the evolution of Catalan industrial society. That is, it was not through a particularly fortuitous model of the family that this group triumphed but rather through the ability of power groups to adapt the family to new settings and problems.

Furthermore, this study relates different levels of power and of conflict. The elite families of Barcelona have been influenced by competition and struggle within Catalonia, by the problem of definition of Catalan hegemony within the Spanish state, and by the status of Catalonia as a productive region within a world economy. These diverse levels have impinged as much upon the family as a unit of procreation and socialization as on its economic and political aspects.

The remainder of this chapter is devoted to placing the issues in the study of the elite of industrial Barcelona into a broader context. The following section introduces some basic concepts of elite research and situates them with regard to work in Barcelona and comparative study. A subsequent section presents the Good Families as elite, and the final section discusses the primary resources and methods that underlie this work.

THE STUDY OF ELITES IN ANTHROPOLOGY

Although most social sciences have scrutinized elites, there is little agreement on theory or terminology to refer to ruling classes. Anthony Giddens has commented:

> No field of sociology has been more subject to vagaries of usage and to nebulous and shifting conceptualizations. Terms are legion: "ruling class," "upper class," "governing class," "political class,"

"elite," "power elite," and "leadership group" vie with each other for supremacy in the literature. Sometimes they are applied as synonyms, sometimes they are deliberately opposed to each other. In some cases terminological usage is merely careless; in other cases terminological variations conceal ambiguities in conceptual formation. (1974:2)

In addition, the field is permeated by ideological perspectives that directly and indirectly add a partisan air to many of these designations. Given these problems it is foolhardy to attempt to redefine elite theory or to impose order upon terminologies and models that have been disputed for so long (Bottomore 1964; Domhoff 1967; Prewitt and Stone 1973:3-28; Giddens 1974:1-2; Marcus 1983; Hansen and Parrish 1983). Instead, I will follow a consistent use of the term that draws upon this debate while adapting it to the realities observed and reconstructed in the field. This perspective refers to a complex of defining characteristics rather than to any single basis for stratification or class conflict. Through this analysis both data and interpretation of the Barcelona case may, in turn, refine the concept of elite for future fieldwork as well as theory.

Throughout this work, the term "elite" refers to a *generalized power-holding group* within a society. "Power" is used in the broad sense of the ability to execute and impose choices on others. By referring to an industrial-financial elite, I have imputed some primacy to economic bases of power. Yet the Good Families are not simply a group of wealthy or successful businessmen. They also include those who held power in land, in experience of political systems, or in prestige—the Catalan aristocracy. No single arena or exercise of power suffices for membership in the group or cohesion of the elite as a whole. Power will be treated as an attribute with a range of family resemblances in its actual realizations and with overlap in its execution, rather than being precategorized into distinct fields. Thus, power may be widespread, encompassing most sectors and subjects, or it may be of varying degrees of specificity. For example, a specific realm of power might be wide, incorporating political administration, or more narrow, including control over education or conversational interaction.

For an elite within Western urban society such a separation of realms is often artificial. Over time, economic and political domination become linked to prestige, cultural expertise, and ideological dominance through the group and individuals who are powerholders. Within this study "elite" refers to such a synthetic group—to a community of limited membership, whose units cohere through kinship, alliance, and ethos as well as their shared domination over key aspects of society.

Analysis of an elite, therefore, must employ multiple criteria. As the French sociologist Pierre Bourdieu writes:

> A class or fraction of a class is defined not only by its position in the structure of production ... but also through indices like profession, income, or even level of education, also by a certain sex-ratio, by a determined distribution in geographic space ... and by a complete ensemble of *auxiliary characteristics*, which, as tacit demands, can function as real principles of selection or exclusion without ever being formally posed. (1979:113)

This does not ignore the fact that there exist different levels of decision making and control within complex societies. The leading citizens of a provincial town or the rulers of a peripheral society only exercise power within a certain domain. Local ruling classes, whatever their sphere of domination, lack the range of power of a central or multinational elite. Lower levels, in fact, will be dominated by these more powerful elites—a dependency reflected in social organization and reproduction. Here again, the concept of family resemblance among the realizations of power permits a more careful phrasing of the study of elites. And in no case is it likely that an elite will have absolute power in any realm: the response of other groups to hegemonic claims is both a commentary and a limit on powerholders like the Good Families, as their history will frequently illustrate.

Recruitment to, membership in, and separation from the group will be determined by a common interest in maintaining undiluted domination of resources or decision making through time. Thus, my usage of elite also refers to a socially and biologically reproductive power group, which may lose or gain member units through time. A synchronic analysis is misleading in that it fails to consider the accumulation of various kinds of capital (in the sense that Pierre Bourdieu uses the term to represent social and cultural as well as economic power) and the meshing of these processes in the formation of a community. Elites exist in and through history and must be understood within a dynamic model.

Elite here is clearly not being used in the confused generic sense of any hierarchy that has often bedeviled comparative theory in anthropology. Elite has been applied cross-culturally to groups that are not strictly comparable in domain or social milieu. Such a classification does not tell us anything about the political and economic processes involved, much less of power groups in general. Nor does it clarify generalizations concerning advanced capitalist societies and their organization of power.

My approach also diverges from the positional approaches to power common in much theoretical literature in sociology and political science. These models are premised on the assumption that power rests in institutions and thus in those who occupy slots within them. Although it is indisputable that some power rests in institutions, and thus in their executives, this view exaggerates structure and ignores other significant facets of power. Analysis can easily become a study of managers, bureaucrats, and administrators; it "dilutes" the concept of a power-holding group—and at times denies its possibility—by emphasizing only the transient holders of positions. Such groups are clearly marked as ambivalent economically and socially in Barcelona. They are not an integrated part of the reproducing elite who ruled the city, even if closely bound to it.

Positional definitions also suggest an essentially static description of elites. By excluding the past and future of the people involved, the circulation of elites is reduced to fluctuations in personnel or in institutional format, while missing what appear to be primary mechanisms of succession and continuity in Barcelona. Economic domination, for example, demands accumulation and management over decades in order to consolidate a position. Social power—the control of prestige symbols, networks, and behavior—is even more diachronic. Again, as Bourdieu has suggested, social power is based on the control of time, the extended memory and reproduction that form a major theme in this study (1979:78).

A diachronic model also entails methodological revisions in elite studies. Thus, this volume is not a description of a reified elite but an analysis of how various power-holding lineages come together into a recognized community. By emphasizing historical depth, I highlight processes of domination more than fixed groups or structures. This approach facilitates a wide range of comparative questions concerning both the powerful and the marginalized (see Hansen and Parrish 1983:273-275).

This use of elite should also be distinguished from those who control the apparatus of the state (Hansen and Parrish 1983:265). It may also be, as in Barcelona, a power group whose organization is independent of the political instrumentality of the capitalist state. The Good Families have lacked specific perquisites of political self-determination or control of a state apparatus. At times, they have competed for hegemony within the state. At other points, they have sought to define themselves against it. This division of power has shaped their history, organization, and ideology.

This vision of an elite, while influenced by Marxist models, also relies heavily on other European social theorists such as Vilfredo Pareto, Gaetano Mosca, Antonio Gramsci, Georg Lukács, and Pierre Bourdieu. This work also recognizes the influence of Marcus (1983), Hansen and Parrish (1983), and Cohen (1981) on the study of elites in anthropology. From the balancing of these sources I have phrased my concern with elites in contrast to power groups defined on the basis of position, reputation, or participation in institutions in a political or economic system. Furthermore, I have focussed on the processes of unification and continuity of an elite group rather than on conflicts between classes. Such a discussion, while important, must be done as a complement to greater knowledge of the actions and beliefs of ruling classes within specific historical contexts. This entails both comparative knowledge and firsthand field investigation.

Systematic anthropological comparison of the Barcelona materials has been constrained by the scarcity of elite ethnographies, although relevant work is present in other fields. While, in general, these comparisons will be appropriately introduced in the text, it is useful to mention those resources that have proved most valuable in shaping this study.

Edward Hansen's work on the rural Catalan elite in the Franco era was a basic reference in preparation of this project (1974, 1977). Because his study was outside of Barcelona and it concentrated on both a narrower time period and a different economic order, his observations are especially useful for comparison of structures and changes within Catalan society. As I have worked in Barcelona, this documentation has been supplemented by more traditional political and economic studies that treat Catalan power groups, especially through major works by Catalan scholars studying their own society. The work of James Amelang on early modern Barcelona society in both writing (1986) and conversation also has been a constant referent for my thought and investigation.

Unfortunately, the richness of Catalan materials is not equalled by data for other areas of Spain. This is particularly troubling with regard to topics such as capital organization, family variation, and ruling-class ideology for Spain's other industrial regions. Fernández de Pinedo (1974) on the Basque regions is a useful exception, as is J. B. Harrison's economic history (1978). While there are suggestive themes to be explored here, often it has proved impossible to do so. Other European studies provide a more useful basis for generalized comparison and for insight into specific themes. Pierre Bourdieu, as both a theoretician and a student of French society has been central to rethinking this work (1976, 1977, 1979; Bourdieu and Passeron 1976). Arno Mayer's provocative work on aristocratic cooptation of the emergent bourgeoisie of Northern Europe (1981) has also helped rephrase and expand questions. Leonore Davidoff's work (1973) on the importance of women in

London society provides a valuable case for discussing a poorly explored area of elite social organization—the role of women (see also Darrow 1979; Socolow 1979; Capmany 1969:61-80; Ostrander 1984). The rise of corporate organization and its relationship to society has been examined for France by Charles Freedman (1979) and for Europe and Japan by David Landes (1965, 1969, 1976). Finally, Carl Schorske (1980) and Allan Janik and Stephen Toulmin (1973), in their work on turn-of-the-century Austria, have raised interesting points on the social models of power in industrial society and the influence of culture on individual mentalities. Abner Cohen's work on a European-influenced elite in Sierra Leone, while published after completion of my original dissertation, has also been suggestive in reevaluating the results of my research.

American ruling classes are probably the subject of the most intensive and extensive historical and sociological examination of any area and thus also provide a framework for comparison. There are major differences between the situation and composition of the Catalan and the American elite: notably, the absence of an inherited aristocracy in the United States, the ideological bias against publicly demarcated ruling classes, and the relatively more powerful position of the American ruling class in the twentieth century. Such differences highlight both the common processes of elite formation and the conditioning factors of their differentiation.

Some American studies nonetheless have identified family as a central unit of analysis. This tradition tends toward social criticism more than social analysis, beginning with Gustavus Myers' *History of Great American Fortunes* (1936) and Ferdinand Lundberg's *America's Sixty Families* (1937; see also Lundberg 1968). This literature includes collective biographies, such as Peter Collier and David Horowitz's excellent portrayal of the Rockefellers (1977), as well as sociological analysis of power-holding communities (Mills 1956; Hunter 1953, 1980; Baltzell 1964, 1979; Domhoff 1967, 1970, 1978). American studies also encompass significant works on specific topics in elite formation. Peter Hall, for example, has written on the relationship between family structure and company in eighteenth- and nineteenth-century Massachusetts (1977, 1982); George Marcus has produced a similar study for Texas in the nineteenth and twentieth centuries (1980, MS). E. Digby Baltzell (1964), James McClachlan (1970), and Ronald Story (1980) have developed the importance of education and socialization of the gentleman in the formation of a ruling class. Social cohesion as well as ideological manipulation are recurrent themes in the works of G. William Domhoff.

The structure of an elite and the manipulation of ideology by those who hold power are intimately linked to the adaptive patterns of workers, as noted by Ignasi Terradas (1978, 1979) for Catalonia, Tamara Hareven (1978, 1982) for the United States, Patrick Joyce (1980) for Britain, and Luigi Guiotto (1979) for Italy. While this study does not explore the depths of such a comparison, the actions of the Barcelona proletariat are consistently present as part of the world—and world view—of the dominant classes. Ultimately, as mentioned in the Preface, the complement of this Barcelona fieldwork is as much the analysis of the poor as it is the powerful. Works on the family and poverty by Oscar Lewis (1959, 1961), Carol Stack (1974), Ulf Hannerz (1969), and Unni Wikan (1980), among others, have suggested to me the range of social structures that exist within capitalist society and the manner in which family and group are shaped by access to power and resources.

In this analysis, then, models of elites as power-holding groups within structures of social inequality have been balanced against theoretical models and available comparative data. For an anthropological study of power, theory must be challenged and refined by the experience of working with elite families. In the end theory and practice have coincided in an investigation of socioeconomic organization, ideology, and reproduction within a closely interconnected power-holding community. The topics suggested by such a sense of elite—individual strategies, family, clientage, alliance, myth, and ritual—are basic to both anthropological fieldwork and theory. Yet this study brings us into direct confrontation with those who control the distribution of power while simultaneously responding to demands within macrosystems. The ethnology of elites combines anthropology and social theory while working towards a new understanding of power.

The Good Families as Elite

The "Good Families" as an emic description of a social category would probably be applied to no more than one to two hundred patronyms in Barcelona today. The exact number of units and members, in any case, like the precise identification of all members through time, is less significant than the way in which these people interact. That is, the Good Families transcend mere ownership or economic position within Catalan society. Their interests, their integration, and their relationships to others go beyond the expression of a common position in the economic structure of Barcelona to encompass a shared style and history that underpins group solidarity. Bourdieu's sense of *habitus* as learned and shared systems of durable yet transposable *dispositions* suggests both their cohesion as a class and their role within a larger society (Bourdieu 1977:72-87).

The Good Families are the result of a synthesis, through the nineteenth and twentieth centuries, of agents who can be broadly classified into two distinct power-holding categories. The bourgeoisie who controlled the investment and accumulation process, the apparatus and the strategy of Catalan industrialization, introduced new economic power into Barcelona. They form the primary axis of my diachronic analysis. Yet an aristocratic establishment, sustained by some economic and political monopolies, held social power throughout the nineteenth century in Barcelona. It was, in fact, an aristocracy that already had been renewed through centuries by assimilating potential rivals, usurpers, and challengers. Its internal differences, indeed, became apparent in coalescence with the new bourgeoisie.

The Good Families do not include all those who are, or have been, economically powerful. Nor does it include all who have held rank within earlier prestige systems. Economic innovation in the nineteenth century produced new leaders, new levels of consumption, and new channels of access to and control of power. These innovations led to redefinition of Barcelona power groups as a cohesive urban community through a unification of economic and symbolic power. The process entailed the success and failure of individuals and families as well as changing structures. This synthesis was largely completed by the early twentieth century, although members units and attributes have continued to evolve within changing contexts. The Good Families are a classic example of circulation and selection within an elite.

The distinctiveness of the elite is clarified also by reference to those groups that coexist with the ruling class yet are not completely a part of it. There exists, for example, a political and economic managerial group that has mediated the relationship of the ruling class to other segments of Catalan society. Such "managers," equivalent in most cases to Domhoff's use of the "power elite" (1978:13), hold a contradictory position within the stratification system of Barcelona (E. O. Wright 1978:61-96). They represent the interests of the elite but only partially share in the ownership and the styles of interaction and consumption that define the group. This is reflected in social and cultural relationships as well: managers form a "marginalized" power group whose presence helps define the limits and power of the Good Families themselves. These managers also highlight the ambiguities of political power in the Good Families' relationship to the Spanish state.

There is also a socially mediating group: that is, a set of families which occupies an analogous position of marginalization with regard to social power. Essentially, many are descendants of a mercantile elite who had moved onto the first rungs of the aristocracy prior to industrialization. This course of social ascent was closed in the mid-nine-

teenth century. These families had committed economic and social capital to the acquisition of patents of nobility of the principality of
Catalonia, yet these privileges were not so highly valued in the later social and economic exchanges that integrated a new upper class in the
city of Barcelona. Unlike the managers, this social group "owns" the
markers of social power, including historical consciousness, but they
are unable to exploit them fully according to their value in an earlier
system. These families, too, are marked by a limited participation in the
Good Families—diminished economic roles, limitations on consumption, and a high rate of endogamy. Those who occupy marginal or contradictory positions with regard to social and economic power provide
crucial clarifications of the limits of power and the alternatives that
were possible historically in group formation.

All these groups have definite relationships to other classes within
Catalan society and to national political activity as well as international economic decision making. These ties will be explored through
the text to clarify levels of interaction for the Good Families as a power
group and the limits of domains within which the group has cohered.

Methodology and Organization

The small and closely integrated community of the Barcelona elite
forms an ideal population for the traditional anthropological method-
ology of participant observation. Yet there is a paradox in this amena-
bility to research that lies at the heart of the definition of the power
group itself. An elite is extremely visible, both in the positions it controls and in its social and economic display. At the same time it is highly
differentiated, actively differentiating itself from other social groups.
The formation of the power group has entailed strict control over access to interaction and alliance. The problem of fieldwork with an elite,
then, is how both to observe from the outside and, at least somewhat,
to participate.

My movement among the contemporary Good Families of Barcelona
was facilitated by the networks of contacts that have been fundamental
to the cohesion of the elite. Entry to the group was gained in 1976
through personal ties and a "friend of a friend" in one family. Since my
introduction was not solely as a researcher interested in the elite, it was
possible to validate my status and inquiry rapidly and to gain access to
formal and informal aspects of elite life.

The initial contacts expanded rapidly and provided a core network
that eventually included over one hundred individuals in many elite
families. This network was highly complex internally; families were
connected by multiple ties, and the same informant often proved to be

a contact in diverse contexts. From this group other members of the family or friends of informants were thus also accessible for brief contact or questions.

Nonetheless, not all contacts and relationships were equal. Some persons limited interviews to office appointments, while others invited me to their homes for meals or took me to the opera. These contacts shaped my life in turn—from the choice of an acceptable field address to dress and presentation of self. They were also juxtaposed to different worlds in the city, from friends at the university to those whom I came to know in the Barrio Chino, a marginal port district.

The elite network and my awareness of it had other advantages. In addition to introducing me to people it situated me in an elite flow of information. Individuals told me about other members of the elite, and in doing so, about themselves. One family, for example, was consistently cited as *the example* of status loss through violation of social norms. I collected information on this family from newspapers, notarial documents, and published genealogies. I also studied the reasons given in different situations by various members of the elite to explain the family's loss of status. They became not only an example of misconduct but a means by which to understand the internal frictions and jealousies of the Good Families.

Also, through the primary group I was able to discuss and test hypotheses in the field with persons internal to the group yet aware of the academic structure, methods, and aims of my work. This was crucial to the evaluation of roles and interests in the sensitive area of family politics. As I have read more recent work on reflexivity in ethnography, such as Dwyer (1982) or Dumont (1978), I have been struck by the differences in working with a well-educated and powerful community in terms of the situation of the fieldworker. Dealing with people who have read anthropology and history and who can respond critically within the same framework as the ethnographer eradicates much of the naiveté of the traditional field situation—and enriches the dialogic elements of an ethnography of power.

Certainly no anthropologist working with a group that has coalesced around domination will accept uncritically either the motivations behind interviews or the emic valuations of his informants. The internal complexity of the network provided one control of interpretive or misleading information, as did my own observations of elite behavior in relation to statements about that behavior. Three other factors peculiar to elite research also enriched my field stay and subsequent interpretations.

First, this study always had sources outside the elite who could expand and corroborate my perception of the information that I was acquiring. These included colleagues in Barcelona's academic community as well as the Barcelona press. Others provided me with a middle-class or lower-class perspective on the Good Families and thus helped me to maintain a critical balance while placing the elite within Catalan society and history. The visibility of the Good Families has made them an object of academic study as well as social comment.

Second, interviews with members of the contemporary elite were not only a source of data on the present but also a bridge to the past. That is, I devoted considerable attention in such conversations to the accurate reconstruction of social historical data—genealogies, linguistic behavior, alliances and business dealings, and political attitudes of the past generation. This oral history was refined, challenged, and completed by archival documentation. Because of their position, members of the elite appear frequently in legal, political, and economic records. These data and resources are described more fully in the Bibliography. While neither oral history nor archives provide "objective" data, the interplay of historical consciousness and historical materials became a central part of my understanding of the elite.

Not all contemporary recollections have archival cognates, however. Extensive talks with elderly women of the elite were especially important since they provided information on female "domestic" power and socialization that generally is lacking in archival and historical materials focussed on public economic and political affairs. These data could then be compared with other recent memoirs as well as behavior in the present.

Finally, my work frequently draws on literature, memoirs, and other written materials as well as archival sources to provide both corroboration and interesting perspectives. Authors as diverse as Dolors Monserdà, a major nineteenth-century Catalan feminist novelist, and Juan Goytisolo, a contemporary Barcelona author who writes in Castilian, forced me to formulate new questions through their insights. Once again the prominence of the elite has made it a common subject for cultivated and popular literature, including many works written by children of Good Families themselves. In all, there is a tremendous and in some ways unique range of materials for social historical investigation of the Barcelona elite. These materials provide a basis for understanding both modern Catalan society and its past.

One final point must be made on the methods employed, since it has required ethical decisions in the field and particularly in my presentation of data. During the period of my active fieldwork (1976-1979), two lineages of the Good Families of Barcelona lost members to extortionist bombings. The visibility of power and wealth and the fear many older informants expressed of turmoil in post-Franco Spain led me to restrict the introduction of personally identifiable data after 1955, unless these had been previously published. This boundary coincides well with a major economic change in the mid-1950s occasioned by the introduction of Spanish and foreign capital into Barcelona and the rise of professionally trained managers (Moya 1970; Pinilla de las Heras 1967; and personal communications). Hence it is a logical analytic boundary as well as consistent with a desire not to directly or indirectly interject current political conflict into the study or into the lives of those who worked with me. In many cases an apt passage from literature or published materials thus has been substituted to discuss conclusions based on interviews and participant observation.

The primary themes of Catalan history that are necessary to situate this study are introduced in Chapter II: the conflicts of politics, economics, and rights to production within which the Barcelona elite took shape. This chapter also treats the variant perceptions of history through which an elite consciousness has distinguished itself from that of other social groups.

Chapter III turns to the meaning of "family" in Catalonia. The discussion serves to place the industrial pattern within a range of household structures—legal, folkloric, and class-based. At the same time these are linked to the themes of ideological manipulation that recur in succeeding chapters.

The fourth and fifth chapters trace the economic evolution of family and group. Chapter IV focuses upon the evolution of the company and household as determined by the interaction of domestic cycles with economic development. Chapter V complements the analysis of the single-family firm with the evolution of economic cohesion. A detailed analysis of a single family, the Güells, and of several organizations will highlight the basic structures and chronology of group coalescence.

Chapters VI and VII mirror the economic analysis of the family with the examination of social power. Chapter VI examines elite assimilation to, and redefinition of, aristocratic norms in socialization. Chapter VII then traces the synthesis of power groups through marriage and the limits of group that this exchange indicates.

Chapter VIII examines the cultural imagery constructed by the ruling class of nineteenth- and twentieth-century Barcelona. Detailed studies of the cemetery and the opera house confirm the centrality of family while illustrating household variation among groups. This discussion returns to the multivalent nature of the family as social and cultural institution, as well as its manipulation by power groups.

Finally, the conclusions suggest hypotheses for future anthropological studies of elites both in Barcelona and in comparative research.

CHAPTER II

BARCELONA IN HISTORICAL PERSPECTIVE

Even though illustrative of general processes of elite formation, the coalescence, reproduction, and decline of the Good Families have occurred within a specific historical context. In order to balance the general with the specific readers unfamiliar with Barcelona may require more information on the major currents of Catalan history. Furthermore, the Catalan revitalization of the nineteenth and twentieth centuries has included frequent references to historical precedents of sovereignty, custom, and culture. Familiarity with the past is a necessary prelude to comprehension of the manipulation of tradition in the present. This overview chapter, therefore, is a foundation for the more detailed historical anthropological analysis that follows. The second section also suggests how historical narrative and the proprietorship of history are directly bound to urban power structures and their transformation.

Three themes of Catalan history are especially relevant to power group formation. The first is the dialectic between national (Catalan) self-determination and association with the Spanish state. This is not a simple dichotomy between an independent Catalonia before 1714 and a region in a larger, centralized state thereafter. The bases of Catalan national identity—territory, economy, political-jural structure, social structure, language, and culture—were all formed in the splendor of the medieval and Renaissance Mediterranean. The gradual redefinition of Catalonia as a unit within the Spanish state, rather than as the head of an independent empire, did not eliminate any of these characteristics so much as it adapted them within new circumstances. Thus, contemporary politicians still debate centurial issues such as law and language. Today, however, this debate encompasses both references to the past and strategies for the present and future of Catalonia within Spain.

A second major theme is the economic development of Catalonia and its capitalist elite within the modern transformations of the European and world economy. Spain has been an intermediate zone in the industrial world.

Backward in comparison with other Western nations, Spain was yet ahead of those other nations whose industrialization began only in the nineteenth century. The case of Spain is less that of a latecomer than that of an attempt, largely thwarted, to join the ranks of the first comers. (Nadal 1973:617)

Within Spain, Catalan industrialization has held an ambivalent position. Catalonia was the primary locale of the Spanish Industrial Revolution for its first half-century. Yet, localized development was shaped by the political and economic conditions of the entire country. The underdevelopment of the rest of Spain, the policies of dependency that emanated from the capital, and the competing claims of other regions all have had direct effects on Catalonia.

Catalonia's response to changing international circumstances thus has been both economic and political, mediated by the intervention of the Spanish state. In the final years of the nineteenth century economic issues spurred the upper class into Catalanist political organization. Other groups have subsequently inherited these questions of political and economic reform, which remain major questions in Catalan life in the 1980s.

Finally, Catalan history encompasses the ongoing transformation of groups and conflicts within that society. Growth in the nineteenth century altered, but did not demolish, social inequality and struggle among social divisions. New classes—capitalists and proletariat—emerged in conflict with older groups as well as each other. This work focusses specifically on the conflicts among elites between this grand bourgeoisie and the preexisting Catalan aristocracies. Yet open and violent struggle between those who hold power and those who do not has also erupted in Barcelona throughout the past century. Workers have fought for their rights through labor organization, political action, and armed struggle. The lower and professional middle classes have emerged in this century as significant voices in Catalan politics as well, especially with the decline of the aristocratized industrial elite. All factions continue to seek their goals within—and even in contradistinction to—Catalan national identity and the organization of the Spanish state.

These themes are neither independent nor sequential. The meaning of nationhood, the linkage of Catalonia as an economic unit to other countries, and the divisions of Catalan society might be addressed as meaningfully to the twelfth or the sixteenth as to the nineteenth century. Rather, the themes guide a synthesis of data and arguments oriented towards an understanding of family and power in industrial so-

ciety. The following section examines these themes in terms of differential group consciousness and appropriation of history.

A Historical Overview of Catalonia

The Background to Industrialization to 1800

In the Middle Ages Barcelona became the capital of a Mediterranean empire that comprised Catalonia (including parts of modern France), Aragon, Valencia, the Balearics, Sardinia, Sicily, and parts of the Grecian peninsula. The kingdom of Catalonia-Aragon developed a sophisticated balance of parliamentary estates and legal codes that endured for centuries. Commerce flourished, enriching the capital. Catalan itself evolved as a language for government, education, and a rich literature within the context of a general cultural florescence.

Barcelona declined from the heights of its power in the fifteenth century. When Ferdinand II of Catalonia-Aragon married Isabel of Castile and Leon in 1469, he brought a nation exhausted by war and economic crises into union with a kingdom about to embark on an era of brilliant expansion. Catalonia became a partner in Spain but not in the Castilian triumphs in Northern Europe and the New World.

As Spain expanded, the gold of the New World flowed to bankers of Flanders and Northern Italy rather than to the merchant bankers of Barcelona. Catalonia retained an independent parliament, law codes, and the Council of Aragon, successor in governance to the Royal Council. While not marked by the same glories of economic or cultural life as in previous centuries, Barcelona remained an active city, whose elite found new roles and interests (Amelang 1986). Yet, in all this, Catalonia shared its king with Castile—and his gaze was directed elsewhere (Elliott 1963).

In the seventeenth century the Catalans rebelled against the monarchy of Spain. This revolt failed, although the terms of the capitulation were lenient. Nonetheless, "during its revolution of 1640, Catalonia was brought to realize, however unwillingly, that it was a part of Spain" (Elliott 1963:552). In 1705 the Catalans rebelled anew but were once again defeated. This second defeat led to new political structures that would shape all Catalan society and culture in subsequent centuries: "This time there was no reprieve. The Crown of Aragon was systematically stripped of the privileges it had preserved for so long, and Catalonia became a mere region of the Bourbon state" (Elliott 1963:548). Among the privileges of nationhood abolished after 1716

Figure 1
Barcelona in the Eighteenth Century

were the elected parliament and the municipal council of Barcelona. The central government moved the university away from Barcelona as well. Finally, attempts were made to limit the domains of the Catalan language. These punishments linked culture and political autonomy; little was done to the weakened economy.

By the beginning of the eighteenth century, then, Catalonia had already experienced a long and complex history as a nation and a state. It had a geographical definition, a legal code that endured even after the dismantling of the system that had legislated it, a well-developed economy, and strong linguistic and cultural traditions. Catalonia had also been shaped by generations of political, economic, and cultural leaders whose heritage could not be eradicated by the state reforms. Since 1716, however, the differentiation of Catalonia as a polity has taken place within the Spanish state. The impetus and leadership for national revitalization, moreover, have come less from the experience of a sovereign political past than from economic development that began in the eighteenth century and continues today.

The Early Industrial Revolution, 1800-1888

At the beginning of the eighteenth century the population of Barcelona was lower than that recorded in 1370; even Catalonia as a whole showed little increase with regard to that earlier period (Table 1). Between 1714 and 1789, however, the population of the city tripled. Demographic increase, which continued apace through succeeding decades, is only one index of Catalan renewal in this century. Agriculture expanded, as did wine production throughout the area. Commerce was reorganized and extended into new markets. Most significantly for the future the cotton industry appeared in the form of small factories along the region's waterways and of cottage production based on one or two looms (Vilar 1962: vol. 1).

This growth took advantage of the new position of Catalonia within the Spanish state. In the eighteenth century Catalan merchants finally were permitted to exploit the opportunities of the New World. Peninsular trade barriers, which had fragmented a Spanish national market, were also lowered, fostering further possibilities for Catalan industry and trade. These changes produced a new capitalist leadership for Barcelona associated with such institutions as the Junta de Comerç and the Theater of the Holy Cross. Even the stereotype of the Catalan held by other Spaniards changed—from a bold and vengeful Mediterranean bandit to a conservative and industrious businessman (Elliott 1963:548; Muñoz Espinalt 1966).

Napoleon's invasion of the Iberian peninsula in 1808 interrupted Catalan expansion. As Spaniards fought the aggressor, new questions arose as well about the organization and future course of the state. In 1810 a parliament met in Cádiz to lay the groundwork for a new liberal bourgeois state; Catalans were active participants. Yet the king returned in 1814 and successfully allied himself with the church, the nobility, and other conservative elements to block such reform. Social, political, and economic divisions were deep and interdependent. Furthermore, the slow and uneven economic recovery of Spain in the nineteenth century exacerbated the split between liberals and conservatives:

> If Spain had recovered rapidly from the ravages of war, the domestic bitterness might have been soothed with time. But no balm of prosperity came to heal the scission of Spanish society. Instead, the scission between progressive anticlericals and Catholic conservative Spaniards, the "two Spains" of recent history, has remained the fundamental problem of Spain. (Herr 1958:443)

Table 1
Population of Barcelona and Catalonia

Date	Barcelona	Catalonia
1370	40,000[a]	400,000[b]
1497	23,000[b]	222,164[b]
1553		279,876[b]
1650	50,000[c]	
1717	34,005[d]	406,274[b]
1787	111,410[d]	814,000[d]
		900,000[e]
1819		829,705[e]
1834	133,545[e]	1,041,222[e]
1842	121,815[e]	1,052,216[e]
1856-1857	188,787[f]	1,673,842[f]
1860	189,948[f]	1,673,842[f]
1877	248,943[f]	1,752,033[f]
1887	272,481[f]	1,843,590[f]
1900	533,000[f*]	1,942,245[f]
1910	595,732[g]	2,394,577[g]
1920	710,335[g]	2,659,033[g]
1930	1,005,565[g]	3,120,179[g]
1940	1,081,175[g]	3,193,186[g]
1950	1,280,179[h]	3,544,984[h]
1960	1,577,865[h]	4,262,389[h]
1970	1,745,172[h]	5,943,052[h]
1975	1,754,714[h, i]	6,045,257[h]

SOURCES: [a] Calculated by Claramunt (1978) from the *fogatge* (census) of 1365-1370.
[b] Calculated by Jordi de Nadal (1971) from censuses of 1497, 1553, and 1717.
[c] According to Nadal, this deceased to 23,000 by 1652 because the plague.
[d] From Vilar (1962), who includes a lengthy discussion of his evaluation of various sources.
[e] From Rebagliato (1978a).
[f] From Rebagliato (1978a). Modern census data appear for Spain beginning in 1856/1857.
[g] From Rebagliato (1978b).
[h] From Rebagliato (1978c).
[i] Although the city itself is no longer growing, expansion has spilled out into the metropolitan area. The county (*comarca*) of Barcelona, for example, reached a population of 2,459,899 in 1975 (Rebagliato 1978c:261).
NOTE: * This figure represents the population after consolidation with smaller surrounding cities.

Within this framework the economic success of the Catalans produced special divisions both internally and in relation to the rest of Spain.

Catalan industry grew rapidly in the 1830s and 1840s. In 1832 a national ban on the importation of finished cotton goods secured a protected market for Catalan manufacturers. That same year, Josep Bonaplata, a Catalan who had studied in England, built the first steam-powered plant for the production of cotton cloth in Catalonia. Another roughly contemporaneous innovation, the limited-liability corporation (1829), helped assemble the capital to build on political and technological improvements. These advances also favored the consolidation of cottage production into larger factories. The owners of these firms formed a core of commercial-industrial power holders.

Consolidation of new power structures became evident in all areas of Barcelona life. The Bank of Barcelona, dean of Catalan finance for nearly a century, was founded in 1844. The Barcelona Savings and Loan opened its doors at the same time. La España Industrial (Industrial Spain), whose very name indicates the ambition of its textilist founders, was chartered in 1847. Major investments were made in machinery, metallurgy, and transportation. Manufacturers founded lobbying groups in Barcelona and Madrid, while speaking out on issues of concern as members of the *Cortes* (parliament). This new wealth and power were also linked to a new quest for prestige and to arenas for social display exemplified in institutions such as the Gran Teatre del Liceu, begun in 1844. This opera house will be considered in more detail in Chapter VIII.

By the mid-nineteenth century the Catalan textile industry ranked "in fourth place in the world, behind Britain, France, and the United States, and ahead of Belgium and Italy" (Harrison 1978:62). Development was not without problems, however. The industrial base was hardly diversified: the capitalization of cotton industries far overshadowed all other sectors into the twentieth century. Moreover, state-imposed limitations on the joint-stock corporation, to be explored in detail in Chapter IV, had a major impact on economic life. Capital that might otherwise have been invested in the expansion of manufacture or in new ventures was diverted by these measures to public corporations, such as the railroads, or to government bonds (Tortella Casares 1968:69-84).

Transportation also plagued industrial development. Spanish railroads bypassed some fledgling centers for industry in order to connect the capital with borders and ports for the importation of foreign goods. Nor did Spanish suppliers profit from the construction of these railroads more than foreign investors. Despite the railway boom, for example, a major Barcelona metallurgical firm, La Maquinista Terrestre y Marítima, received no contracts for railroad cars until 1882. On the whole, the Catalan rail network was more efficiently designed as an industrial grid than that of the rest of the nation. Yet Catalonia was bound by the dependency of the state as a whole.

Despite Catalonia's successes, therefore, it is fair to say that Spain *became* increasingly underdeveloped with respect to northern core economies in the course of the nineteenth century (Sánchez-Albornoz 1977:8; Jordi de Nadal 1973a). That is, the gap between Spain and the industrial vanguard nations widened rather than narrowing. Catalonia was caught in the policies and decisions of the Spanish state and limited by the markets it provided. Such contextual factors are clear in the divergence of Catalan economic cycles from those of the rest of industrial Europe. The Spanish Revolution of 1868, for example, initiated a six-year period of instability that climaxed in the eleven months of the first Spanish Republic (Izard 1979:206-223). The restoration of the Bourbon monarchy in 1874, therefore, opened an era of stability and perceived prosperity that coincided with the Great Depression of Northern Europe. Spanish colonial markets were also lucrative possessions in this period, and the phylloxera that ravaged French vineyards favored their Catalan rivals. Thus the Catalan economy seemed triumphant while the rest of Europe suffered.

Political change, however, had not kept stride with the economic changes of Catalonia. Carlist reactionary bands drew on the support of conservative rural Catalans in intermittent wars. Despite a series of nineteenth-century reforms, including an elected state parliament and extended male suffrage, localized political bosses (*caciques*) and coalitions of traditional interests dominated Spain. While Catalans lobbied in Madrid they did not generally enter these coalitions. Ironically, the limited influence of bossism in urban and educated populations isolated Barcelona even more from the rest of Spain: "In the end, Catalonia rejected the Andalusian set of controls and became the first area to break away from the Restoration style of politics" (Kern 1974:30).

Even if Catalonia's political identity and power were moot, economic success did revitalize its cultural and linguistic identity. Literature reached a new florescence: by mid-century, novels, theater, and poetry in Catalan found new creators as well as support from newly literate audiences. Art and architecture were also patronized by the emergent elite. The cramped medieval Barcelona that lingered into the industrial period was converted into a modernist city. The walls were replaced by broad avenues, and palaces designed by major architects such as Gaudí and Puig i Cadafalch changed the cityscape. The image of the city in the early part of the century (Figure 2) contrasts sharply with that of only a half-century later (see Figure 33, p. 183).

Figure 2
Map of Barcelona in 1855

The Triumph of Bourgeois Catalanism, 1888-1923

At this pinnacle of industrial Catalonia—and of the industrial elite of the area—Barcelona hosted the international exposition of 1888. This fair announced Catalan economic and cultural success to the world:

> The streets were filled with a swarming multitude that had come from all over the world to know the powerful spirit of nascent Catalan industry, the beauty of the city, and the titanic effort of a people who were able to raise a superb exposition in such a short time—to their own pride and to the admiration of foreigners. (*Barcelona y sus exposiciones* 1929)

Yet, the relationship of Catalonia and the state was called into question by events at the end of the century. In 1890 phylloxera reached the Catalan vineyards, rapidly and thoroughly destroying that sector and producing chaos in agricultural Catalonia. In 1898 war between Spain and the United States led to the loss of the last major colonies that had once constituted Castile's empire. This was a spiritual as well as an economic and political blow to the nation.

TITLE

SHELFMARK No. | **BARCODE No. (8 DIGITS)**

FOR LIBRARY USE ONLY

DATE RESERVED | **NOL** | **COL** | **RECALLS**

Figure 3
Entrance to the Barcelona Universal Exposition of 1888

Devaluation of the currency and the repatriation of capital and con-
sumers from the colonies alleviated some immediate economic problems. Yet, Catalan businessmen recognized problems ahead and acted
to deal with them. They first chose General Polavieja, a military hero,
to champion their program in Madrid. Their suggestions included a
free-trade zone from Barcelona, state-financed technical education,
government support in the search for new markets, and a new taxation
system favorable to industry. The Madrid government not only rejected these ideas but also proposed an income tax levied on industrial
contributions. This was met in Catalonia with a taxpayers' and shop-
keepers' revolt. As the economic historian J. B. Harrison notes, the
state's stringent repression of this strike "with imposition of martial
law throughout the region and the imprisonment of its leaders" provoked a counterreaction that "finally convinced the business community of the desirability of pursuing a specifically Catalan form of political activity" (Harrison 1978:83).

In 1891 four Catalan businessmen were elected to the Spanish Parliament on a regionalist platform. The new commercial-industrial families seemed to take political charge as well as to commandeer economic
and social dominance. Their primary political institution, the Lliga Re-

Figure 4
Barcelona in the Nineteenth Century

gionalista, was presented as an "interclass party" of national vindication. A general strike in 1902, however, undercut this claim to unity.
Thereafter, radicals became "for the Lliga the principal enemy, the enemy of class" (Riquer 1976:306). The identity of Catalonia and of Catalan nationalism in this century cannot be understood without further
exploration of this division in Catalan society.

The first years of Catalan industrial consolidation in the 1830s and
1840s had also spurred proletarian consciousness and organization.
The earliest attempt at collective bargaining in Barcelona took place in
1834. Luddite violence appeared the next year in the burning of the
Bonaplata factory. A formal labor organization began in 1840. By the
1850s workers were able to present a structured and powerful representation of their claims in a general strike supported by forty thousand
workers (Harrison 1978:104-122).

Later in the century Catalan labor divided between anarchist and socialist leadership. The Tres Clases de Vapor of the Catalan textile industry worked with owners during economic crises to safeguard jobs.
Anarchists took a more radical stance. When their movement weakened in the 1890s, some turned to terrorism, giving Barcelona an international reputation as "The City of the Bombs."

In the early twentieth century many workers turned to the centralist
republican party of Alejandro Lerroux. The anarchists stayed apart
from political action. In 1910, however, they founded the National
Congress of Workers (CNT) that would be a strong force in strikes and
reform for the next decades.

In spite of these deep divisions within Catalan industrial society elite
regionalism had some strategic successes. In 1914 the Lliga secured the
Mancomunitat de Catalunya, the first government with limited auton-

omy for all four Catalan provinces in two centuries. Its first president was the lawyer, author, and politician Enric Prat de la Riba, whose writings on industry will be analyzed in Chapter IV. The Mancomunitat encouraged the Catalan language and made improvements in such areas as transportation and communication.

World War I, in which Spain remained neutral, stimulated Catalan development. Catalan manufacturers overcame a lack of stocks to fill the vacuum left by the nations at war, supplying belligerents, capturing foreign markets, and at last controlling the Spanish national market without fear of competition (Harrison 1978:88-99; Casals and Sans 1972:30-33). Once again, Spanish politics differentiated Catalonia's economic life from the rest of the industrial world.

Challenge and Changing Power Structures, 1923-

The aftermath of the war boom damaged both Catalan industry and Catalan unity. Money had not been invested in modernization or re-capitalization of older factories, nor had plans been made to deal with oversupply and recovering competition. Even before the war's end inflation sparked renewed discontent in the working class. Union membership increased, especially in the more radical anarcho-syndicalist groups. In 1919 a general strike closed 70 percent of Barcelona's industry. A settlement was reached, only to be sabotaged by the military forces in the city who refused to accept it (Boyd 1979:121-135). A biennium of almost open class warfare in Barcelona followed, among gangs of gunmen sponsored by manufacturers and unions. Eventually the elite abandoned the pretense of Catalan unity and appealed to Madrid for help. By calling on the civil governor, Martínez Anido, to brutally repress war in the streets, Catalan businessmen and their aristocratic allies chose between Catalan self-determination and their interests of class and social stability. A Madrid newspaper commented:

> As bourgeoisie, as conservatives, and as patrons, they not only sympathized with Martínez Anido but almost all of them had publicly congratulated the governor on his policies. But if as bourgeoisie, patrons, and Somatenistas [members of a Catalan civil militia] they could celebrate the repressive policies of Martínez Anido, as Catalanists and adversaries of the state they could not do so. Politically, this would have had the effect of recognizing a functionary of the hated central authority in Catalonia. (El Imparcial, 12 December 1921)

As they became committed to the central government for protection of class interests the Good Families steadily lost power in Catalonia. In

1923 they strongly endorsed the national coup of General Primo de Rivera, then civil governor of Barcelona (Boyd 1979:269). One of the dictator's first acts was to limit the use of Catalan, and in 1925 he abolished the Mancomunitat. Nonetheless, the elite tolerated his regime until the effects of the world depression began to be felt in Spain. In 1930 the Primo de Rivera government collapsed. Within a year the Spanish monarchy followed. When the second Spanish Republic was proclaimed in 1931, other socioeconomic strata had taken control of Catalanism.

A few hours before this proclamation, Francesc Macià announced a Catalan republic in the framework of a Spanish federation of states. Leaders of the central government soon convinced Macià to accept an autonomus regime within the state, the Generalitat. This was chartered by law in 1932 and a regional parliament elected. In contrast to the Mancomunitat republicans of the middle class and the working class were in control of the new autonomous polity. This government emphasized reforms in education, the economy, and society that threatened the position of the older elite. Economic depression and political uncertainty, however, limited the success of such reforms.

Many events coincided in redefining the position of the Good Families in the 1920s and 1930s: class conflict, the collapse of the Bank of Barcelona (1921), the policies of the Primo de Rivera regime, and world depression. Ironically, the Republic forestalled some of the early effects of the depression because of the lowered price of raw materials and the incipient redistribution of agricultural wealth. "Catalan industrialists went so far as to argue that Spain was experiencing no economic crisis at all, simply a political crisis" (Harrison 1978:142). While the upper class had lost power within the new political structure of Catalonia, it retained its economic and social status.

By 1934 this situation, too, was ending. The demand for manufactured goods declined, while unemployment and calls for real social and economic reforms increased. A right-wing government had taken power in Madrid in 1933; the Lliga, inspired by this class-linked success, planned for the upcoming local elections in Catalonia. Yet, the Catalan government remained in the hands of a coalition of leftist nationalists. Once again tension between Barcelona and Madrid erupted. On October 5, 1934, President Lluís Companys of the Generalitat proclaimed a Catalan republic, repeating Macià's words in a ritual of protest against the central state (Balcells 1974:126-132). The reaction of the central government was not the same as in 1931. The Generalitat was suspended and its leaders imprisoned.

The next elections, in 1936, further manifested the divisions within Catalonia and the Spanish state as a whole. The Front Català d'Ordre, a heterogeneous right-wing coalition representing industrialists and financiers, pitted itself against the leftist Popular Front. In Catalonia the Popular Front won 59 percent of the vote (Balcells 1974:134-135). In Spain as a whole the vote split 50.5 percent for the leftist coalition, 43 percent for the right, 5 percent for centrists, and 1 percent for Basque nationalists (Jackson 1965:193).

This new government faced regional and national polarization with little opportunity to satisfy either the expectations of leftist workers and peasants or criticisms of rightist elites. On July 17 and 18 the Spanish army under General Francisco Franco rose up in rebellion. The Spanish Civil War had begun.

The military rebellion failed in Barcelona; Catalonia was a mainstay of the Republic during its final three years. The class tensions latent in industrialist society erupted immediately. Members of the Good Families found themselves the targets of political and personal reprisals. Their strength was further undercut by economic reforms, such as the collectivization of factories (Thomas 1961:187-192, 424-429, 565-578). Upper-class families withdrew to inconspicuous or clandestine lives, fled into exile, or joined the forces of General Franco.

Barcelona resisted the insurgents until 1939. This struggle traumatized Catalan society and devastated its economy. After the capture of the city the Franco regime also hindered regional recovery. The dictatorship emphasized national self-sufficiency rather than trade and expansion. Indeed, it had few outside allies after the collapse of the fascist regimes of Germany and Italy, and little hope for foreign aid.

More significantly, the dictatorship singled out Catalonia for a savage repression directed against the entire society, regardless of class or politics. By the end of the war

> the use of Catalan was identified with separatism. . . . The Falangist press invented an artificial antisemitism: the region's inhabitants were repeatedly described as *judeo-catalanes* and Companys (and Cambó) and the leaders of the *Lliga* were claimed to be secret Jews. . . . Draconian punishments for Catalonia were demanded; the precedent of Sodom and Gomorrah was cited as a fit fate for Barcelona, and there were serious suggestions that the region revert to an agricultural livelihood, exacting war reparations from Catalonia by physically removing its industries to the rest of Spain. (Jones 1976:239-240)

External repression forged a new Catalan unity. This negative definition of the nationality resulted in the destruction of Catalonia's political rights, limitations on its economy, and the prohibition of the use of its language in schools, mass media, and public assemblies. It even entailed the manipulation or concealment of historical events and personages. Catalan identity was thus reshaped in reaction to this negative imposition from outside.

Franco's definition of Catalonia trapped the Good Families of Barcelona whether or not they had supported him. They were weakened economically by both losses in the war and restrictions on rebuilding and supplies. They were also marginalized politically:

> For the majority of the upper middle class, who had supported the *Lliga*, exclusion from power and indeed from any form of public office was the rule. Even the names of many could not be mentioned in the press during the 1940s. . . . The *Lliga haute bourgeoisie* had turned to Franco in their dismay at the social revolution in Republican Spain, and at the end of the war they recovered their decollectivized factories, their law practices, their fortunes and estates; but their original sin as catalanists made them ineligible for public life. (Jones 1976:237)

This period marked the decline of the Good Families as a dominant political and economic group. While they did recover partially, and have continued as visible power holders, their industrial and financial resources have since lagged behind new construction in Madrid and the rest of Spain built with government intervention or foreign capital. The largest employer in Barcelona today is SEAT, the Spanish Fiat subsidiary. Banks with headquarters in Madrid or the Basque provinces have swallowed independent Catalan institutions. Until the prolonged economic crisis of the 1970s the descendants of the entrepreneurs of the nineteenth century retained wealth, commercial interests and land, and social prestige, including close intermingling with the older aristocracy. But they could not control the political economic system in which they might exercise this prestige.

Catalonia as a whole began to recover after economic restrictions were eased in 1955. The area attracted tourism and foreign capital. The population grew as immigrants arrived from poorer regions of Spain. Collective political activity gained momentum in the 1950s and 1960s, although it faced continuous centralist harassment and punishment (Jones 1976:247-256). Catalans also revived their language and culture. Books in Catalan had been reauthorized in 1945; in 1959 the Abbey of Montserrat, traditional spiritual center for Catalonia, took advantage of a law that exempted church publications from censorship to bring out a Catalan language magazine. The 1960s and early 1970s saw continued economic and cultural growth with some liberalizations of the Francoist regime—who nonetheless maintained controls on groups perceived as leftist or separatists.

Following the death of Franco in 1975 the pace of reform and recuperation of a Catalan identity has quickened, within a generalized process of political and social reform in Spain. In 1977, after forty years in exile, the Generalitat was reestablished in Barcelona. The Catalan language reappeared in public assemblies and mass media: a Catalan television channel was active by 1984. The language has slowly been reintroduced to education, while local regimes support literary and cultural events. In 1980 the Catalans overwhelmingly accepted a statute of autonomy that legalized the competencies of the new Generalitat. A new parliament was elected, led by a conservative middle-class Catalanist. In later elections socialists took the mayoral post in Barcelona. While reforms remain slow, Catalonia is searching for a new order in politics, economics, and society.

Many issues of Catalan nationalism and national identity remain in flux. The economy faces the difficulties of an international recession with noncompetitive plants and scant resources. The delineation of political powers has been agonizingly slow. Nor have social reform nor even cultural revitalization achieved their ends. A fervent campaign for "normalization" of the Catalan language, for example, still faces the difficulties of defining what normal usage is in a bilingual society and how language and identity will intermesh in a new polity (Woolard, in press; DiGiacomo 1984).

Catalonia's problems are based in internal diversity as well as relationships to the Spanish state and world markets. Class conflict is intertwined with ethnic divisions. At the turn of the century immigrants from rural Catalonia and nearby provinces were already arriving in Barcelona, attracted by industrial wages and opportunities. Through the century more workers have come from Andalusia, Murcia, Galicia, and other non-Catalan speaking provinces. Between 1940 and 1975 over 1,600,000 immigrants arrived in Catalonia. They differ in language, culture, and political affiliations as well as class patterns. Their children or grandchildren may or may not speak Catalan or identify with the polity. The position of these "other Catalans" has become one of the major questions of Catalan politics and contemporary self-definition (see Candel 1964; Jiménez Losantos 1979).

This summary of Catalan history has provided a schematic survey within which elite development can be situated. Yet, this objectification removes the past from a matrix of power conflicts that is never absent in Barcelona. In fact, one of the pillars of elite unity is its shared consciousness of history and of the class proprietorship of Barcelona history. An anthropological appreciation of Catalan history thus demands reflection upon various perspectives and their interplay in social definition.

History and Historical Consciousness

Interviews with members of the elite, as well as the writings of earlier generations, consistently portrayed a group-specific sense of history. This was the product of an elite position of domination, as well as the legitimation of that position. It was also strongly personal: history was recounted in terms of heroes who were ancestors. History was not only property, it was inherited property. At the same time, in Catalonia social and political reformists were raising arguments over different versions of past events, with slogans like "*Recuperem la nostra història*": "Let us recover our history." In the heated debate over political rights, economic responsibility, and linguistic-cultural identity, this slogan signalled the significance of history as a component in the struggle for power.

"History," whether in Catalonia or in any other complex society, varies according to the social groups that claim it and the ways in which they use it. That is not to say the events themselves change, so much as the interpretation, narration, or expectations of historical experience (see Jameson 1981:17-58; Rosaldo 1980; Sahlins 1981; John Lukacs 1985). This differentiation also encompasses the extent to which any interpretation is heard, that is, can compete with other versions, or can be imposed upon other groups. The appropriation of history as an interpretation of the past in the present reflects—and is shaped by—the interactions of all power groups within a society, as well as their multiple ties to other academic, political-economic, and social communities. In Barcelona the Good Families felt that their special rights as actors in history eclipsed other groups and movements. This ownership correlated with their interpretation of the past and its value in the present: their historical consciousness. The structures of this consciousness, such as the three-generation model of industrial-familiar expansion and decline, will be analyzed further in subsequent chapters. By contrast, those who called for "our history" also recognized the meaning of history in the definition of social groups, in the establishment of an identity, and in the grounding of collective action. Their call to consciousness confronted the elite appropriation of the past.

Nonetheless, like many other politically weighted slogans of modern nationalist controversies, "*Recuperem la nostra història*" is indeterminate or ambiguous with regard to its referential meaning. At a basic level this slogan refers to the recovery of both academic and popular rights to history as commemorated in festivals and monuments, as taught in schools, as researched in universities, and as preserved in archives and museums. Such a claim responds to the "scorched past" policy of the Franco regime that Hispanicized historical interpretation and even eliminated Catalan historical landmarks. At another level, however, the slogan refers to political actors and economic classes in Catalonia who have been denied depiction within a ruling-class historiography. Both themes merit discussion.

History and Power within Catalonia

The development of historiography in modern Catalonia has reflected that of economic and political life. As the eighteenth-century economy of the polity revived, historians such as Antoni de Capmany (1742-1813) looked to the past for a charter. His *Memorias históricas sobre la marina, comercio y arte de la antigua ciudad de Barcelona* (1779-1792) saw Catalan as a dead language and the former wealth and political autonomy of the area as past. Yet the very act of writing about these themes produced a crucial statement for the mentality necessary to economic revitalization.

In the nineteenth century academic historiography was often the preserve of elite amateurs or more serious scholars with upper-class associations. Their writings were enlisted in the progressive vision of the emergent industrial-commercial power holders. Both manufacturers and companies subscribed to Pi Arimón's 1854 history of the city (1,131). In 1878 the city sponsored a competition for the best essay on the "Past, Present, and Future of Barcelona" in which major historians like Antoni de Bofarull (1829-1892) oriented the city towards a glowing future of industrial expansion (1878). This ideology of history underpinned the Exposition of 1888 as much as the renascence of elite Catalanism.

History followed the bourgeoisie-aristocracy into the twentieth century. Even under Francoist repression elite historians such as Ramón d'Abadal and Ferran Soldevila continued to research the history of Catalonia, although often publishing on royal or noble themes. In the 1950s Catalan historiography was revivified by the introduction of "international" canons of scientific history. The leader of this movement was Jaume Vicens Vives, whose vision was still influenced by a bourgeois background. His *Industrials i polítics* (Industrialists and Politicians), the final volume of his *Biografies catalanes*, for example, viewed the forebears of the Good Families as heroic figures. Moreover, the nineteenth century became a period of rediscovery, of a revolution in mentalities, of "the eternal springlike return of Catalonia" (1958:4).

The contrast between these men and the new history that has arisen since the 1960s and 1970s is evident in both fresh interpretations and changing interests. Catalan historiography has shifted from eulogistic accounts of great men towards socially based history. The laudatory portrayals have also been revised by more critical accounts. In the introduction to a critical study of the Catalan bourgeoisie written in 1972, Antoni Jutglar uses history to make claims about contemporary politics, attacking the bourgeoisie whom Vicens Vives had praised:

> The fundamental thread of the contemporary evolution of Catalan history evidently requires a clear and demythologized history of the role of the bourgeoisie. From whatever angle, this knowledge is basic: the history of political movements, the history of the working class, the understanding of cultural phenomena, of social conflicts, etc. (p. 29)

Jutglar orients the study of bourgeois-dominated society away from the buorgeoisie towards a utility in the history and struggle of other classes. The shift in academic/political interests is evident in the whole corpus of investigation and publication in such fields as history, sociology, literature, politics, and economics in contemporary Catalonia. Rather than continuing a focus on the bourgeois leaders of nineteenth- and twentieth-century Catalonia (although strong revisionist work continues), topics are influenced by democratization and politicization of Catalan society: labor history, the history of leftist parties and ideology, women's history, and critical reexamination of the bases and failures of nationalist revindication.

This shift in academic interpretations reflects the declining hegemony of the older elite. As the Good Families have lost their public domination of Catalan society since the Civil War, however, they have clung to this personal "ownership" of history as a genealogical foundation of group identity. Their claims are increasingly limited to an almost "domestic" circle. Yet it was through such a viewpoint that my work was consistently reinterpreted by them as genealogy or family biography rather than anthropology or social history. This comprehension reflected their sense of self-importance as well as of the task of history.

Politicized history similarly pervades current popular culture. One of the first Catalan films of the post-Franco period, *La Ciutat Cremada*, was a historical docudrama on the period from the Spanish-American War to the Tragic Week of 1909. The plot revolved around a bourgeois family caught up in these events. Yet a critic noted that

> the most profound lesson I have learned from this script by Sanz i Ribas is that which contemporary Catalan history confirms. It is the proletariat and the artisans who really confronted the oligarchic and imperialist government of Madrid. . . . In any case, as in the best cinema of Eisenstein, the pedagogical evocation of the

political past is sufficient to understand, in depth, the present.
(González Casanova 1976:8)

Accuracy, in such a context, is less meaningful than effect, than the call
to historical consciousness.

These class divisions in Catalan historical consciousness have existed
within their national and even international context. Whether politicized or private, each of these interpretations was shaped by centralist
attempts to recast events and figures in different modes.

Catalan History and the Nation-State

The struggle for a Catalan valuation of the past within Catalan identity
has been waged in many areas of writing, oral tradition, and action.
Every school text, for example, carries a message reflective of the concerns of identity and power. These messages are changed in accord with
those who control the educational system (for similar cases see Fitzgerald 1979; Bourdieu and Passeron 1976).

A Catalan elementary school textbook of the 1890s exemplified the
elite Catalanist spirit of the Lliga Catalana and the turn-of-the-century
autonomy movement. It valued the Catalan spirit of events as a separate and glorious tradition: "Catalans have always been distinguished
by their love of liberty, their respect for past traditions, their heroic
courage, their greatness of spirit under suffering, over which they have
always triumphed . . ." (Font Sagué 1899:19). The book further noted
the role of history in establishing a national consciousness: "If we wish
to underline the most important factors that have intervened in the revindication of Catalan Nationality . . . undoubtedly we would find
that, even more than the discords and vexations of centralism, they
have been historical studies" (Font Sagué 1899:9). The rhetoric was
calculated to unify a divided Catalonia by reference to a past dominated by merchants and financiers: the medieval bourgeoisie.

After the triumph of Franco in 1939 history was rewritten under
state control to glorify centralism and devalue national minorities. One
nationally used 1950s text on political formation lists among the evils
of the era of the House of Austria "the birth of Catalan separatism,
promoted by France, which, like England, had no other goal than to
precipitate the agony of Spain, whose power prevented them from
being rulers of the world" (*Formación Política*, n.d.:154, 163). Another 1950s text noted:

> And, nonetheless, the men who lived in regions so different in their
> accidents—soil, race, language, folklore, etc.,—were united in re-
> alizing a collective endeavor in History. This collective enterprise

of Spaniards is the destiny of Spain, the essence of the History of our people, that to whose service we must be disposed, and united in turn, although enjoying at the same time the variety of the accidental in each region. Without forgetting that all together we form Spain. (Mendoza Guinea 1954:10-11)

The opposition of essence and accident drew on scholastic categories to subordinate national movements to that Spain which is truly and eternally united.

Since the death of Franco not only academics but political parties have entered the fray by rediscovering distinctive versions of Catalan history. This struggle has been especially intense in the university. Historians such as Jordi Solé-Tura, who have moved from teaching to politics, have vigorously participated in Catalan definition against the Spanish state. Parties have also sponsored historical commemorations and even texts for children.

Yet, in addition to the academy, the struggle for history as a component of national revindication needs mass support and communication. The Franco regime extended its repression of history to popular culture. Festivals like the commemoration of the Siege of Barcelona (September 11), the Catalan Fourth of July, were banned: the reinauguration of that holiday in 1977 attracted one million people to Barcelona. Francoist writers and censors eliminated heroic figures from public view or denatured them as Hollywood stereotypes.

The renaming of streets epitomized this relentless erasure of meaningful structures of history. Barcelona's avenues had long been a mnemonic record of Catalan history, commemorating institutions, possessions, and heros. After 1939 the Avinguda de les Corts Catalanes, commemorating the Catalan parliament, became Avenida José Antonio Primo de Rivera, designating the founder of Franco's Falange. Most Barcelona residents called it the Gran Vía, resisting the latter association, but losing, in the process, a continual reminder of another part of their history. In most cases pre-Civil War names have only been resurrected in the last few years.

The importance of this street-naming process was not lost on Catalans. Streets in Barcelona already had been christened during the Spanish Republic with appropriately Catalanist names (Fabre and Huertas Claveria 1976). In a 1978 meeting in a mushrooming Barcelona suburb, political and economic interests clashed over which history new names would revitalize. Existing names, creations of the Fascist regime, were acceptable to few. One local historian offered universal figures, like Dalí, Miró, Picasso, and Albéniz, who might instructively be honored. A second, linked to the local elite, spoke of noble families, including his own, who had influenced the village. Discussion afterwards divided along rather different lines from Castilian versus Catalan—without reaching any compromise. It pointed to the underlying fragmentation of class and political loyalties that were growing apparent in the village in the post-Franco period. When history moves from besieged opposition to a positive statement of identity, other divisions of power become much more evident.

Conclusions

Historical consciousness in Catalonia embodies both the confluence and divergence of various levels of political and social conflict: local, national, and international. While the crux of the use of history has been the first two, the Catalan past *and* the interpretation of that past have obviously been influenced by international politics, economics, and culture. As a cosmopolitan center Barcelona has received ideas from London, Paris, and New York, and Catalonia has been the subject of investigations and publication by outsiders: anthropologists, political scientists, historians, and linguists. Appeals to outside scholars—and readers—have been made by both the state and Catalan groups, often with strikingly different interpretations.

As these examples suggest, the recovery of history in contemporary Catalonia is a complex process related to the reformulation of Catalan identity and the cohesion of power groups within Catalan society. In the four decades of Francoist rule (and, to varying degrees, in earlier periods of centralist domination), history was a polemical element in the definition of Catalonia as a nationality. History was not only a study of conflict but also a weapon in that study. Since the death of Franco and the liberalization of the Spanish regime the struggle for history has been realized in research and writing, in the renewal of commemorative markers and events, and in the protection of historical resources. Yet in this more open arena divisions within Catalan society have become more evident in competing claims for the legitimacy of a particular interpretation of shared past events. An understanding of these histories entails a sense of dynamic distribution of power in Catalonia while it contributes to the analysis of power struggles among various groups.

History and historical consciousness interact throughout the study that follows. While the primary import of this chapter was to set forth the major events and currents of the Catalan past necessary to an understanding of family and power, it has been impossible to isolate these themes artificially from a context of power. As the subsequent chapters will show, elite development has been reflective on itself as history in the making and has used that reflection within a struggle for hegemonic control. In an analysis of the cohesion and reproduction of power it is vital to remember that history, too, is power—and evokes the same sorts of responses from the disenfranchised.

CHAPTER III

FAMILY AND VARIATION
IN CATALONIA

In 1854 José de Manjarrés y de Bofarull, a Catalan pedagogue, admonished young ladies entering society on the importance of the family:

> The family is the basis of society, and it reflects exactly the customs of that society. All the categories, all the considerations, all the interests—in short, all the elements of that society—have their origin in the family. If the bonds of the one be corrupted, the other will not long avoid decay. Strip the family—from the parents, authority and government; from the siblings and relatives, sincerity and mutual relations; from the servants, honesty; and from all, affection—and respect for public power will disappear; dishonesty will be the soul of all contracts, fraud the only means of speculation, and treason the remedy for miscalculation.
>
> This is the reason that the individuals who constitute the family sacrifice within this circle a part of their natural liberty, which sacrifice represents propriety and good education. (P. 32)

Both the ideal of the family that Manjarrés favored and the importance that he imputed to it reflect his upper-class heritage. The industrialists and merchants of nineteenth-century Barcelona, like the aristocratic elites that preceded them, relied on extended households and strategic alliances to consolidate, distribute, and reproduce their resources. The structure and dynamics of the family through time are therefore basic to any understanding of cohesion and change in Barcelona society.

Basic sociocultural meanings of the family in Catalonia have been determined both by legal codes and by customs of alliance and succession. The chapter begins with an overview of the *typical* Catalan family, emphasizing the interplay of tradition and adaptation within the household. Adaptation here includes changes in the formal structure of the household as well as in the attitudes of those who live in and react to it.

A second section looks beyond the law codes at the urban industrial family itself. Urban power-holding families generally have resembled the landed and aristocratic families of Catalonia in their internal stratification by generation, age, and gender. The elite families of industrial

Barcelona appear conservative beside their European neighbors in terms of family size, authority, and distribution of inheritance. Nonetheless, interesting developments have taken place in family strategies, such as the division of the patrimony or the interaction of fathers and heirs—changes directly related to these families' new economic foundations. Furthermore, these modifications have been shaped by the political and economic relations of Catalonia to Spain and wider markets.

Finally, this chapter deals with the family as a political symbol. The social value of the family in Catalonia has consistently been enmeshed in the ideological implications of "tradition." The industrial upper class of turn-of-the-century Catalonia seized the family as a unique response to two political threats. On the one hand, the patterns of marriage and inheritance enshrined in the Catalan Civil Code expressed the unity of the Catalan people in counterpoint to other ethnic groups in Spain. Catalanists placed the family in opposition to state centralism: "By virtue of its natural essence, regionalism favors the family, while unionism perturbs it" (Torras Bages 1967:67). On the other hand, the household as an embodiment of hierarchy was used as an image through which to order the proletariat. In the work of the jurist and politician Enric Prat de la Riba Sarrà workers were portrayed as "children" with filial obligations towards their patriarchal employers. In this sense "family" became a mold for internal unity as well as a key symbol in external politics.

These three aspects of the family—structure, practice, and ideology—are flexible rather than rigid in response to changing circumstances. This chapter introduces basic dispositions of the Catalan family that have endured over centuries. The changes of the industrial period will be explored within this framework in subsequent chapters.

CIVIL LAW AND CHANGING TRADITION

In the days of Catalan independence, rights of marriage and succession were established by law codes continuously modified by legislation and practice. The reforms of 1716 froze the law code in form, while maintaining its authority. Thus, the Catalan Civil Code, which covers all legal ramifications of alliance and succession, is one of the few institutions of an independent Catalonia to have retained its authority into modern times. As such, law is evoked as a cornerstone of Catalan identity:

> If one says, as did one of our most distinguished jurists, Manuel Duràn i Bas, that the essence of a people is made manifest in their

language and their law, then, in the Catalan Civil Code we recognize one of the most important aspects of our personality. (Roca 1977:7)

In the nineteenth century, regional laws became a rallying point for various nationalist groups in Spain. Proponents ranged from rural Carlist reactionaries to cosmopolitan jurists influenced by European Romanticism, who searched in folklore for their quintessential national character (Trias de Bes 1960; Pi Sunyer 1960; see also Bard 1982:41-58; 172-211 on Navarra). In the twentieth century, legal scholars have undertaken further studies on local practice and other aspects of family law throughout Catalonia (Faus Condomines 1908; Maspons Anglasell 1907, 1935, 1938; de la Fuente Pertegaz 1921). The current codification (1960) was compiled from older statutes as well as from sociolegal studies (Font Rius 1960). The Generalitat de Catalunya has recently published a new and accessible paperback edition (*Compilació* 1982).

The economics of the traditional legal family have depended on an extended coresidential and coproductive household, often personified in the large rural homestead (*masia* or *casa pairal*). The *masia* sheltered a large agricultural family, its stock, and its major economic activities. The edifice itself, with stables and cellars for the storage of wealth, and space for a large family, was a physical symbol of lineage continuity

Figure 5
A Typical Catalan Farmstead: Casa Fluvià, Hospitalet d'En Bas

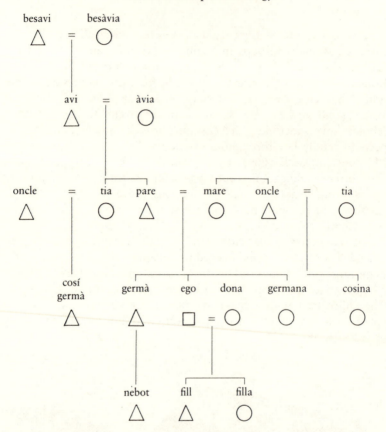

Figure 6
Catalan Kinship Terminology

and solidarity. Massive *cases pairals* still dominate the Catalan countryside, although some have been redeveloped as summer homes for new urban elite families.

In this type of household property and possessions are transmitted from generation to generation through a single, designated heir, the *hereu* (male) or *pubilla* (female). This heir generally is the firstborn male; in most parts of Catalonia the female inherits only in the absence of male issue, where she acts as a "substitute male" in the preservation of her patrilineage. If considerable property is involved, her husband (the *pubill*) and children may be required to adopt her surname as a patronym (Elliott 1963:37; Ferran Soldevila Zubiburu 1936:12). If the eldest son abandons the land, or otherwise proves unsuitable, his father may pass over him in favor of a brother or even a sister. Kin terms are schematized in Figure 6.

The heir's part is slightly more than three-fourths of the total estate. The Catalan Parliament raised this base share from two-thirds in 1585 as a strategy to consolidate property in the midst of a prolonged economic crisis. The remaining one-fourth is divided equally among all children, including the heir. This division constitutes the *llegítima*, the minimum portion for each child. For daughters the *llegítima* becomes the dowry through which their claims to the patrimony are bought off. Males are expected to use their portion to begin a career. Siblings who do not marry leave their share in a common household fund and participate in the everyday life of the *masia*, although in a position inferior to that of the heir. These relations are presented in Figure 7.

The *capítols matrimonials* (marriage contract) of the heir settles the inheritance for all childen of the family. This written agreement establishes both the exchange of wealth between newly allied families and the arrangements of succession within each family. The father legally contracts to pass on his estate to his heir. The heir, in turn, promises it to his firstborn son or future progeny. The continuity of both tenancy and labor are insured since the *hereu* and his wife, the *jove*, have vested interests in the prosperity of their future home (Maspons Anglasell 1907:7-74; Hansen 1977; Breton and Barruti 1978:56-61).

The marriage contract also ensures a continuity of authority. Although the father relinquishes ownership in the *capítols*, he retains control in the household and farm. This leads to certain domestic problems. While noninheriting children tend to escape domination through their socialization and careers, the relationship between the mother and the intruding *jove* is often tense. Even this is overshadowed by the male owner-producer axis: the status of the son-heir as owner *and* servant can lead to conflict, particularly in a situation in which the heir perceives innovation, rather than reproduction, as his primary survival strategy. If the structure does not change, behavior may conflict with legal patterns.

This basic stem-family varied according to its geographic or historical environments. In a period of legislative and practical autonomy legal change was a stimulus to social change. J. H. Elliott, for example, has commented on the far-reaching alterations that arose from the simple redefinition of the *llegítima* in the sixteenth century:

> By making it more difficult for the second and third sons to live on inherited wealth, the law of 1585 played its part in creating another one of the stock characters in Catalan family life—the so-called *fadristern* or *cabaler*, the younger brother who leaves the family home in search of his fortune. While the elder brother, by remaining at home to tend his estate, has helped to give Catalan

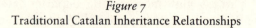

Figure 7
Traditional Catalan Inheritance Relationships

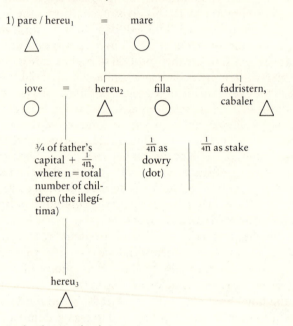

Inheritance relationships:

1) pare / hereu₁ = mare

jove = hereu₂   filla   fadristern, cabaler

¾ of father's capital + $\frac{1}{4n}$, where n = total number of children (the illegítima)

$\frac{1}{4n}$ as dowry (dot)

$\frac{1}{4n}$ as stake

hereu₃

In the absence of male issue:

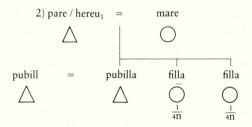

2) pare / hereu₁ = mare

pubill = pubilla   filla   filla

$\frac{1}{4n}$ $\frac{1}{4n}$

society its fundamental stability, the younger brother, forced to fend for himself, has injected into it a dynamic element. (1963:38)

The success of the *fadristern* also depended on historical circumstances. When opportunities contracted, he suffered. Thus, "some of the most serious cases of social tension in sixteenth and seventeenth century Catalonia may be traced to a family system which dispossessed younger sons and threw them out into a world that could not employ them" (Elliott 1963:39).

After 1716, however, changes were limited to the internal dynamics of the family rather than to legal forms. The tension between old forms and new strategies became particularly evident in periods of rapid progress. This strain, for example, is a major theme of a classic novel of nineteenth-century Catalonia, *La família dels Garriga*. Josep Pin Soler portrayed a wealthy rural family caught in the modernization of the Camp de Tarragona, a fertile agricultural plain south of Barcelona. Given that such a *casa pairal* was viewed as an archetypical representation of the legal ideal, the depiction of stress is significant. As in the customary model the father personified Catalan patriarchalism:

> He was ruled by the lofty ideal of authoritarian paternalism. In his house he never laughed. He often repeated, "Don't show your sons love, lest they cause you pain." He was convinced that a father should not speak to his sons except to reprimand them.
>
> The farm hands called him "Master," his children, "Father," and his sister, "Hereu." (Pin Soler 1980:22, first pub. 1887)

This father reproduced the socioeconomic relationships of the preindustrial *masia* in which he had been formed. His son, however, held a different awareness of the world and could not accept his role as owner-servant:

> Father and sons were victims of exaggerations. Ramon, raised by a rigid father at the beginning of the century . . . believed, as his father believed, that while there were Parliaments, Constitutions, newspapers, and, above all, soldiers . . . all was not well. Secular studies, he maintained, destroyed faith. The abolition of privileges, the division of goods, the even partial emancipation from *patria potesta* would make men disrespectful, without law or control.
>
> Ramon Junior . . . saw in all authority an enemy of public and private liberty and in his father the *summum* of all tyrannies. (1980:30)

Pin Soler favored a dialogue between generations: "Father and son needed a third party, since they understood each other so little, to tell them it is good to keep the learning of the past and to discard the errors" (1980:30). But this was not to be; instead, internecine conflict destroyed the family.

Echoes of such conflict remain in contemporary capitalist agricultural development. In the 1960s Edward Hansen studied changing economic and social structures of the family in Vilafranca del Penedès, a modernizing viticultural region south of Barcelona. New values of land, career, and education emanating from the metropolis had challenged the strategic divisions of rights by age, sex, and generation that underlay the traditional stem-family. In sibling relationships, for example, Hansen found that *cabalers* with specialized training were becoming successful in industrial and business careers, while the heir remained bound to the land. Children perceived the land to be declining in value and to lack any future. Furthermore, the father ruled the heir, whose economic prospects were also constrained by potential demands on the *llegítima*. One result of this conflict between traditional valuations of sibling roles and a new economic environment was a marked increase of law suits among siblings over rights and expenses (Hansen 1977:101-104).

The father-heir relationship was even more problematic. Some heirs chose to abandon their status entirely, opting for the potential success of a professional career. In other cases tension and negative feelings emerged:

> The heir's period of deprivation may last into very late manhood, depending upon the longevity of his father. "I have only ten years of life left that I could enjoy, and that guy . . . is as strong as an oak," said one middle-aged man to me. In these cases where the father becomes a tyrant, the heir sullenly waits for the old man to die. Although I do not know the statistical frequency of this phenomenon, it is frequent enough to have a name: "the heir's curse." (Hansen 1977:101)

The chronological sweep of these examples points to the confluence of personal and historical factors in the situation of any heir. Tension might erupt because of a despotic father, but the economic basis of the family would still remain intact. When the context is changing rather than stable, however, the need for innovation within a legally fixed system augments intergenerational problems. In industrial families changes in both the mode of production and the pace of innovation have thus complicated traditional generational transitions.

The Practice of the Urban Industrialist Family

While living within a historical legal framework shared with rural and noble families, the urban industrialist family has represented a special interpretation of the *casa pairal*. Residence exemplifies the pattern of change. In the urban upper classes of the nineteenth century residence became separated from the place of production. While an eighteenth-century textilist like Erasme de Gònima might build his palace next to his factory, by the end of his career he had acquired a country farm for retreat from the city. Bankers and industrialists of the nineteenth cen-

nerships of the period also tended to incorporate all male siblings, as did later family corporations.

This step was a major transformation of the stem-family model. The *masia* reproduced itself via a cycle of expansion and contraction in each generation; both the patrimony and the number that it supported remained relatively constant through time. Inclusion of all males established a geometrical progression in the numbers of owners and managers. This change was facilitated in part by new forms of commercial organization. It also drew upon a transformation in economic mentality that transcended individual family fortunes.

Capital, rather than land, constituted the urban industrial patrimony. The elite perceived this capital as more easily divisible than property, especially as the concept of stock gained popularity. Furthermore, the upper class saw industrial wealth, unlike land, to be capable of almost indefinite expansion. An aristocratic historian expressed this view in 1878 for the city as a whole:

> Is it by any means possible to imagine that the successive increment of Barcelona, in the sum of all its parts and in each single one of them, will not continue? That it will be detained on the road so majestically begun towards material greatness, given its richness, its constancy, and the character and intelligence of its children? Never! It has been great since the dawn of history, is greater now, and will be still greater in the future! (de Bofarull i Brocà 1878:58)

This vision of capital did not influence strategies concerning resources neither expandable nor easily divisible, such as the opera box or the family mausoleum. There, the designated heir retained sole possession, as in the *casa pairal*.

This generalized inclusion of male offspring did not eradicate the privilege of the firstborn. In his detailed study of the Serra Feliu family, Ianasi Terradas has noted that the eldest son always held a controlling advantage in company stock (1979:104-111). Both the cultural stress on sibling cooperation and the continuation of dominance—and reaction by the younger siblings—erupted in Narcís Oller's *Febre d'or* (Gold Fever, 1890-1892). In this classic novel of the Catalan industrial revolution a businessman has assembled a new brokerage with his brothers and affines in subordinate roles. One brother not only avoids the firm but even the family Christmas dinner. Responding to the possibility that the sibling might be ashamed, the businessman retorts:

> "Ashamed? Of what? Of working for a brother who loves him and who is trying to improve his lot? Ashamed to spend Christmas with his siblings? Are you ashamed?"

tury lived near their office, but their children were more likely to establish their residences in the new prestige districts of the city. In the twentieth century the idea of the coresidential household has faded, as heirs have sought distinct apartments in the palace, or even independent residences. Nevertheless, they often maintain close contact through meals or vacations. One informant suggested that the country house has become a more meaningful center for family unity than the scattered urban apartments. Thus the spacial representation of the household may return to the *casa pairal* within a building totally divorced from any productive functions.

While the physical unity of the family as productive unit dispersed, the economic unity of the household continued in new forms. The simple household gave way to the family corporation, yet intensive usage of alliance and succession remained prominent. The urban bourgeois family has reinterpreted, but not abandoned, the basic axes of the Catalan family—generation, birth order, and sex. In order to understand this development, however, it is necessary to review the dynamics of the family as well as its apparent formal structures.

Fathers and Sons

Patriarchalism, grounded in authority and succession, is still one of the most striking aspects of the urban elite Barcelona family. A young businessman with extensive experience in both Catalonia and Madrid characterized the difference between the two societies: "The Catalan family is like the Castilian family, but with more interference." This interference can encompass decision making within the family or firm and control over actions and plans. The depth of the father-son bond has long been idealized in Barcelona by the identification of the sons as the "second existence" of the father (Sanpere Miquel 1879:31). This epithet appears in family biographies from the eighteenth century to the present (Pourret 1796:26, rev. ed. 1844:7; Prat de la Riba Sarrá 1898:158-159; Moreu Lacruz 1921:49). The obituary of the nineteenth-century textile magnate Claudio Arañó expounds upon this concept:

> Father of a numerous family, he attended to it with exquisite care, taking pains to give his children, primarily males, a complete education on moral, religious, intellectual, and physical principles with the efficient aid of his loving wife, an exemplary mother. . . .
>
> He did not ask what the desires of his children were in order to satisfy them, nor did he look for ways to spare them suffering. He studied their natural dispositions in order to convert them into talents and abilities, and he tried to uncover their righteous senti-

ments and impulses in order to convert them into inclinations and habits. . . . He showed himself in these areas to be severe without hardness, soft without weakness, as a father should be. . . .

He would put his sons to work in the factory when they reached adolescence, continuing their education in special classes. . . .

As a model husband and father, Arañó exemplified the perfect citizen. (Torelló Borrás 1888:17-22)

Even though characterized as a paragon of self-sacrifice, this ideal paternal role has entailed a complete domination of sons in education, career, and personality. The similarity to Pin Soler's nineteenth-century agricultural patriarch is striking.

These past observations concur with the opinions of many contemporary Barcelona businessmen. One factory owner whose thirty-year-old sons have had much more specialized training in law and management than he nonetheless insisted: "I may ask for their opinions. But the one who makes the decisions around here is ME." In case of his sudden incapacity power would pass to his wife, acting *in place of the father* rather than as an independent female and extending his control.

Within the family corporation, even more than in agricultural work, there have been no inevitable mechanisms for retirement. Thus, in the case of the Bank of Barcelona, a major public corporation, Manuel Girona Agrafel held firm control from his foundation of the bank in 1844 to his death, at the age of 90, in 1905. Towards the end of his tenure he resisted innovations. Thus, the bank proved ill-adapted to the business climate of the new century and collapsed only fifteen years after Girona's death (Cabana 1978:87-110). This pattern recurs in contemporary family businesses. A manager, for example, criticized the sons of a well-known textile firm: "The first day those sons ever made a decision there was the day that they carried the old man out of the factory, dead."

Sons may react in many ways to the authority of the father. Within a continued structure of paternalism the heir can reproduce the attitudes of the father, wait sullenly for control, or leave the business. Generally, while structures of inheritance and control have changed only slowly, interpersonal dynamics have nonetheless been an index of the tension between conservatism and innovation. In a contemporary novel one such heir muses by his father's deathbed: "He never paid any attention to my projects. From now on, all this is mine" (Benguerel 1955:10).

Other sons leave for professional careers—a reaction more common in the bleak economic situation of Catalan industry in the 1970s. Even so, these new professionals tend to maintain frequent contact and exchange with their families.

Finally, some sons may rebel more completely. Many [ ]ist artists and their clique in turn-of-the-century Barcelo[ ] industrial families rejecting the business world of their fa[ ] artist-writer Santiago Rusiñol, dealt with his own escape [ ]ineering industrialist grandfather in the popular *Auca d[ ] teve* (novel 1907, play 1917; see Pla 1942:19-39; R[ ] 1950:6). The title character continued the shop of his fathe[ ] father, yet ultimately admitted that "I have worked hard i[ ] I have done no more than that: work. . . . I have never liv[ ] not know what life is. I have passed through, no more[ ] 1968:119). Esteve's son, Ramonet, rejected business to beco[ ] ist. He was admonished, however, to

keep in mind now and forever that you had a father who w[ ] ing in this world, so that you might be something; wh[ ] money so that you would have it . . . and that if you ever do [ ] work on the road that you have undertaken, you could n[ ] done it without me. (1968:119-120)

Clearly the father-son bond was not completely broken for the [ ] The modernist artist renounced his bourgeois forebears on th[ ] dation of wealth and power. Moreover, he established bonds [ ] style and tastes of the aristocracy that suggest the ongoing synth[ ] power groups into a cohesive elite.

As the next chapter shows, the extent and channelling of tensio[ ] shaped by forces extrinsic to the family as well as by interaction a[ ] its members. Behind the continuous facade of an impersonal com[ ] conflict has been a constant evolutionary force. Moreover, paterna[ ] has taken on new meanings for both sons and workers.

Brothers

While patriarchalism has remained a constant motif modified by [ ] extent and direction of conflict, the relationship of elite male siblin[ ] has changed with industrialization and new patterns of capitalizatio[ ] The major shift in sibling relationships in the industrial family, appa[ ] ent even in Arañó's obituary, was the replacement of the single hei[ ] with the inclusion of all sons. This was *not* a change in the legal cod[ ] so much as one of elite practice. In such major families as the Jovers [ ] (AHPB: Bellsolell 1865, 2:306), the Villavecchias (AHPB: Moreu 1872: [ ] 2,059; AHPB: Pallós 1877), the Gironas (AHPB: Planas Compte 1855, [ ] 1857), and the López (AHPB: Pallós 1855), more equal distribution re[ ]placed the *hereu*'s role after the mid-nineteenth century. Family part-

"Not I, but he, poor boy, still dresses like a worker."
"What of it? In *germanor* [brotherhood] there are neither poor nor rich." (1948:302, first pub. 1890-1892)

As in the case of modernist rebels this brother becomes an artist.

Sibling ties changed much more in response to new opportunities and mentality than did father-son bonds. These changes, in turn, extended the father's control within the family and the factory, while expanding the range of the household as an elite unit of production. These male roles, however, were complemented by equally interesting continuities and changes in elite females.

Sisters and Wives

While new economic circumstances changed male roles, the economic status of females has remained relatively unchanged until recent generations. As widows and mothers, wives have achieved economic power, but only as an extension of their husband's control, which they held temporarily until a son came of age. Certain women of the Barcelona elite were said to have held onto such power after a son had reached his maturity—but such conduct was severely censured.

Until the 1940s this limited potential for power as an affine was much more than an upper-class woman might expect from her lineal inheritance. Daughters were "bought off" with dowries that cut their ties to family production; property was favored over stock as the appropriate coin of the *llegítima*. Even after the Civil War, in a major familial textile firm daughters were given a share in the corporation only to be bought out by private agreement. Their *llegítima* was enlarged, but they were excluded from patrilineal ownership. A family member lamented: "You don't want to *have* to work with your in-laws." There has been a continuous exchange of women among such families: social cohesion balances the competition of independent units of production. This is reflected in an interesting fashion in marriage ties, which will be discussed in Chapter VII.

Women did become heirs in the absence of male siblings. In no elite cases that I found, however, did this *pubilla* emerge into the active role of the widow, much less the male heir. Instead, marriages have been arranged with a man of known managerial skills, even more than class position, who is subsumed by the reproduction of his wife's family company.

Two important corollaries qualify these limitations on women's public economic roles. First, the social importance of women in the cohesion of the Barcelona elite has been paramount not only in social and cultural life but in economic and political action. The social/symbolic capital dominated by women has cemented the group force within which men acted. This pattern is also repeated in other European industrial elites, as noted by Davidoff (1973) for England and Goblot (1967) and Darrow (1979) for France. Thus in order to accurately portray the cohesion of the elite, I juxtapose the economic organization of males discussed in the next two chapters with the privatized social networks of the salon and visit in Chapters VI and VII.

A second and more easily neglected point is that women did not necessarily accept the roles into which the economic and social system of the elite placed them. Women of the first, upwardly mobile generations had the experience of rural or lower-class life in which their contributions to the household economy were significant. In subsequent generations their daughters may have had the experience of acting as "corporate widows." In my conversations several older women expressed regret that they had been excluded from a more active public life.

As in earlier examples, reactions can also be channelled into emotion and awareness without any surface change in family form. This is glimpsed in a novel by the Catalan Dolors Monserdà de Macià (1845-1919), herself from a bourgeois family. In La fabricanta, originally published in 1904, she portrayed a woman of the early industrial revolution, marginalized by social custom from the family firm in which she earlier had participated actively:

> Once the business reached its maximum and the house was bought and opened, providing large warehouses for the sale of items, Pere Joan, who ranked among the largest industrialists of Barcelona . . . no longer felt it appropriate that his wife continue to work in public view. Protesting that she deserved a rest, he deprived her of her career. But Antonieta, removed from behind the counter and from contact with the workers in whose sorrows and joys she had always participated, with her son on partial board at the College, . . . despite her large and luxurious home, did not know how to resign herself to the life of a parasitic plant amidst the velvet and trappings that surrounded her. Having passed her entire life in the shop, she did not understand the attraction that other women of her new position felt for walks and visits. . . . Moreover, the thought that her intervention was unnecessary for the good of her house hurt her deeply. (1972:166-167)

The evolution of urban capitalism, then, did not necessarily open new opportunities for women of the elite. In fact, as this citation suggests, it may have opened a new awareness for them of the opportunities they were being denied.

This section has reviewed the urban industrialist-financier family forms of Barcelona in relationship to the more commonly described idealized rural-legal stem-family. The most striking structural change in the urban industrial pattern, although still not embodied in a legal alteration, was the expansion of sibling inheritance. Yet, even in relatively constant areas such as the prohibition of women from economic life industrialization has influenced the balance of public and private roles or the changing perceptions of relatively unchanging status. An understanding of the relationship of traditional and adaptive family forms, however, remains incomplete without consideration of the manipulation of cultural values. Even as the elite lived within a malleable social system, it made political use of very traditional models.

SOCIAL STRUCTURE AND IDEOLOGY

The *masia* was important as a symbol in Catalan political discourse in addition to its social functions. In particular, turn-of-the-century Catalanists used the family as an emblem of a historically homogeneous Catalonia in opposition to the encroachments of the centralist state. At the same time these writers evoked the household *within* Catalonia as a template for social relations. The Good Families responded to popular unrest with the imagery of Catalonia—and the Catalan family firm—as a collective, sentimental, and disciplined household. That unit which was fundamental to elite social organization became a cornerstone of their ideological manipulation of industrial society.

Like the customary forms and legal structures of the Catalan family, the political symbolism of the household has a long history. In the autonomous Barcelona of the early modern period J. H. Elliott has pointed out that

> with every individual as part of a family, Catalan society was a society of interlocking families, rising in a pyramid at the summit of which stood a patriarchal king. "Hijos míos," "my children" was the phrase with which Philip IV addressed the Catalans in the Corts of 1626. Down from the king ran the ties of dependence, linking family to family to the very bottom of the social scale. (1963:40)

The nineteenth-century rediscovery of the family by Catalan jurists, politicians, folklorists, and national apologists reinvigorated earlier political usage. Some apologists treated the family as the foundation of a peculiarly Catalan social order. This position was synthesized in the writings of Josep Torras Bages (1846-1916), Bishop of Vic and ideologue of the conservative Catholic sector of upper-class Catalanism. In his influential *La tradició catalana* (The Catalan Tradition, originally published in 1892), he wrote:

> The family is the substance and base of social organization. Social decadence supposes decay in the family. Social regeneration, social reconstruction, must begin with the reconstruction of the family. We turn our eyes to our Spain, and we will see that the spirit is strongest in those nationalities [*països*] that have the strongest regional spirit. Love for the homestead [*casa pairal*], the desire to conserve the patrimony, the order of the family hierarchy . . . all is superior where regional life has been maintained, even in decayed form, as opposed to those areas which are confused with that great mass, the nation. (1967:67)

Torras Bages' views echoed those that Manjarrés had expressed some thirty-five years earlier. Yet, in contrast, for Torres these words were linked to national identity, not etiquette. His was not an emotional statement of traditional values but an explicit and reasoned political conservatism.

Other ideologues of bourgeois Catalanism championed reinstatement of older institutions as well as the creation of new laws adapted to the needs and values of Catalonia rather than all of Spain. These men were not blind to variation and conflict within their society. Nonetheless, nationalism was a cause that had to dwarf internal differences (Solé-Tura 1974:233-263; 285-294). As the journalist Gaziel put it: "Bourgeois Catalanism had a serious internal contradiction: it wished to radically reform Spain without causing even the slightest disturbance in Catalonia" (cited in Solé-Tura 1974:290).

It was in this vein that an appeal to the sentimental values of the family could become particularly effective within Catalonia. For reformers the family was the ideal template on which to arrange the hierarchy of class interests that had emerged in industrial Catalonia:

> The issue of the moment is the reconstruction of social structure accommodating it in all aspects to the natural and spontaneous development of social life. It must start from the unity of industry . . . and must take as a foundation the gradation, natural as well, of natural territorial societies—that is, the community, the county, and the region.
>
> The industrial corporation must be the family of labor. In it, all who participate in any branch of production must fit, each in his place. (Prat de la Riba Sarrà 1898:46-48, cited in Solé-Tura 1974:240)

The full meaning of this use of family imagery is apparent in the career of one major Catalanist politician, Enric Prat de la Riba Sarrá (1870-1917), one of the central figures in the rebirth of Catalan nationalism and the foundation of the Lliga. He wrote for and edited a Catalanist daily, *La Veu de Catalunya* (The Voice of Catalonia). A linguist, a philosopher, and, above all, an astute politician, he was the architect of the Mancomunitat de Catalunya, as well as its first president until his premature death.

Prat de la Riba was also a pragmatist. He wanted to ground Catalan industry in an ordered society that would link owners and workers according to the pattern of the traditional household. In this he resembled certain other European social thinkers of his day, notably Frédéric Le Play, who popularized the term "stem-family" in his writings on the social organization of labor in southern France (1866; 1871). Le Play, indeed, saw the Catalan family as an ideal model for industrial organization, and his influence, in turn, was felt in Catalan industrial sociology (1871:30). Yet these ideas extended beyond sociological reflection: Prat de la Riba's charter for the industrial mill town (the *colonia*) became a basic organizing device for capital and labor in industrial Catalonia. This was set forth in his *Ley jurídica de la industria* (Judicial Law of Industry 1893).

The expressed aim of the *Ley jurídica* was to derive industrial society from the family: "Some embryo of industrial law must have already existed in the primordial family. . . . Just as political and religious aspects were dominated by the patriarchal family, so, too, was the economy" (1898:4). On this foundation Prat de la Riba moved to modern business. En route, the image of the family was so strengthened that all national industry took on the visage "of an immense family" (1898:45; see also Bofill Matas 1979:72).

Within this collective consciousness

> the word *house [casa]*, applied to all classes of industrial exploitation, is in itself a revelation. It manifests the nature [of industrial activity] with more precision and clarity than the most detailed and careful analysis. *Casa* means family, and thus, the *industrial house* will be the *industrial family*, the primary industrial society. In this society we distinguish a personal element, grouped in a hierarchy under the patron or entrepreneur or owner [individual or collective], and a material element—a locus, material, or instrument of industry. (Prat de la Riba Sarrà 1898:76)

The identification of family and factory became clearest in the areas of control and succession. The industrial household is organized under a patron: father and patriarch. While his death ends a phase in the genealogy of the business, it does not terminate either the company or the family, which enter new generations (1898:157). To mold this continuity, Prat de la Riba explicitly evoked Catalan tradition:

> These considerations suggest to us an observation on the excellence of a popular Catalan custom that has a tremendous impact on industrial life and is one of the causes of the relatively flourishing state of agriculture and even of the progress and development of other sectors. We refer to the institution of the *heir [hereu]*. . . . The *hereu*, continuation of the personality of the father and the unity of the family, is the patron *par excellence*—who maintains the house, saving it from that dissolution which is, for it, synonymous with death. (1898:161)

Prat de la Riba, in effect, was transposing the *casa pairal* to the factory. In so doing, he retransformed an instrument of elite capital organization into a national symbol.

The sections of the *Ley jurídica* devoted to labor also work within a traditionalist framework of Catalan identity and history. In these, Prat de la Riba referred to medieval or archaizing structures such as the revival of guilds. Moreover, in his conceptualization of the *colonia* or mill town he tended to adapt the feudal manor to a new setting.

The *colonia* was conceived as a self-sufficient nucleus of production near an energy source such as a river but isolated from any urban agglomeration. The owner would provide all facilities for work as well as for the life of the workers: schools, housing, nurseries and hospitals, chapels and recreational facilities. He would also maintain a family home there in which to pass time each year. In return for creating this home for the workers the owner would expect total control:

> All or nearly all of the faculties that the patron needs are established in his rights of property. He can rely on this faculty to forbid in his *casa* anything other than certain fixed practices and customs and to expel from the house those who deviate from them. He can prohibit the entrance of persons and things—newspapers or magazines, for example—that do not agree with him. The head of the household, the chief of the industrial family, fixes a certain regimen. On entering the industrial family, workers voluntarily accept this regime. If they tire of it, they can leave. (1898:262)

These theoretical statements are all the more significant because of the prevalence of mill towns in Catalan industrial organization. Even today, these towns dot the landscape. The *colonia* did more than link owners and producers into a traditionalized unit, however. It also isolated laboring groups from each other and undercut the potential for organized opposition to capitalist owners.

Working with the members of a colony in Ametlla de Merola, near Barcelona, Ignasi Terradas found that the ideology of the family was even internalized by workers. He observed "a continuum established between production and consumption. The relations of social reproduction, expressed mainly in kinship, neighborhood, and friendship relations, become embedded in labor relations." Furthermore, he noted "a tendency to self-exploitation resulting from both the exclusive factory-family link and from the expectations of promotion derived from paternalism" (1979:46-47). Workers even adopted kin terminology in speaking with each other.

The colony became the *casa pairal* writ large. Yet this model also was linked to the relationship of Catalan industrialists to their weak and dependent state. The *colonia* rose with the attempt of the industrialists to become a political ruling class and has faded with their economic decline: mill towns were no longer built in this fashion after the Civil War. Terradas summarizes the relationship of local organization and the state:

> It is perhaps not altogether pure coincidence that the greatest theorist of Catalan nationalism, Prat de la Riba, was also the great theorist of the colony system, arguing for the privatization of public authority in the face of the decaying Spanish state. The industrial bourgeoisie needed to provide an alternative superstructure for capitalist accumulation. However, it very soon realized that it was better to rely on the Spanish state to protect and reinforce the conditions of a market economy than to construct a political superstructure on its own, i.e., an independent or autonomous Catalonia. (1978:48)

Despite its perdurance in the popular imagination of former mill town inhabitants, though, this imagery of the family has declined in political utility and emotional impact since the collapse of the Lliga. As the Good Families have been replaced by newer politicized elites, their symbolic manipulation of the family has been overshadowed by new themes. In 1960, in fact, Franco felt the *casa pairal* so neutral an element in Catalan identity as to permit the formal codification of the Catalan Civil Code in the heyday of cultural repression. Today, despite the republication of this code by the Generalitat and ongoing investigations by the academic community into traditional farmsteads, other symbols—language, education, and "culture"—have emerged as more powerful and widespread indices of Catalan political identity.

Conclusions

This chapter has placed the primary structures and values of the Catalan upper-class family within their social and historical contexts. The
Good Families emerged within a particular social and cultural heritage,
while adapting this heritage to new political and economic circumstances. The kinship patterns of Barcelona in themselves are generally
familiar from other European societies. To understand these structures
in class formation, it is necessary to see kinship as strategy and practice
as much as any formal code. Moreover, strategies are bound to the ideological reproduction of the elite and its interactions with other groups
in Catalan society.

While these patterns are intrinsic to the social and economic formation of an upper class, other classes did not show the same patterns.
Marriage contracts as well as the contemporary practice of Barcelona
workers suggest the class foundations of an elite world view that led to
the adoption of the *casa pairal* as an inclusive national symbol. The
elite maintained its cohesion and dominance through ideological projection and manipulation as well as through its internal and institutional organization. "Family" synthesized representation with organization, although the relationship between public and private, practice
and ideology, became complex—as the work of Prat de la Riba illustrates.

In order to understand the ideology of the family as it has been used
by the elite we must follow the economic and social value of the household, too, within this group. Family, here, has been presented as the
nexus of interactions between old legal codes and landed power groups
and the creative strategies of new businessmen. This same process has
also been crucial in the history of the organization of management. The
following two chapters will develop these relations of economic reproduction and alliance.

CHAPTER IV

LA CASA INDUSTRIAL:
HOUSEHOLD AND COMPANY IN
THE INDUSTRIAL ELITE

The last chapter explored the general meanings of the family in Catalan society with regard to structure, strategy, and ideology. This chapter and the next will focus on the evolution of the family as an economic institution in the grand bourgeoisie. Although "family" has pervaded the economic, social, and political organization of Barcelona power groups for centuries, structures of capital accumulation and reproduction have dominated the transformations of the past 150 years. These structures include not only the biological and social family but also the factory, bank, and other enterprises in which the elite family participates. The relationship of family and factory may be as "businesslike" as the recruitment of the sons as managers—or as intimate as the choice of marital prospects for the daughters. In Catalonia all these economic ties can be subsumed by the label *casa industrial*, the industrial household.

A composite analysis of elite family histories from Barcelona suggests a regular pattern of socioeconomic development from individual entrepreneurs to limited-liability corporations in which ownership is divorced from day-to-day operation of the company. This pattern has been formed by organizational, demographic, and economic pressures. Law codes and preindustrial business practices provided nineteenth-century Catalan businessmen with basic structures for capital organization. These codes have been modified through strategic interaction in legislation as well as economic use. Birth, marriage, and kin ties also have influenced industrial organization as entrepreneurs passed on their patrimony. Finally, this evolution has been linked to Catalan participation in a world economy as mediated through Spanish national economic policies.

Despite my analytic separation these factors share an interdependent evolution. As George Marcus has shown in his studies of Texas elites, legal institutions such as the corporation deeply influenced the organization of the upper-class family:

A legally devised plan to transfer and conserve patrimonial capital in one generation becomes in the next generation an organizational framework for extended family relations—actually a formal model or surrogate of the family with law, rather than the founding entrepreneurial patriarch, as its source of authority. (1980:859)

This intermeshing of social structure, corporate forms, and macroeconomic development has been equally significant in Catalan history.

The present chapter draws on individual cases and synthetic models to clarify the changing industrial household and its role in Barcelona society through time. Analysis begins with the legal framework for Catalan industrial-commercial organization as formulated by the Spanish commercial code of 1829, which introduced the limited-liability corporation into the Iberian Peninsula. Modifications in both law and custom—notably, the development of a paralegal close or family corporation—are then examined to follow organizational evolution for Barcelona in relation to national and international changes.

On this basis, discussion turns to social and cultural changes. The reproduction of wealth in Barcelona long has been represented by a folkloric "Law of Three Generations" still current among members of the upper class. This historical paradigm traces a family from a founding grandfather, through the sons who expand a business, to the grandsons who ruin or abandon it. While such a generalization does not coincide with the career of every family, or with every sector of Catalan industry, it is a revealing ideological interpretation of elite history. Furthermore, it has reverberations beyond economics: the acquisition of prestige examined in Chapter Six presents an almost direct inversion of this three-generation model.

Commercial Law: Codification Versus the Practice of the Company

The Principality of Catalonia was the birthplace of the first mercantile-maritime code of modern Europe, the thirteenth-century *Llibre del Consulat del Mar* (Book of the Tribunal of Maritime Commerce). This code, like the Catalan Civil Code, retained its force even after the reforms of the Nova Planta in 1716. Its application, however, was never uniform throughout Catalonia: cities and districts were free to establish their own variants. Until 1829 a crazy-quilt of local customs and rules governed commerce in the Spanish dominions (Gómez de la Serna and Reus García 1869:29).

Mercantile enterprise before the nineteenth century was organized on the basis of individual economic responsibility or simple partnerships in which two or more investors shared profits and risks (Vilar

1962, 3:144-187). The "privileged" or protected company, forerunner of the modern corporation, emerged throughout Europe in the seventeenth century, under the patronage of monarchs seeking profits from overseas expansion (Freedman 1979:xiii; Garrigues and Uría 1953:59). British imperial expansion, for example, built on the East India Company (1599-1858), while Dutch colonialism relied on the Dutch East India Company (1602-1798). In Catalonia the privileged company did not appear until the eighteenth-century thrust of Catalan commerce into the New World. In 1709 Catalan merchants banded together in the short-lived Companyia nova de Gibraltar. In mid-century Catalans formed the Companyia de Comerç de Barcelona, dedicated to the Latin American trade. This company was consolidated in 1785 with a parallel Basque venture to form the Compañía Guipuzcoana de Caracas. These were the last privileged companies formed to exploit the Spanish colonial empire; their rights ended with Latin American independence in the nineteenth century (Vilar 1962, 3:464-486; Molas Ribalta 1977:121-171).

In the early 1800s two major changes swept through European commercial law. First, regulation became relatively standardized on a national and even continental level. These new laws shared both a new economic environment of burgeoning industrialization and the pervasive political influence of the Napoleonic Code of 1807 (Gómez de la Serna and Reus García 1869:27-29; Freedman 1979:12-15). Among the provisions of this code was the second major change: the creation of the nongovernmental limited-liability firm. The American historian Nicholas Murray Butler described this innovation as "the greatest single discovery of modern times. . . . Even steam and electricity are far less important than the limited-liability corporation, and they would be reduced to comparative impotence without it" (cited in Cataldo 1953:473). The joint-stock corporation became a vehicle for the assembly of capital for buildings, energy, machinery, and transport. In Catalonia it transformed cottage industry and house banking into an imposing new form of production. The corporation, in turn, shaped the structuring of power-holding classes.

The establishment of the corporation marked a shift in the impetus of capitalist economic exploitation from government patronage to associations of private investors. European governments, in fact, soon came to see private corporations as a threat to national sovereignty:

When businessmen in the nineteenth century chose the corporation as the most appropriate instrument for the immense industrial potential that capitalism was discovering, they found this very instrument viewed askance by the state. The state did not wish to abandon to its citizens an instrument that was dangerous because of its economic power and the potential abuses of which shareholder and creditors might be victims. (Garrigues and Uría 1953:59-60)

The relationship between private associations and the state depended upon economic development as well as each state's legislative process. In core industrializing societies like the United States and England, with their common law tradition, the corporation was defined through court cases and legislation over the entire first half of the nineteenth century (Dodd 1948; Gower 1953). In France the 1807 code was dramatically replaced by contrary legislation before a stable code was reached in 1867 (Freedman 1979; Treillard 1953). Spanish development followed the French model; changes in the peninsular corporation, however, have been both more extreme in their range and more susceptible to external interest groups.

The first attempts to write a uniform national commercial code for Spain began in the early nineteenth century. Wars and government instability delayed the ratification of any text until 1829. Nevertheless, Spain preceded nations such as Portugal (1833), Holland (1834), Austria (1842), and most German and Italian city-states (by 1865) in this reform. As in the French code, Spain had a minimal definition of and control over the newly created corporation. Instead of a comprehensive examination of the organization and responsibilities of such bodies the government relied on commissions of authorization to restrain the company. As in the United States and France each limited-liability firm required individual authorization from the government (Freedman 1979:15-18; Dodd 1948).

The Spanish code of 1829 recognized three basic forms of the company. The first is the simple partnership, or *sociedad colectiva*. Here, all participants share equally in the ownership, management, and responsibilities for loss of the company. Second is the limited partnership, or *sociedad en comandita*. In this form a simple partnership expands through the presence of a silent or loaning investor, the *comanditario*, who is isolated from the management of the company but also protected from its liabilities. A variant of this form, the *sociedad en comandita por acciones*, divides the loan into negotiable shares. Finally, there appears the limited-liability corporation, or *sociedad anónima*, in which the extent of participation as well as loss is limited to a stock investment.

Of these formats the joint-stock corporation was the most unfamiliar in the nineteenth century and therefore was viewed most warily by state governments. In 1848 Spain followed the actions of France and England in banning most authorizations for new corporations. Two primary motives underlay these prohibitions. Governments that used corporations "in the public interest" were chary of those devoted to basic manufacturing (Dodd 1948:1,352-1,353; Freedman 1979:46). At the same time, fraudulent companies, with abuses of power or serious inaccuracies in their reported assets, alarmed both rulers and investors (Freedman 1979:44, 46). The depression of 1846/1847 finally precipitated drastic legal reform.

The Spanish ban on the corporation was both more complete and more enduring than that of its European neighbors. In France the *société en commandite par actions* remained a useful alternative to non-limited-liability investment (Freedman 1979:112-114). In Spain this form, too, was prohibited (Tortella Casares 1975). The English relied on companies ostensibly chartered elsewhere prior to reestablishment of limited liability in 1856 (Freedman 1979:132-134). Spain, however, did not derogate its ban until the liberal revolution of 1868.

For two decades Spanish investment was forced into public works such as railroads and mining. These investments made huge profits for foreign investors, while Spain fell behind other industrial nations with regard to its own basic manufacturing. In an industry like textiles, basic to Catalan prosperity, this legal morass evoked even more complicated countermeasures:

> The government had an ambivalent position towards the textile industry. On the one hand, it banned joint-stock companies, thus closing off the most important route to the capital market. On the other, as an insufficient and demogogic compensation it conceded a tariff protection to textiles that permitted the industry to survive and that was, in reality, a regressive subvention directly paid for by the nation. (Tortella Casares 1968:76)

After 1869 Spain revived its 1829 code, omitting the review tribunal that had earlier put some check on corporate activities. Again, this reaction was more extreme than that of most other European nations. France, for example, while eliminating the tribunal, balanced previous controls against free incorporation (Freedman 1979:140-144). Spanish regulations were much weaker with respect to both independent organizations within the nation, such as the Catalan family firm, and manipulations by foreign investors. This legal impotence reflected the declining political economic status of the Spanish state within a world capitalist system.

Although the laissez-faire code was criticized within the state, reform projects consistently failed. In 1926 Spanish reformists established committees and discussed plans, only to be defeated "through the determined opposition of financial groups and bankers" (Garrigues and Uría 1953:68). The heritage of this long phase of "nonlegislation" remains problematic.

> Through the work of the Spanish legislators of 1885, a bizarre concept of liberty was built into the core of the law. From the technical legislative viewpoint it was inadmissible. In business practice it led to no few abuses. Above all, it contributed to the diffusion among businessmen and financiers of an atmosphere of hostility to any coercive norm. (Garrigues and Uría 1953:61)

Only in the 1950s was Spanish commercial law revised in conformity with that of other Western states. Such reforms may have characterized a new stage of Spanish dependency. The economic reconstruction of Spain since the 1950s, through tourism and foreign investment, required some control on previous corporate abuses in order to attract new capital as well as to restructure the state-planned economy. Since the death of Franco abuse of existing laws has also become a major theme in investigations of Spanish business. In repeated cases, such as MATESA and RUMASA, the state has been forced to intervene in order to continue the operations of the company.

The Spanish commercial code has thus been both a structuring device for business organization and a means of response to political and economic change. Nowhere is this more apparent than in the family corporation, where Catalans exploited the potential of the code even more than its written provisions.

To understand this, it is helpful to reframe the company formats of Spanish commercial law in terms of two characteristics, control and limitation of liability. *Control* is defined by the extent to which owners participate personally and directly in the management of the company. In the simple partnership, for example, all owners are managers, with a direct personal involvement in the firm, its profits, and its failures. In the other forms at least one owner is *not* a manager. In the limited partnership this is the *comanditario*. In the corporation elected representatives of all owners form a board of directors that appoints a salaried managerial staff. While individual board members generally hold stock in the company, their power exceeds their private holdings. Managers need not have any stock in the company.

Limitation of liability is the degree to which an investor is sheltered from loss in company actions. In a simple partnership all owners share responsibility for company debts. If these exceed their investment or even the company's total capitalization personal wealth may be attached. In the limited partnership this responsibility coexists with that of the "silent" partner, whose liability does not exceed the sum of his loan. The principle of limitation on loss receives full meaning in the *sociedad anónima*, where no owner loses more than his stock investment.

This combination of characteristics suggests a possibility for commercial organization not chartered by nineteenth-century legal codes. This company, a *sociedad anónima familiar* or close corporation, would be defined by personal (familiar) control achieved through the identification of owners and managers, yet it would be protected by limited liability. Thus it would retain family dominance in conjunction with organizational innovation. This corporate format emerged to prominence in turn-of-the-century Barcelona and has remained central in textile and retail sectors to this day. It is a format, however, derived from practice rather than from a legal code.

To understand the social organization of economic life, we must view the usage of each format as it changes through time. The Mercantile Register of Barcelona, which inscribes every new company founded in the city, provides substantial data for such an analysis. Volumes from 1850 to 1888 were not accessible during my fieldwork, and volumes postdating the Civil War were not open to academic inspection. Table 2, however, presents the relative importance of companies in each format founded at twenty-year intervals from 1846/1847 to 1926. This is complemented by Table 3, which considers the percentage of total capital invested in each format. Together these tables tell how Catalans experimented with and developed within the possibilities offered them by a national legal code.

As Table 2 indicates, partnerships were clearly the most frequent type of organization in early Catalan capitalism. In 1846/1847 simple and limited partnerships together encompassed more than 90 percent of all companies chartered. Only six corporations were founded in the last biennium before their prohibition. Capital distribution, as shown in Table 3, inverted these proportions: the six corporations represented 92.4 percent of all inscribed capital. Nonetheless, some caution is advisable in weighing these figures. While the Bank of Castile and Catalonia, for example, was permitted to issue stock up to a maximum of 67,000,000 pesetas ($12,931,000), there is no indication of how much the company actually ever raised. It disappeared without any impact on the city and is thus a telling example of the "anonymity" and secrecy possible in the *sociedad anónima*.

In 1886 usage patterns still resemble those of 1846/1847, despite the intervening prohibition and relegalization of the corporation. Most companies were partnerships (Table 2); most capital, however, was in joint-stock corporations (Table 3). A major bank, the Crédito Mercantil (50,000,000 pesetas; $9,650,000), and the railroad line from Madrid to Zaragoza to Barcelona (100,000,000 pesetas; $19,300,000)

Table 2
The Changing Use of Company Formats, 1846-1926

Company Format	Percentage of Total Companies Founded			
	1846/47	*1886*	*1906*	*1926*
Partnership	67.7%	77.5%	69.1%	32.5%
Limited partnership	22.6	19.7	22.5	7.7
Limited company	—	—	—	18.1
Corporation	9.7	2.5	8.2	35.1
Family corporation	—	—	—	6.6
	(N = 62)	(N = 324)	(N = 314)	(N = 376)

SOURCE: Old Commercial Register (1846-1847) in the ACA and RM.

Table 3
The Changing Capitalization of Company Formats, 1846-1926

Company Format	Percentage of Total Capital Inscribed			
	1846/47	*1886*	*1906*	*1926*
Partnership	3.4%	1.7%	15.5%	2.6%
Limited partnership	4.2	1.0	2.0	.1
Limited company	—	—	—	21.5
Corporation	92.4	97.3	83.5	54.2
Family corporation	—	—	—	23.4

SOURCE: Old Commercial Register (1846-1847) in the ACA and RM.
NOTE: The 1906 and 1926 sample refer only to the first fifty companies inscribed.

were inscribed. Both played important roles in Catalan development, in contrast to the corporations of 1846/1847. In 1886, as in 1846/ 1847, the corporation and the partnership served different functions. Small, experimental ventures or self-capitalizing enterprises became partnerships. Grandiose schemes of development were chartered as limited-liability corporations. Both formats had their own social concomitants as well.

In 1906 Catalonia was recovering from the loss of colonial markets, so overall capitalization remained depressed. Two changes had occurred, however. Partnerships held a larger share of capital than in any previous sample year (Table 3). The corporation had also become proportionately smaller. In 1846/1847 the mean size of the corporation was 176 times that of the average partnership. By 1906 this ratio was reduced to 60:1 and by 1926 would decrease still further to 16:1. In

1906 the largest corporation chartered proposed a capital of only 10,000,000 pesetas ($1,930,000). Yet two partnerships achieved a capital of 1,000,000 pesetas. One of these was a family firm in its second generation that would soon incorporate.

Usage patterns suggest that the needs of the family firm and other historically reproductive partnerships were converging towards the economic potential of the corporation. Old family firms had accumulated wealth far beyond that previously exposed to risk in partnerships. Meanwhile, corporations involving fewer investors and limited projects were becoming more common. Catalonia was ready for experimentation with a family corporation.

By 1926 this development had taken place. Partnerships represented only 1 percent of all officially inscribed capital and were even less numerous than limited-liability formats. Two new forms had emerged in the interim as well. One was the *sociedad (de responsibilidad) limitada*: the limited responsibility private company. This was essentially a modification of the limited partnership that allowed partners to fix a limit on their liability and to distribute it by private contract. The concept had developed in Germany as a way to encourage small investment in new companies, but it spread rapidly through Europe (Treillard 1953:551-554). It did not play a major role in Catalonia.

The other innovation was the close or family firm. Close corporations were still not designated as a separate category, although they can be identified through the kinship bonds of their founders. As Table 3 shows, in 1926 these family companies accounted for 23.4 percent of new company capital. On the average they were larger than other corporations founded that year, although not so large as the mean corporation size of earlier periods in this sample. These firms held the accumulation of generations, now sheltered from the uncertainties of market and labor that followed World War I. They also manifested the adaptation of state codes to the Catalan social and economic experience.

The family firm continued to coexist with associative and multinational corporations after the Civil War. In the 1950s it was finally recognized as a distinct legal form (Ngô Bá Thanh 1963). Yet such corporations were already part of a new economic world. Many *sociedades anónimas familiares* have found themselves swamped in recent decades by changing markets, competition and consolidation within their fields, and their own internal tensions. To understand these problems we must retrace Catalan capital organization in terms of its internal familiar organization.

THE LAW OF THREE GENERATIONS

The biography of one of Barcelona's major twentieth-century textilists, Eusebio Bertrand Serra, includes the stereotypical generational model of the Catalan industrial family:

> Great houses have their crisis or fall in the third generation. The grandfather creates the enterprise amidst hardships. The father, who participates in the work of the founder, completes the work. Then the sons, who have not witnessed the struggles and who have become soft with the goods that their progenitor provided them, fail to comprehend the value of goods. (Aliberch 1952:26)

This model recurs in other family biographies (Fluvià 1970) and historical analyses (Vicens Vives 1958:127). Members of the contemporary Good Families also refer to it in conversation. Today, it is often a commentary on the failure of Catalan firms in recent economic crises. Reflecting on his own situation as the descendant of a once-illustrious family, for instance, one young man thus added a fourth generation— "with nothing at all."

The Bertrand biographer situated the three generations within a definite chronology, marked by the lifespan of Eusebio Serra Clarós (1820s?-1904), his son-in-law, Manuel Bertrand Salsas (1840s-1912), and his grandson, Eusebio Bertrand Serra (1877-1945). In more general terms the author refers to the entrepreneurial generation who reached maturity in 1840-1860 and the succeeding generations of boom and reorganization. Yet the model is not merely another genealogy of history; it also schematizes stages in the organization and reproduction of capital. The distinguished Catalan jurist José Puig Brutau has explicitly linked this sequence to company practice:

> A small business was exploited by the grandfather as an individual merchant; his sons continued, forming a simple partnership. Finally, there appears a corporation that is merely the judicial disguise for a familiar reality, since those who have obtained a participation in the business do so by rights of succession. With the passage of time and the succession of generations, it becomes difficult for family branches somewhat distanced to live in perfect harmony as the directors of the same enterprise. (1958:575)

This model will be used here as a framework through which to discuss the adaptation and evolution of the industrial household. Obviously, the paradigm itself is an ideological representation, a selective structuring of elite experience that speaks to social and cultural influences beyond economic history. Therefore it must be refined, even while bridging to the earlier discussion of historical consciousness and genealogical appropriation.

Entrepreneurs and Founders

The economic accumulation that initiated family mobility in the nineteenth century usually began with individual businessmen. Such entrepreneurs, who successfully exploited innovations in technology and management, are today recalled as founders of major industrialist lineages. Yet despite family records and academic research it is difficult to construct the social history of this generation. Personal documentation is fragmentary, and crucial ideas, plans, and activities may not be extant in public records. Furthermore, any sample has been skewed by the uncontrolled selection of later events. Successful entrepreneurs are more accessible than failures, or than those whose descendants failed to build on an early success. Other early businessmen have been so polished by their descendants that available information reveals much more about later generations than the founder-ancestor, a frequent phenomenon in the anthropological investigation of myths.

Within these limitations, however, one may draw an impressionistic portrait of the founding generation in the mid-nineteenth century. The governing committee of the Universal Exposition of 1888 provides an indicative set of those recognized for their power and leadership among the Catalan *grand bourgeosie*. Two members were not in business. Francisco P. Rius Taulet, mayor of Barcelona and president of the exposition, was the son of a modest provincial merchant. Manuel Duràn i Bas, one of the three vice-presidents of the exposition, was dean of the University of Barcelona Law School, head of the bar, and scion of a legal dynasty in the city. He was also the only member of the committee whose father was born in Barcelona. The remaining three officers— Manuel Girona Agrafel (Royal Commissioner) and vice-presidents Claudio López Bru and José Ferrer Vidal—exemplify three typical paths to success in the early Catalan industrial revolution.

Manuel Girona (1818-1905) was the son of the merchant Ignasi Girona Targa (1780-1867; see Figure 43, Appendix). According to family tradition, Ignasi Girona was a watchmaker in the inland village of Tàrrega who came to Barcelona after the Napoleonic wars. By 1828 he was included in the register of merchants of the city; at mid-century Ignasi Girona ranked twelfth on a list of Barcelona's wealthiest taxpayers (Solà 1977, 1:24).

As his sons matured, Ignasi Girona organized his business into a family partnership, Girona Brothers, Clavé. In 1855 this became a limited partnership, with Girona's daughters and younger sons as silent part-

ners (AHPB: Planas Compte 1857, 1:87, 187). Later, each son moved
into a different economic sector. Ignacio Girona Agrafel became a major figure in metallurgy and machinery. Jaime founded the Bank of Castile in Madrid and became Count of Eleta in 1893. Casimiro married
Elvira Clavé, a relative of their family partner, and dedicated himself to
agriculture. Esperanza, a daughter, married Pablo Henrich. Their son
became an important publisher and mayor of Barcelona.

Manuel Girona Agrafel was perhaps the most important figure of his
family. In 1844 he founded the Bank of Barcelona, a key financial institution of Catalan industrialization, which he ruled for sixty years. In
addition to other important corporate posts he was also founder-pres-
ident of the Barcelona Chamber of Commerce, mayor of Barcelona,
and senator for life (Cabana Vancells 1978:11-15). He was a cultural
patron, personally financing the completion of the facade of the Barcelona cathedral. From all these roles his name became a symbol of
wealth in Catalonia: the phrase "*ric com En Girona*" (rich like Mr. Girona) eclipsed powerful and wealthy names that had been used before.

The Girona family were provincial Catalans who made a small fortune in commerce only to expand it dramatically in the second half of

Figure 8
Manuel Girona Agrafel

the nineteenth century. Their ascent was, if anything, earlier than that of most industrial families. Manuel Girona was the only member of the 1888 Exposition committee to have served on a previous industrial exposition in 1844. Their subsequent move from industrialist to artistocratized businessman was also atypically early, as suggested by the 1867 will of Ignacio Girona Agrafel, who advised his sons

> from my own experience not to take part in mercantile societies, and to occupy themselves with their own affairs. Thus they will acquire honor and advantage, and their reputation will not be besmirched. (AHPB: Moragas Ubach 1867:461)

Nonetheless, the Gironas continued to be involved in Catalan business. A great-grandson of Ignacio was listed in 1978 tax records as the wealthiest man in Barcelona (*Fomento de la Producción* 1980:16; see also the Appendix).

Claudio López Bru, by way of contrast, was the son of a self-made Castilian from the mountain village of Comillas in Santander. Antonio López left Spain at an early age to make his fortune in Cuba in fields open to immigrants from the peninsula—transportation, commerce, and, according to Barceleona tradition, slave trading. In 1849 he married Luisa Bru Lassus, daughter of a Catalan with Cuban investments; López returned to his wife's native city to establish himself in Spain. His relationships with his affines were poor: his brother-in-law, Francesc Bru, publicly accused López of bastardy, fraud, embezzlement, and attempted murder (1857;1885). López nonetheless became a civic leader. His corporations, discussed in detail in the next chapter, attempted to renovate colonial exploitation in Spain's remaining colonies, Cuba and the Philippines (Izard 1974:47-89). In 1878 López became Marquis of Comillas; in 1881 he was raised to the status of Grandee of Spain. This title, along with control of his companies, was inherited in 1884 by his only surviving son, Claudio. Claudio López Bru expanded his father's companies, while developing new interests in energy and banking. He also became a patron of the Jesuits, who later supported unsuccessful efforts to canonize him. Claudio López died childless, and his positions passed to his nephews, the Güells.

The López's were particularly notable representatives of the *indianos*, Spaniards who found wealth in the New World. Cuba and Puerto Rico figured in the foundation of several leading families of Barcelona. The Güells, affines to the López family, became successful in Cuba after failure in Santo Domingo. Josep Xifré Casas, the largest property owner in mid-nineteenth century Barcelona, also built his fortune as a Cuban merchant (Pons Gurí 1976; San Pedro 1952). So did Miguel Biada Bunyol, builder of Spain's first railroad—an interest sparked by

the success of Cuban trains (Wais 1974:95-107). Carolina Vidal Qua-
dras, wife of Manuel Girona, was also from an *indiana* family, as was
José María Serra, Girona's colleague in the Bank of Barcelona.

Indianos have acquired a folkloric status in Barcelona, however, that
must be carefully evaluated. Many emigrants failed in the New
World—including the fathers of both Biada and Güell. Others stayed
there rather than returning; some fought against Spain for Cuban independence. Hence while the López story is again suggestive of the entrepreneurial generation, it may only be placed in context by further
studies in Spain and Cuba.

José Ferrer Vidal, the third vice-president of the exposition, was the
only one of these three industrialists to have made his fortune in his
own lifetime. His father had been a barrelmaker in Vilanova i la Geltrú,
a coastal village fifty kilometers south of Barcelona. Ferrer Vidal began
work in a textile factory in Vilanova; by 1839 he was manager. He consolidated his position through marriage with Concepción Soler Roig,
daughter of an *indiano*. In 1844 the factory became José Ferrer and
Company (Virella Boada 1977:22-23). Although perhaps not so
wealthy as Girona or López, Ferrer Vidal diversified his investments in
banking, rails, and trade. He was a deputy and senator in the Spanish
parliament and president of the Foment de Treball Nacional, the lobby
for Catalan manufacturing. At his death he was praised as the "honor
of his nation, pride of Catalonia, and preeminent figure of our troubled
times" (Puig Alfonso 1907:21). Ferrer Vidal's son, José, married Josefina Güell Bacigalupi, and was thus an affine to Claudio López. A second son, Luis, was founder and president of the Caja de Pensiones y de
Ahorros de Vejez (Savings and Loan for Old Age) and president of the
Foment. He was also a prominent Catalan nationalist.

All these men and their families—Girona, López, and Ferrer Vidal—
shared three major characteristics despite their differences in origins
and mobility. First, all three managed new capital from sources crucial
to Catalan industrialization in the nineteenth century. Girona and his
brothers built on their father's success by taking advantage of opportunities in metallurgy and large commercial banking. The colonial fortune of the López family and Ferrer Vidal's interest in textiles derived
from other major areas of Catalan expansion.

Second, all three men transformed their capital from individual
wealth into more stable companies. Personal capital was always limited, and the isolated businessman risked the welfare of his family as
well as his enterprise. The Gironas expanded from a family partnership
into one of the first major corporations in Barcelona history, through
which Manuel Girona controlled the wealth of many families. The López group stabilized more slowly, with some partnerships continuing

Figure 9
José Ferrer Vidal

until the 1920s amid huge López corporations. Ferrer Vidal rose from salaried employee to partner to diversified investor. In all three there is a clear trajectory from entrepreneur to participant in more complex, but safer, companies. Peter Hall has documented a parallel trend in Boston merchants (1977:40).

Finally, all three men established families. Their children were both heirs and new associates. The case of Josep Xifré provides an apt contrast here. Xifré maintained his wealth in private investments and properties in North America and Catalonia. His wife, though, moved to Paris, while his son sold off the property piecemeal to maintain a courtly life in Madrid. The family established neither social nor economic continuity in Barcelona, and its name is largely forgotten today. To appreciate this failure, though, we must look at the second generation and its roles.

Sons and Partners

The defining characteristic of a *sociedad colectiva* is its total sharing of resources, control, and responsibility, which in turn necessitate cooperation and limit size. Analysts in Catalonia (Prat de la Riba Sarrá 1898: *passim*, especially pp, 156-165; Piñol Agulló 1956:300-310; Puig Brutau 1960:845-858), the United States (Hall 1977; Marcus 1980), and Latin America (Lomnitz and Pérez Lizaur 1978, Socolow 1979) have pointed to the ideal and culturally "natural" potential of the family for such an organization. Family ties uniquely reinforce confidence and mutual interest: associates are "born into" the business, and they have a vested interest in maintaining it as their future inheritance. Sentiment confirms this unity. To what extent, however, was family-based business actually practiced in Catalonia?

Data from the mercantile registers on kin relationships in company organization show the early association of the partnership and familiar organization (Table 4). In 1846 no limited-liability corporation evidenced kin ties. Nearly one-third of all partnerships, by contrast, were exclusive to a single family. An additional 8 percent consisted of a family with additional investors. Limited partnerships also used kin ties, although they tended towards inclusion of nonfamily members, especially as silent investors.

In 1886 family and partnership continued to be strongly associated, and no familiar strategies were manifest in corporations. The 1926

Table 4

Kinship and Company Formation in Barcelona, 1846-1926

Date	Form	Percentage of All Companies Per Form Based on Kinship			Percentage of All Kinship-Based Companies in Each Form	
		All Kin	Mixed	No Kin	All Kin	Mixed
1846	Simple partnership	31.5%	7.9%	60.5%	59.1%	13.6%
	Limited partnership	9.1	36.4	54.5	4.5	22.7
	Corporation	—	—	100.0	—	—
1886	Simple partnership	22.2	22.2	55.6	40.0	40.0
	Limited partnership	6.2	37.5	56.3	2.8	17.1
	Corporation	—	—	100.0	—	—
1926	Simple partnership	—	25.0	75.0	—	21.4
	Limited partnership	100.0*	—	—	7.1	—
	Limited company	7.6*	15.3	76.9	7.1	14.2
	Corporation (including family corporation)	16.0	22.0	61.0	21.4	28.4

SOURCE: All data are from RM.

* Only one example of this type founded.

data from Table 4, however, show a striking change in the use of kinship. Of all kinship-based companies in the sample for that year, more than half exercised some form of restriction on liability. Seven of the 50 were corporations; 3 were limited-responsibility companies. Meanwhile, only 4 partnerships were founded on the basis of family ties. At this point the major lineages of the Catalan industrial revolution had reached a more advanced stage of capital organization.

A survey of 99 elite partnerships from the Mercantile Register, 1886 to 1932, showed that 70 percent relied on exclusive (49) or partial (21) familiar ties. Siblings were the most common associates: 47 companies used such ties. Often these were brothers refounding the family firm after a parent's death. Parent-son bonds occurred in 25 cases. In 10 cases inscription marked the loss of a father or male director, with the mother appearing in the company of her sons. Affinal relationships, by contrast, were rare: chiefly husbands who appeared in the absence or illness of males in their wife's family.

In none of the general samplings from 1846 to 1926 were the majority of *all* partnerships grounded in kinship. Cooperative ventures among friends, or patron-client relationships in which an investor sponsored an inventor or a shop, were also vehicles of elite investment. Generally, though, these were peripheral or short-lived undertakings. The role of the partnership in the long-term history of the family firm was quite different.

In a family enterprise partnerships have tended to be serial. Status changes within the family lead to new and yet continuous companies. Thus, while the partnership was characteristic of a particular stage of capital accumulation and generational succession, any single generation might encompass multiple partnerships. The case of the Sala family (Figure 10) exemplifies these processes. The family's original woolen mill was founded in 1838 by Joan Argemí (Joaquinet 1955:34). The founder died in 1860, leaving a wife and several daughters but no male heir. The company was transformed into a simple partnership, "Widow of Argemí." The widow soon acquired the assistance of two *fadristerns* from nearby Sallent, Antonio and Pascual Sala Sallés. The company was reorganized to recognize the contribution of the brothers as well as new outside capital under the name "Alegre, Sala and Company."

The Sala brothers fixed their position in the firm by marrying two Argemí daughters. By the time the partnership was again liquidated in 1886 the brothers controlled two-thirds of its capital. Alegre left, and the company became "Sala Brothers." When Antonio died in 1890, his place was taken by his son Alfonso, and the partnership "Sala and Nephew" was established. This ended in 1894 with the death of Pas-

Figure 10
Generations and Organization in the Sala Family, 1838-1910

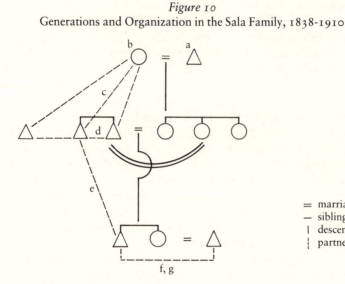

= marriage
— sibling
| descent
¦ partnership

SOURCES: Joaquinet 1955 and RM.
NOTES: a) Joan ARGEMI as entrepreneur, 1838-1860.
b) Widow of Argemí (partnership).
c) Alegre, Sala and Company, 1860-1886 (limited partnership: two
siblings and common mother-in-law plus an outsider).
d) Sala Brothers, 1886-1890 (partnership).
e) Sala and Nephew, 1890-1894 (partnership).
f) Sala Badrinas, 1894-1910 (partnership with brothers-in-law).
g) Sala Badrinas, S.A., 1910- (close corporation).

cual Sala. Alfonso Sala Argemí then formed a company with Benito
Badrinas Poll, a textile engineer. Sala contributed 91 percent of the capital but drew only 70 percent of the profits in recognition of Badrinas'
managerial role. In 1896 Badrinas married Sala's sister, Ana, repeating
the strategy of the previous generation. This partnership lasted until
1910, when the factory was converted into a family corporation.

   The Sala-Argemí factory passed through at least six successive partnerships before reaching a personnel-transcendent corporate form.
Other elite family firms have shared the Sala pattern of succession.
Table 5 lists fifteen companies on which a relatively complete series of
partnerships can be assembled. Most are textile firms; Rivière, S.A. is
in metallurgy, and Garriga Nogués is a bank. Most of these firms became corporations in the 1920s or 1930s. While the number of partnerships per family ranges from two to eight, the mean time span from
foundation of the first partnership to incorporation in the third state

was seventy years: two generations. While the change was influenced by capital accumulation and political-economic circumstances, incorporation tended to take place as the Law of Three Generations suggests. Yet this law, in turn, serves to create a unity out of diverse histories and therefore to substantiate the cohesion of the final group formed.

Variations on the partnership phase, finally, served special functions within the family firm. It could allow the self-capitalizing family enterprise to receive some outside assistance without losing—or sharing—control. It could also permit family members with rights to capital to oversee their investment without actually running the company. The industrialist Pedro Gual Villalbí recalled the complex manipulations possible within his own family experience:

Table 5
Partnership Succession in Catalan Firms

Company	Foundation	Incorporation	No. of Partnerships	Avg. Duration (in years)
Textile firms				
Comella Soler, S.A.	1847	1926	6	13
RIFA, S.A.	1838	1929	4	22.8
Anónima Rifá[a]	1838	1936	4	24.5
Colonia Güell, S.A.[b]	1840	1921	5	16.2
Hijos M. Rius	1884	1935	2	25.5
Manufacturers Isidro Carné	1896	1925	2	15.15
Banca Rosés[c]	1838	1945	7	15
Antonio Aparicio	1900	1931	2	15.5
Industrias Montalfita	1843	1929	5	15.6
Viladomiu, S.A.	1869	1934	5	13
CA Bertrand	1884	1924	3	13.3
Sala Badrinas	1838	1910	6	12
Non-textile firms				
Rivière, S.A. (metals)	1864	1935	3	20.3
Garriga-Nogués (bank)	1831	1941	8	13.8

SOURCES: *Espíritu y fuerza* and RM.
NOTES: [a] Both RIFA, S.A., and Anónima Rifá spring from the same original partnership, Rifá Sabates. They split in 1886.
[b] Taken from various sources on the Güells. See Appendix.
[c] Originally inscribed as a textile firm, this became a bank without any new registration of company purpose.

With such indications of my favorable aptitude for the control of
a company if necessary, my father began to talk of retirement. He
was tired of the load he was forced to bear and expressed this every
time he praised the results that he had obtained through his les-
sons. But I did count on the double conditions that my father imposed in order to realize his retirement. The first condition was
that I should marry, to give him some guarantee of reforming my
disorderly life. . . . Of course this guarantee meant for him marriage with a woman who had his complete approval. The second
part of his conditions came down to the transformation of the firm
into a limited partnership in which I would be a working partner
in tandem with the chief accountant, the respectable Mr. G., who
had been with my father since the beginning. Now, as a reward, he
would get a part of the firm's capital. The silent partnership would
belong to my father and represent most of the firm's capital. This
arrangement was further constrained so that if my conduct at any
moment did not meet my father's expectations, and the business
suffered, it would return to his control as lord and master.
(1923:54-55)

The association of economic maturity and marriage as a social rite of
passage accords with the jural model of the Catalan family. It also coincides with social values of marriage to be discussed in Chapter VII.

    In short, the partnership—whether simple or involving a silent inves-
tor—was a crucial stage in the growth of family firms. Despite modern
elite historical consciousness it cannot be strictly limited to a single generation or company. In a broader sense, though, it marks a transition
stage between the entrepreneur and the corporation. Where the
founder mingled personal and business wealth, the partnership established a preliminary separation between these realms. The distinction
was not complete insofar as partners remained liable from their personal fortune and as capital organization was subordinate to social organization. In a third stage, the close corporation, family and business
would be legally divided, while remaining linked by moral and opera-
tional ties.

The Family Corporation

The *sociedad anónima familiar*, according to the Mercantile Register
and company histories, emerged in Catalonia in the first decades of the
twentieth century. Figure 11 charts the foundation of such firms from
1890 to 1939 for industry in general and for textiles specifically. The
number of incorporations, practially absent before 1909, peaked in the

decade 1920 to 1929. This substantiates the confluence of family history and economic context suggested by Table 5. The first family corporations appeared as the expanding Catalan economy of the 1880s/1890s faced a major setback with the loss of the Spanish colonial markets and the phylloxera infestation in the vineyards. When a new and serious slump occurred after World War I, established family companies moved towards incorporation to protect family assets from business risk. Demographic developments and the increase of capital in firms by this period probably facilitated rapid acceptance.

The interaction of generations and political economics is confirmed in the 1920s by founders and firms who rose to prominence *after* the first consolidation of major industries. Their successors have tended to pass through the same *stages* of capital organization as other industrialist lineages, but the generations themselves have been foreshortened. Doctor Salvador Andreu Grau (1841-1929), for example, did not begin his career in pharmaceutics until the 1870s. The fame of his work against yellow fever and the success of his preparations established him in international production and trade. Before his death, though, his investments in both pharmaceutics and land were converted to close corporations (RM 1927, 227:16,637; RM 1899, 48:4,219). His sons changed from partners to officers, forming a second generation in power, organized according to the characteristics of the historical "third generation." A similar foreshortening is apparent in the later

Figure 11
Foundation of Close Corporations, 1890-1940

Column 1 lists close corporations in any sector with elite participation founded in that decade; column 2, those in textiles in the RM survey; and column 3, all textiles in RM and *Espíritu y fuerza* (1945).

	30		
		18	
			15
8	9		
	6	5	
2			
1	1 1 1		1
1890-1899	1900-1909	1910-1919	1920-1929	1930-1939

firms found in Table 5. In such circumstances the family might repeat the stages of older families' organization but did not need to repeat their experiments. By the present all of these variations have been re-formed by elite historical consciousness into "three-generation" models.

In the family firm, as the last chapter discussed, owners, managers, and family were one and held their interests by virtue of succession. There was little differentiation of home and work place, at least for males. Above all, paternalism reigned. The family firm continued the patterns of the traditional upper-class family, while adopting new innovations in capital management. Through usage rather than legislation Catalans responded creatively to external ideas and business cycles.

The third generation, therefore, was actually a synthesis of several interdependent processes. The capital of family businesses, even when limited by self-capitalization, had grown through two generations. Demographic expansion meant that sons and males of cadet lines were available as managers—and held competing claims to control. At the same time the uncertainties of the Catalan and world economies favored institutions that would protect personal wealth from business risks. The corporation offered such an alternative, with some modifications. Once established, though, the corporation itself became a determining factor for future generations. As in the United States, family and firm became intertwined within shifting legal, political, and economic constraints (Marcus 1980, MS; Collier and Horowitz 1977).

The Fourth Generation

The career of family firms since the Civil War has been troubled. The policies of the early Franco regime hindered Catalan economic recuperation (Ribas Massana 1978:21-153). Those family firms that recovered were often overshadowed by competition from foreign branch offices in Spain. In all sectors Catalan companies were absorbed by larger corporations, Spanish or foreign.

Since the close corporation was not a legally protected form, there were no restrictions on sale of stock to outsiders. Puig Brutau wrote on the potential dilemmas he had observed:

> Even apart from the natural centrifugal tendency of the controlling nucleus, we see the corporation with limited organization who, because of the need to expand capital, has had to admit a new associate who is no longer a small capitalist investing all or part of his reduced capital but rather a major capitalist or a smart busi-

nessman capable of giving the firm the impulse it needs to fight new and powerful competition. (1958:575)

Worse, the organization of family firms held few protections against transformations by an outside capitalist:

The company enters a new life, under the same judicial guise and the same legal structure, although it faces new problems. Perhaps the new group which, in fact, has come to dominate the company, if not by capital than by the technological dependency that now exists towards other group companies, imposes a capital amplification in which the former small capitalists have no right of preferential acquisition. (1958:575-576)

Such expansion dilutes the original family's power in ownership and management. It may separate them entirely from the management role as professional executives are hired. In this situation the company no longer cements the family together, and cousin branches may separate.

Professional managers may threaten the traditional spirit and operation of the firm and family. The contemporary humorist Pere Calders has satirized such effects on both owners and employees. In one story he ironically echoes the law of three generations from the standpoint of management analysts, when a grandson of the company's founder laments to the workers that economists

have shown me with impeccable numbers that the factory lost money since its foundation. We have invested erroneously, they say, and for twenty-five years we have operated with negative consequences. As if we were to say we are alive only by miracle and according to them my grandfather should have gone bankrupt. . . . They have shown me in an irrefutable fashion that I am superfluous, too: a dead weight. And that my father should have retired long ago (for the good of the firm). (1984:20-21)

Not all companies were reorganized or absorbed. One of the notable results of the continuing economic crisis of the late seventies was the collapse of many remaining family firms. In 1983 a businessman joked that my fieldwork had been well-timed, since "all the families involved have since gone bankrupt." Burdened by an authoritarian ownership that often precluded innovation, and limited in their adaptation by self-capitalization, centurial firms have proven unable to compete. In some cases, at least, the family fortune also went in an effort to prop up the company. In others, control of the family name has passed to larger companies or foreign investors.

As Spain becomes associated with the Common Market, older and noncompetitive Catalan firms may be further decimated. A Catalan banker commented on the future plight of the family firm:

> The family company, unless it has been able to create or establish a special niche in technology or service, will not be able to compete with the glut of mergers, consortia, acquisitions, conglomerates, et cetera, that are coming in the near future. Industries or businesses that are marginal are condemned to disappear because they cannot maintain their position against those national or foreign firms who operate with more efficiency. . . . The continuity of localist operations necessarily will be reduced to affairs of minor consumption or service. The sad reality is that we have an endless array of companies that do not know how to die, and that continue, day by day, without pain or glory their pseudopaternalism and their musty concepts of production and marketing, inspired by an inefficient and simplistic mercantilism. (Gibernau 1976:4)

Thus the evolution that began with the emergence of industrialization has reached a new stage. Yet it remains incomplete until complemented by the acquisition of symbolic capital. Even those members of the fourth generation "who have nothing" have an education, social connections, and inherited homes and possessions that make them members of a social elite with aristocratic styles of consumption. Even if they must rebuild, they do not do so from scratch. As in the past prestige has been a bridge to a renewed circulation and exchange among elite groups.

CONCLUSIONS

This chapter has traced four phases in the economic organization of the Good Families of Barcelona. The analysis entailed a preliminary understanding of legal codes and company practice through the industrial revolution. These, in turn, could be related to family dynamics, capital accumulation, and national as well as international economic changes. Commercial regulation itself has embodied a delicate balance between Spanish autonomy and dependency on foreign investments.

Catalans followed a somewhat independent trajectory in relation to the state. The result was the creation of a familial industry subsuming traditional Catalan values and the kin-based cohesion of the elite. This form, however, has since been challenged by other investors, often non-Catalans. Even surviving family firms are now small units within a large and complex economy. The decline of the Good Families is reflected in their current lack of nationalist leadership and their dependency on the central state.

Like the family itself, the organization of capital also has been part of Catalan ideological identity. The family firm has had an intense symbolic value in Catalonia, whether in the Law of Three Generations as an elite interpretation of their own historical experience, or in the wider manipulations of "the family" in elite politics.

For many, the "single-family" firm was a stem from which the elite diversified their holdings and established associations with other families in larger companies. Thus, an economically cohesive power group emerged, based on interlocking directorates and multiple connections among bourgeois and aristocratic families. These relationships, in turn, were bound to exchanges of symbolic capital with the aristocracy through kinship and friendship. To understand these phases, we must move to a more social view of the economic organization of the industrial elite.

CHAPTER V

FROM FAMILY TO OLIGARCHY: THE COHESION OF ECONOMIC POWER

The Catalan family firm defined and reproduced the basic units through which a new elite organized itself. Yet, individual lineages generally have not limited their investment to a single company, nor has group cohesion arisen from parallel and discrete ventures. Major corporations and projects, economic lobbies, political parties, and even social institutions like the Opera House have relied on the integration of capital and talent from many families. At the same time families and their multiple connections have provided the matrix for the coalescence of both an economic and a social power group.

This chapter employs two complementary perspectives on elite economic development. First, it traces the diversification of investments and networks within a single lineage, the Güells. Juan Güell Ferrer, the founder, established himself in Barcelona in the 1830s; his descendants have been eminent in industry, politics, social affairs, and cultural patronage over five generations. This study focusses on strategies through which a family establishes economic associations in both public and private life and the changes in such ties over time. The complementary social and marital history of the Güells will be taken up in more detail in Chapter VII.

The second half of the chapter provides an analysis of three major economic institutions. This perspective reveals not only the recurrent mechanisms of group formation but the historically specific processes of elite cohesion through time. These processes are especially evident in the history of the oldest continuing financial institution in Catalonia, the Caixa d'Estalvis i Mont de Pietat de Barcelona (Barcelona Savings and Loan). Since its inception in the 1840s the Caixa has been dominated by members of quite different power categories: its story recapitulates the evolution of the Good Families as an economic power group. The Caixa continues to be an arena of contention for competing power groups today.

A series of corporations founded by Antonio López y López in the late nineteenth century provides the focus for the second part of this section. During this time, the corporation was more widely used as an economic form, and the industrialists of Barcelona were also more established and interactive than they had been in the past. López and his descendants built a group whose stockholders and directors united powerful families throughout Spain in common interests of colonial and national development. Social intercourse and kinship solidified these interests: the López network was not only an *interlocking* directorate but also an *intermarrying* one. Ultimately the difficulties faced by this group pose anew the questions raised earlier concerning the relationship of Catalonia and its localized oligarchy to the Spanish state.

The chapter ends with a more recent phenomenon previously mentioned in the historical overview of Catalan industrial evolution: the professional manager. As founders and heirs retired from an active interest in industrial expansion, new power holders came forth to manage Catalan interests—and those of other investors. Francesc Cambó, leader of the Lliga after Prat de la Riba and manager within the banking network of the Arnús family, was a forerunner of this process. His position echoed the interest of regional and state politics raised by the López group but within a distinct political context. The technocratic power group also serves to highlight the boundaries to social cohesion of an elite: while they shared economic interests with owners, they did not establish the connections of marriage or kinship that otherwise unite the Good Families.

These institutional studies also form a historical sequence. In the first, elite formation is traced through successive stages of circulation and synthesis. The second case focusses on more developed strategies of elite cohesion, at the apogee of Catalan industrial domination of Spain. The final study shows the decline of direct economic interaction, as industrialists became owners and moved from the factory floor to the board room—and the club. These perspectives complete the portrayal of the Good Families as an economic power group that was introduced in the last chapter.

THE GÜELLS: 1800-1980

The Güells have been a prominent family within the Barcelona elite for over a century. By nature of their economic and political power, they are also an extraordinarily well-documented family. Both the founder and his heir are the subject of multiple biographies (*Colonia Güell* 1910; Llorens 1960:326-332, on Juan Güell; d'Esplugues 1921; Gual Villalbí, 1953, on his son). Fluvià (1970) has published a detailed composite genealogy of the family. Finally, family members themselves have published various works: Juan Güell Ferrer (1866, 1871) on politics; Juan Güell López (1928, 1932); and Eusebio Güell López (1947) in autobiography. In conjunction with archival materials and intrviews these sources make possible the reconstruction of an extremely complete portrait of the family over time. The emphasis on males follows the characteristic lineality of the Barcelona industrial household. Females, in fact, have been extremely important in the social networks and prestige of the family, as will be apparent in discussions of marriage strategies. However, their economic participation, and that of their offspring, generally has been linked to the enterprises of their affines. The Appendix includes a comprehensive schematization of the family history (see Figure 41).

The First Generation: Founders

The founder of the family fortune was Juan Güell Ferrer (1800-1872). An official family biography describes him, in English, as a "self-made man" (*Colonia Güell* 1910:9). He was born in the coastal village of Torredembara, south of Barcelona. From there he went to Santo Domingo and joined his father in an unsuccessful business venture. At the age of fourteen he returned to Barcelona to study as a pilot. When he completed his studies, he went back to the New World, to Cuba. This time he was more successful. He finally resettled in Barcelona in 1836, having used his travels to observe industrial centers in the United States and northern Europe (*Colonia Güell* 1910:10; Fluvià 1970:3-4).

Güell invested his Cuban wealth in a textile factory outside Barcelona. In 1848 he bought a new site in the Barcelona suburb of Sants and founded the partnership Güell, Ramis and Company. This firm relied on the most modern equipment and energy resources to capture the market for cheap cloth. By 1851 the plant had 200 mechanical looms, powered by an 80-horsepower engine, and it employed 360 workers (Carreras Verdaguer 1980:62). This family firm remained the cornerstone of the Güell fortune for a century.

Güell also participated in other corporations. He was a founder of the Maquinista Terrestre i Marítima, which built machinery for Catalan industry. He served on the boards of the Bank of Barcelona (1845-1849) and the Barcelona Savings and Loan (1847-1850). He also lobbied for Catalan industry: as a member of the Spanish parliament he defended Catalan rights to protected markets in Spain and Cuba (Güell Ferrer 1866; 1871; 1880). Moreover, in 1849 he founded the Institut Industrial de Catalunya, whose newspaper fought the partisans of free trade. This organization was the forerunner of the Foment de Treball Nacional, the most effective lobbying organization of industrial Catalonia (Graell 1911).

Güell married late in life to Camila Bacigalupi Dulcet. After her early death he wed her sister, Francisca. At his death in 1872 he left an estate of 7,255,498.34 pesetas ($1,400,311.18), to be divided between his two children from these marriages. His daughter, Josefina (1853-1874?) received one-third of the estate. She married José Ferrer-Vidal Soler, son of the president of the Foment (see Chapter IV). The primary heir was Eusebio Güell Bacigalupi, who inherited the active business interests and such indivisible resources as the box at the Opera House (AHPB: Martí Sagristá 1877).

The Second Generation: Consolidation

Eusebio Güell (1846-1918) expanded his family's economic and social position. The motto that he took on his acceptance of the title of Count Güell in 1910 epitomized this transition: *"Ahir pastor, avui senyor"* (yesterday a shepherd, today a lord/gentleman).

In 1891 Güell converted the family factory into a *colonia* further away from the city (*Colonia Güell* 1910:53-62). The Colonia Güell encompassed work place, housing, schools, hospitals, and recreational facilities. The chapel was designed by Antoni Gaudí, the most famous Catalan architect of the period, whom the Güells patronized in the construction of their own palaces. Güell's reputation and his involvement with the development of the *colonia* concept are confirmed by the fact that Prat de la Riba dedicated his *Ley jurídica de la industria* to him (1898).

An incident in 1905 dramatizes the patriarchal relationship that the Güells projected onto the family firm. A child fell into a vat of hot dye, suffering severe burns that threatened the loss of both legs. Residents of the *colonia* were asked to donate skin for transplants. As manager of the factory Claudio Güell López was the first of twenty donors to be operated on; his brother Santiago followed (*Colonia Güell* 1910:72-84). Both men received noble titles for their actions.

Eusebio Güell diversified the business interests of his father. He was a director of the Barcelona Savings and Loan—a position almost continuously occupied by a Güell from the foundation to the present day. He was a founder and a director of companies in insurance (Banco Vitalicio La Previsión) and railroads (FFCC Alcantarilla a Lorca, Caminos de Hierro del Norte). He was also involved in various smaller and less successful ventures. Yet his major advancement of the family's position linked economic and social action: this was Güell's entrance, by investment and marriage, into the López group.

In 1871 Eusebio Güell married Isabel López Bru, daughter of the merchant-financier Antonio López y López. As López reorganized his business interests into corporations, Güell became a stockholder and

Figure 12
Eusebio Güell Bacigalupi, as Depicted by the Satirical
L'esquella de la torratxa, 1911

director in each. His capital participation was small at first: at the foundation of the Philippine Tobacco Company in 1881 López held 14.75 percent of the stock and Güell 1.25 percent (Izard 1974:55). The Güell position was later enhanced by inheritance from the López line. Antonio López divided his wealth among his three children. His successor, Claudio López Bru, died without issue, so the Güells inherited leadership in the López group.

Like his father, Eusebio Güell was active in politics as alderman and parliamentary deputy. He supported the elite regionalism of the Unió Catalanista and the Lliga, although he was not the leader his father had been. His affine Lluís Ferrer Vidal Soler and his son-in-law José Bertrán Musitu, however, were both officers in regionalist parties (Riquer 1976:174-175). As family ties extended, power was increased and diffused.

Finally, Güell became an aristocrat, solidifying the social position of the family. The title of count recognized his economic, civic, and cultural leadership (Fluvià 1970:5). A Barcelona newspaper reaffirmed the status of the family in Güell's obituary:

Great was the father and great the son. The royal title that ennobled the final years of his life was, as much as an act of grace, an
act of justice that bore the confirmation of the nobility that his fellow citizens had always attributed to him—whatever their class or
conditions. (*La Veu de Catalunya*, 9 July 1918)

Eusebio Güell consolidated the family's presence in Barcelona society. That society itself distinguished his career from the life and strategies of his father. Whereas Juan Güell had returned to a Barcelona in
which new entrepreneurs were reforming the economic life of the city,
Eusebio Güell knew and cooperated with the children of those entrepreneurs, already established in business as well as in social life. He
moved among politicians and nobles, increasingly interested in the
changing power structures of Barcelona.

The Third Generation: Incorporation

Eusebio Güell and Isabel López had ten children—four males and six
females. Alliances with families of the old aristocracy began in this
third generation via the marriages of the Güell daughters. As economic
power continued to grow, it was enmeshed in social power. The grand
bourgeoisie provided an economic foundation through which the
Good Families became a kindred.

Güell Bacigalupi's oldest son, Juan Antonio (1874-1955), inherited
the titles of Count Güell and Marquis Comillas. He became the head of
the López companies on the death of his uncle Claudio, giving him a
diversified and strong economic position. Politically, he was an active
monarchist and Catalanist. In 1930 Alfonso XIII appointed him mayor
of Barcelona: one of Güell's first acts was to reintroduce Catalan into
civil proceedings, ending Primo de Rivera's ban. During the Second Republic, Güell was a Lliga candidate in Catalan elections. After the Civil
War he went into exile, a punishment attributable to both his Catalanism and his monarchism. He died in exile in Mallorca (Molas 1972,
2:316).

The Güell López brothers were involved in the family firm as well as
the López group and other businesses. In 1921 the brothers incorporated the Colonia Güell, with Santiago Güell López as president, thus
exemplifying the Law of Three Generations. In 1943, however, the
Güells sold the colony to another textile family, the Bertrands. It ceased
operation in 1972. The Güells, meanwhile, could no longer be defined
by reference to a single family corporation but rather by their position
in a network of businesses.

In the 1920s family action reappeared in urban development. The
family had previously called on Gaudí to urbanize an area northeast of

Figure 13
The Barcelona International Exposition of 1929

the city. That attempt failed, although various constructions remain to-day as the Parc Güell. The International Exposition of 1929 focussed the expansion of the city on the northwestern plain (Solà-Morales 1976:137-148). The Güells, like other elite families, owned land in this area that they had previously used for recreation. All the siblings, male and female formed the company Urbanizaciones Güell to develop this now choice real estate. The Güell sisters were also stockholders. Land was a stable, socially acceptable resource as well as one at the heart of the household so that women could share in its profits. Public participation in the company, however, was left to their husbands.

In the third generation the Güells had become one of the most eminent families in Barcelona. Their power, however, was solidified in a different way from that of their father or grandfather. Rather than resting on individual accomplishment or a family firm, the Güell siblings occupied diverse roles within a more economically and socially cohesive power group. They had become a unit in the Good Families as elite.

The Fourth Generation: Dispersal

Claudio Güell López, First Viscount Güell, died a bachelor. Each of the other male lines established itself, albeit distinctively. In the fourth generation the Güells became a national as well as a Catalan family, with concomitant changes in their economic and social situations.

The line of the Count Güell, for example, settled in Madrid. Juan Claudio Güell Churruca (1905-1958) served on many corporate boards as the last Güell to preside over the declining López empire. He also founded a new bank, the Banco Atlántico, although control passed from his hands. Politically, he was identified with the Franco regime, despite his father's relation to it. He served as president of the Provincial Delegation of Barcelona under Franco.

The baronial line, founded by Santiago Güell, passed to his daughter Adela, who married Pedro Ibarra Mac-Mahon, of a noble Basque family. That branch is now settled in Vizcaya, a northeastern industrial center.

The line of the Viscount Güell has remained in Barcelona. Eusebio Güell López, who inherited the title from his brother, married the heiress to a Catalan shipping fortune. He continued the families' traditional roles in Barcelona economic and social life. His son, the current viscount (b. 1904), maintains an extremely active life as a businessman, socialite, and cultural patron at the time of my fieldwork. Through this line the Güells have revived their role in Catalanist politics. Carlos Güell Sentmenat, son of the current viscount, became involved in business lobbies before the death of Franco. After the legalization of political parties he formed the Centre Català with other industrialists and civic leaders. Although conservative, the party insisted on recognition of Catalan identity. Güell served as a deputy in the first parliament (1976-1978) but did not seek reelection. Instead, he ran for mayor of Barcelona as the candidate of a center-right coalition, losing to the socialists. He became an alderman and lieutenant mayor (Giral 1972:89-114).

In many ways the Güells exemplify the patterns of the family firm discussed in the last chapter. Yet, they have reached beyond their original factory base into new economic, social, and political connections. Since 1943, in fact, there has been no central family company. The Güells' roles within multiple elite associations, however, have reinforced the family's high visibility. To further understand the meaning of family it is necessary to look at these associative contexts and their evolution through time.

INSTITUTIONS AND POWER GROUPS

The Caixa dels Marquesos

The Barcelona Savings and Loan was chartered in 1841, although it did not officially open until 1844. It is the oldest financial institution in continuous operation in Catalonia. Its $3 billion in assets make it the largest savings and loan in Spain—larger than many of the commercial and investment banks that dominate Spanish finance and industry (Muñoz 1969; Voltes Bou 1965; Caja de Ahorros y Monte de Piedad de Barcelona 1945). As such a major resource power groups have naturally struggled to use and control it.

The Caixa was founded as a civic and charitable institution as well as a financial one. It aimed to guarantee the small savings and dowries on the working class. This capital has supported housing projects, libraries, and other social or cultural projects. Since 1977, for example, a similar Caixa has subsidized paperback editions of Catalan literary classics. Capital has also been available for industrial and mercantile projects and political campaigns.

Until recently the popular nickname "The Treasury of the Marquesses" (*Caixa dels Marquesos, Castilian. Caja de los Marqueses*) summarized class and control in the Savings and Loan. Post-Franco advertisements evoke the more democratic image of *"La Caixa de Tots"* (Everyone's Caixa). For its time, though, the first epithet was substantially accurate: in 1955, sixteen of the twenty-nine directors had noble titles; ten actually held the title marquis. In fact, the Caixa epitomized an elite bound by kinship and social category. The president, Carlos Sanllehy Girona, Marquis of Caldas de Montbuy, was a direct descendant of Manuel Girona, married to the Countess Solterra, whose title dated to 1671. He was related by descent or marriage to one-third of the other board members. Three other directors had nephews on the board, and their were four pairs of brothers-in-law. One director, Eusebio Güell Jover was both brother-in-law and first cousin to the Marquis Sentmenat.

Despite surnames like Güell, Girona, and Sanllehy, the board was not primarily dominated by industrialists. Many names recall the landed aristrocracy of the countryside: Salas, Fontcuberta, Casanova, Ponsich, Montoliu, and Sarriera. These families, however, had not held continuous control of the board since its inception. They had assumed control in the latest phase of a succession and redefinition of elites. Their role, in fact, was made possible by the coalescence of industrialist and aristocrat that defined the Good Families.

Table 6 depicts the history of the Caixa in four phases: mercantile aristocracy (1841-1876); industrialists (1877-1913); the Good Families (industrialists and aristocrats, 1913-1977); and managers (1977). The succession of presidents from each category determines the dates. This election was generally a watershed in the composition and action of the board as a whole.

The first board of directors was mixed. Two presiding officers stabilized operation and control. Ramón de Bacardí Cuyàs was a director

Table 6

Groups Represented in the Directorship/Presidency of the Barcelona Savings and Loan

Mercantile Aristocracy (1841-1876)	Industrialists (1877-1913)	The Good Families (1913-1977)	Managers (1977-)
José Xifré Casas (1841-1844)?	José M. Ferrer Vidal (1877-1878)	Benigno de Salas Carbajo (1913-1919)	Eusebio Diaz-Morera Puig-Sureda (1977-)
Ramón de Bacardí Cuyàs (1844-1845)	Salvador Maluquer Aytés (1879-1888)	José Franquet Dara, Baron Purroy (1919-1928)	
Erasme de Janer de Gònima (1845-1860)	Pelayo de Camps Matas, Marquis Camps (1888-1889)	Luis de Dalmases Olivart (1928-1937)	
Sebastian Antonio Pascual Inglada (1860-1872)	José M. Ferrer Vidal (2 terms, 1889-1893)	Luis E. de Alós Matheu, Marquis Alós (1939-1945)	
Rafael Maria de Durán de Ponsich (1873-1876)	Francisco Romaní Puigdengolas (1893-1900)	Carlos de Sanllehy Girona, Marquis of Caldas de Montbuy (1942-1962)	
	Delfín Artós Mornau (1900-1903)	Luis de Desvalls Trias, Marquis of Alfarrás (1962-1977)	
	Luis Sagnier Nadal, Marquis Sagnier (1903-1913)		

SOURCE: Caja de Ahorros y Monte de Piedad de Barcelona 1944.
NOTE: The title of the post has changed: until 1900 it was director of savings (Caixa), from 1900 to 1933, joint director, and from 1933 onwards, president.

for a year, before heading the Mont de Pietat (loan division), which he
ran until 1866. In his place the directorship was assumed and occupied
for nearly twenty years by Erasme de Janer de Gònima (see Table 6).
Both Bacardí and Janer were nobles of the Principality of Catalonia.
Their ancestors were successful entrepreneurs who had acquired patents of nobility in the eighteenth century (Barcardí in 1789; Gònima in
1791). Many of these families had converted their investments from
commerce and industry to more stable rents—which would be
swamped by the expansion of the industrial economy. Yet they formed
a powerful and cohesive group: Ramón de Bacardí and Erasme de Janer were also brothers-in-law (see Chapter VII).

The Savings and Loan was practically the only economic association
in which these families figured, perhaps because of its patronal ambience. The Caixa also controlled the capital of others rather than re-
quiring investment that might have been difficult for some such families. The contrast drawn by the industrialist's Bank of Barcelona at this
period is interesting:

> For the bank the Savings and Loan was "an establishment that
> gathers together the savings of the poor classes of society." (Mem-
> oir 15-II-1846). The bank [adopted] a typically paternalist attitude
> toward the Caixa. The expression it uses leads us to believe that
> the bank was to gather the savings of the "well-to-do." (Cabana
> Vancells 1978:21)

While the sources of the capital differed, so did those in control. The
Bank of Barcelona and the Caixa suggest incompatible domains in
which an elite establishment and an emerging group of challengers distinguished themselves.

In 1877 José Ferrer Vidal became president, inaugurating a new
phase in the Caixa. Ferrer Vidal was an industrialist, as were the majority of his fellow board members. Between his two terms as president
of the Caixa he served as president of the Foment del Treball. He alternated economic power in Catalonia through the Savings and Loan with
lobbying for Catalan industry in Madrid. Francisco Romaní, director
from 1893 to 1900, was also the brother of another president of the
Foment. This association of economic development and political action
typified the Catalans of bourgeois nationalism.

A third phase of control took shape at the turn of the century. Although Delfín Artós and Luis Sagnier came from families who had
gained power in the nineteenth century, both were related to the older
aristocracy as well. Benigno de Salas Carbajo, elected in 1913, was the
first president without an industrial family background. At the time of
his election ten of the twenty-six board members were old aristocracy;

three others held new titles. By contrast, at the previous election only seven members of the old nobility were on the board, and an industrialist was elected as president. In 1919, when the Baron Purroy (title granted 1609) took charge, fully half the board held titles that antedated industrialization, in addition to five ennobled industrialists. The Good Families formed an aristocratized controlling bloc, uniting industrialists and nobles.

This was a period of synthesis rather than replacement, as the following social chapters will corroborate. Nobles rarely entered Catalan board rooms before 1900. This gradually became more acceptable and important to them as a social and an economic role, while businessmen sought political support and prestige from the landed aristocracy. The 1920s were also the period that this new elite turned to Madrid for support in their class interests in Barcelona.

The Civil War interrupted the elite domination of the Caixa. Afterwards it was reconstituted as an aristocratic industrialist oligarchy, which remained stable except for lineal replacements of deceased board members until 1974. The entry in that year of Carlos Güell Sentmenat, aristocratic industrialist and active manager, foreshadowed a new pattern. He was soon followed by other managers without any direct connections to the Good Families. When the last aristocratic president, the Marquis of Alfarrás, retired in 1977, a technocrat replaced him. Eusebio Diaz-Morera Puig-Sureda, the new president, is a graduate of the Harvard Business School's Barcelona affiliate and the youngest president in the history of the Caixa. He has led a re-Catalanization of the institution after years of identification with a Castilianized elite:

> His designation supposes the incorporation to the post of greatest responsibility of a person of recognized professional prestige and deep awareness of the problems of savings and loans. He takes up his position with the desire to take all the necessary initiatives so that the Caja can figure as a financial institution of the first order in the service of Catalonia, in the current period of historical transcendence. (Caja de Ahorros y Monte de Piedad de Barcelona 1977)

Since the death of Franco, the Caixa has taken on new importance both as a support for the promotion of Catalan culture and development and as a resource for loans to political parties. The Savings and Loan was also the focus of a constitutional crisis in 1980, when the Generalitat de Catalunya claimed regulatory power over all such institutions as part of its autonomous powers. Control of the Caixa is clearly still a central issue in the structure of power in Barcelona and Catalonia: the retrocession of the Good Families before middle-class managers and politicians reaffirms their continuing decline as a power group. Yet, like earlier power elites, they have not surrenderd all positions, economic or social.

The history of the Caixa over 140 years signals the succession and circulation of elites in Barcelona. Economics, kinship, and social category have all shaped the constitution of a controlling bloc within the Caixa, as in the redefinition of urban elites. The study of the López group allows more detailed exploration of kinship and cohesion in the emergence of an elite.

Interlocking and Intermarrying Directorates: The Trasatlánticos

A sardonic observer of mid-nineteenth-century Madrid claimed that anyone building a corporation would attempt to assemble a directorate that encompassed every power group in his society: "A banker as respectable as our founder, or more so, and three or four noble titles of the realm, and an ex-minister or two among the directors of the society . . . and capital will be reached in an extremely short time" (Flores 1968:178-179). Nicolás Sánchez-Albornoz's work on the Crédito Mobiliario Español from 1856 to 1902 supports these observations (1977:155-183). The strategies of corporate formation that Sánchez-Albornoz outlines are especially telling in comparison with Catalonia, as exemplified in the Caixa and the López group. In Madrid the adaptation of interest groups facilitated radical shifts in corporate leadership; in Barcelona the reification of economic ties in social bonds was stabilizing but less flexible in periods of rapid economic change.

The Crédito Mobiliario was founded as a subsidiary of the French Crédit Mobilier. The Mobiliario funnelled foreign capital into profitable public works in Spain, such as railroads, and into service and transformation industries. It did not support primary production. The Mobiliario was thus, at least indirectly, an instrument in the underdevelopment of Spain. While it did not divert Spanish capital from primary industry, its profits influenced Spanish investors and planners to follow the example of the foreign capitalists. Spanish industry also suffered from the Mobiliario's intervention in government for policies useful to its French owners (Sánchez-Albornoz 1977:180-181).

The directorate of the Mobiliario changed repeatedly during its fifty-year history. These changes were invariably responses to new political conditions and international demands. Sánchez-Albornoz has identified in the board room of the Crédito Mobiliario a state and international elite centered in Madrid but outside the institutions of the state itself:

In the directorate of the Mobiliario Español politicians and men of money sat down with nobles of ancient lineage. . . . Men of various backgrounds rubbed elbows with the liberty that comes only from belonging to the same class. The Mobiliario served this fusion by offering a framework independent of that in which such interaction had previously taken place. Alongside various institutions of the state, in which the amalgam had once been produced, an alternative arose. . . . Sánchez Toca denounced the domination of the state by a bourgeoisie enfeoffed to foreigners. As he wrote, it is hard to imagine that he did not have in mind the men of the Crédito Mobiliario. (1977:182-183)

While the owners of the Crédito Mobiliario manipulated competing elements in Spanish politics for half a century, it was not inevitable that this group would form the origin of a national economic elite. Barcelona was more of an economic center than Madrid, especially in production and transport. The groups coalescing there, while often localized, nonetheless developed national and international connections. In the López group an oligarchy united Madrid, Barcelona, and the Basque provinces in control of a formidable diversity of investments. The striking difference between this group of directors and those of the Mobiliario, however, was the family structure that reinforced cohesion and reproduction.

Although Antonio López y López moved from Cuba to Barcelona in the 1840s, he did not begin to incorporate his interests until 1875. In that year he founded the Banco Hispano-Colonial to promote the economic interests of Spain in Cuba—including bonds for the wars to maintain those interests (Cabana Vancells 1972:9-10). The bank's original capital of 75,000,000 pesetas ($14,475,000) was divided equally among investors in Madrid, Barcelona, and Cuba. Antonio López and company invested 10,250,000 pesetas ($1,978,250). Only the Bank of Castile, which bought the Madrid shares, had a larger investment. Antonio López became president; Manuel Girona Agrafel, whose brother led the Bank of Castile, was vice-president. Other directors were prominent Catalans, Cubans, and influential Madrileños such as José de Salamanca, exminister of the Treasury. Eusebio Güell, López's son-in-law, also served on the board, although he was not listed among the original investors (Cabana Vancells 1972:12-15).

Antonio López founded two more corporations before his death in 1884. The Compañía Trasatlántica (1881) extended López's shipping interests in Cuba and Barcelona to serve all the Hispanic world and the United States (Compañía Trasatlántica 1950; Cossió 1952). Tobacos de Filipinas, founded the same year, exploited the agricultural possibil-

Figure 14
Antonio López y López

ities of the Philippine colonies, which had previously been given only cursory attention (Izard 1974:48). In the third company half the capital came from López and the Hispano-Colonial Bank. The other half came from foreign investors, including the Crédito Mobiliario and the Banque de Paris (Izard 1974:52-56).

Antonio López relied on his experience of the colonies and his connections at the court to build multinational firms within Spain's imperial possessions. The loss of the colonies in 1898 changed Spain's situation, although all three companies continued successfully. López's son and heir, Claudio López Bru, developed his father's enterprises in a new direction: towards the exploitation of raw materials within Spain. In 1893 he established the Sociedad Hullera Española to mine coal and oil in Asturias, in northwestern Spain (RM 1893, 30:2,349). The Sociedad General de Asfaltos y Portland, S.A. (ASLAND), which specialized in ce-

Figure 15
Pavilion of the Compañía Trasatlántica, Barcelona Universal
Exposition of 1888

ment, followed in 1901. Both were attuned to Spain's new needs in the second Industrial Revolution. Finally, in 1921 the short-lived Banca López Bru incorporated the private banking operations of the family in Cuba, Mexico, and Spain (RM 1921, 130:13,697).

As the group of corporations expanded, the same investors and directors were repeatedly recruited. Table 7 schematizes the overlap among directorial families in five of the six companies of the López group. The Banca López Bru is omitted since it would occupy only one slot, with 100 percent overlap. In general, from 60 to 100 percent of the directorial families served on the board of at least two corporations. The fewest interconnections took place in Tobacos de Filipinas, where "outside" capital was prominent. Even the Hispano-Colonial Bank, which also drew in such capital, eventually paralleled the others. By the turn of the century this interlock wavered between 80 and 100 percent.

The process illustrated here is important. At the formation of the Hispano-Colonial Bank and the Philippine Tobacco Company López and his close associates formed an alliance that dominated the investments of a much larger group of stockholders. Within a few decades this alliance became more consolidated through inclusion of new elements and reinforcement of ties, as evidenced at the foundation of

Table 7

Interlocking Directorates in the López Group: Percentage of Company
Directors with Patrilineal Kin in Another Group Company

	Foundation				
Company	1880-1890	1893-1901	1921	1950	1962
Banco Hispano-Colonial	48.4[a]	*	91.6[f]	50.0[g]	—
Trasatlántica	81.3[b]	80.0[c]	81.2	71.0	*
Tabacos de Filipinas	45.5[b]	35.0	31.3	47.0	*
Hullera Española	—	100.0[d]	100.0	*	63.0
Asfaltos y Portlands (ASLAND)	—	90.0[e]	80.0	*	66.0

NOTES: — Company not in existence.
* Information not available.
[a] In 1877.
[b] In 1881.
[c] In 1905.
[d] In 1893.
[e] In 1901.
[f] In 1919.
[g] In 1943.

ASLAND. Interconnection peaked in the 1920s. As the Good Families of
Barcelona have subsequently declined, the companies have changed,
turning to new investors or influential government figures. Today those
companies that survive show much more separation and diversification
of control.

Figure 16 schematizes the connections among the core group referred to in this discussion. The López, Güell, and Arnús-Gamazo lines
were involved in all six companies; the Ferrer-Vidals, Sotolongos, Satrústeguis, and the Oñate-Gils in four; and the Carreras, Miralles del
Imperial, Gironas, and Diaz-Quijanos in three. The accumulation of
ties illustrated in the diagram were linked to a strategy of kinship
within the board room.

The Güell-López marriage (1871) and the Güell-Ferrer-Vidal marriage (1874) preceded the establishment of the Hispano-Colonial Bank.
Social coalescence continued throughout the life of the companies. Not
until 1881, for example, did Claudio López marry María Gayón Bar-
rie. Gayón was the daughter of an old associate of López in Cuba (a
group that also included the Roberts, Sotolongos, and Satrústeguis).
Her sister had married Manuel Arnús, and her godfather was Clemente
Miralles del Imperial. Thus, one key marriage cemented four sets of ties

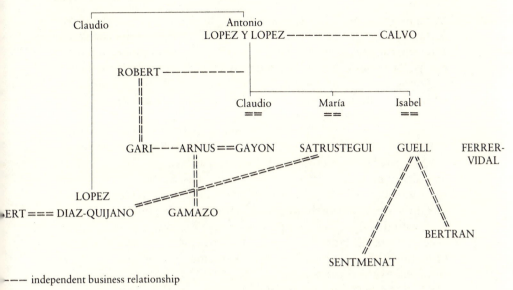

Figure 16
Kinship and Company Formation in the Trasatlánticos

within the López group—perhaps not independent of the second phase of expansion that took place at the same time. After the first alliances occurred, the group continued to be a social circle for endogamy. Subsequently, for example, two Barcelona Güells have married women of the López-Satrústegui family.

Not all ties were reified by marriage. Anastasio Oñate Salinas was a friend of López, for example, with easy access to the court. Yet, the Oñate-Gil family has never been connected by marriage to any López branch. Nonetheless, social interaction produced a "pseudo-kin" ambience. Similarly, when asked about the Sert family, one elite woman born at the beginning of the twentieth century immediately responded that they had been part of the "Trasatlánticos." That is, the name of one company in the López group was extended as a social categorization of all those who shared in the company.

Summer residence also reinforced group ties. Although the directors were scattered throughout Spain, all shared the tradition of moving their families from the cities during the hot summer months. In the case of the Trasatlánticos, the village of Comillas on the northern coast of Spain became a sociocultural nucleus. Comillas had no national or international stature as a spa, and it was far from Barcelona, although closer to the summer royal court in San Sebastian. As the birthplace of Antonio López, however, it was favored with a new seminary and public buildings, as well as a family palace. Soon López's kindred and associates followed suit, and in 1927 the society notes of the *Diario de Barcelona* spoke of nineteen palaces occupied by elite families and their guests. "Various other estates and resort houses are now being built" (7 August 1927). The guest lists also provide insight into the ongoing strategies of the group: among those at Comillas was the Spanish minister of finance, Calvo Sotelo.

López built a nationally based elite that was an alternative to that assembled by the Crédito, which it in fact outlasted. Yet, political power in Spain resides in Madrid, not Barcelona. The Hispano-Colonial Bank was absorbed by a more powerful Madrid-based bank in 1948 (Cabana Vancells 1972:52). The Compañía Trasatlántica underwent serious difficulties during the Republic when a new regime restructured preferential routes. The company survives in a weak form, with its headquarters in Madrid (Compañía Trasatlántica 1950:58). The other companies survive in Barcelona, but their familial complexity has been curtailed. In 1972, for example, Alfonso Güell Martos was president of the Trasatlántica and a director of ASLAND. Yet the Güells were the only link to Tobacos de Filipinas.

The López group epitomized a pervasive Catalan ideal of industrial organization applied to a state, even multinational, corporation. This strategy was successful on the local level or in times of relative stability. Yet this reinforcement of economic ties with social ties, as in the organization of the family firm, was potentially less flexible in dealing with new power groups. As the story of the Caixa shows, the twentieth century has become increasingly the century of the manager, with profound implications for both the economic and social life of the Good Families as an elite.

Entrepreneurs and Investors: The Arnús Group

A pamphlet published shortly after the collapse of the Bank of Barcelona in 1920 named a conspiratorial oligarchy as secret manipulators of Catalan finance—"The same names are repeated everywhere: Cambó, Estruch, Arnús, Güell, Ventosa, . . . and when these names are absent, their trail is still evident to the astute observer" (Oligarquía 1921:10). Apart from the Güells, however, these men often were primarily managers: a power elite whose power rested in the administration of the investments of others.

Stock and investment specialists already were well-established among the small banking houses of nineteenth-century Barcelona. After the turn of the century, however, their power became more noticeable within the operation and financing of industrial firms them-

selves (see Kotz 1978:23-71 on the United States). In one such company, the Marsans Bank,

> exchange alone led to an ever greater interest by the banks in the
> operation of industrial enterprises. All offerings that were sold to
> the public had to rely on the aid of some agent who morally guar-
> anteed the integrity of the enterprise's directorship. From that
> guarantee to a direct participation in the companies so promoted
> was a simple step. (Cabana Vancells 1972:159)

Banker-managers became industrialists. When Lluís Marsans Peix died
in 1923, he presided over eleven major industrial firms in addition to
his banking roles.

Banks also acted as corporate treasurers. In 1929 the Arnús-Garí
Bank was the treasurer for no less than fifty-six major enterprises.
Again, the power of the families involved transcended individual and
corporate assets, resting on "the volume of its trade and the political
power that it had, directly or indirectly, over the actions of various enterprises" (Cabana Vancells 1972:169).

The action of these banks and the families who controlled them differed from the patronal stance of Manuel Girona at the Bank of Barcelona, or the entrepreneurial attitudes of the López group. The associates of Arnús-Garí "were not promoters of new enterprises. They
were technicians of financial operations and stock ventures, but they
did not know anything about the industrial world" (Cabana Vancells
1972:170). These companies managed, and solved problems, without
attempting to expand or develop the Catalan economy:

> Arnús-Garí knew how to resolve the financial problems of com-
> panies after these companies had been set in motion by people who
> deserved economic aid. Thus, they were linked to companies as
> different as Barcelona Traction and CHADE, or the city government
> of Cádiz. In all these cases the common denominator was financ-
> ing. (Cabana Vancells 1972:171)

The entrepreneurs of nineteenth-century Catalan industrialization
were active as individuals and nuclear families in economic and social
change. Their heirs at the end of the century shared economic and social enterprises, which emerged as a platform of political and economic
concerns for Catalonia as a nationality. In the 1920s, however, the
third generation was retiring from an active role in the family firm as
well as the general economic and political life of Barcelona. Instead,
spokesmen for Catalanism and Catalan business emerged from other
positions within Catalan industrial society: unifamily businessmen (especially textilists) and professional managers. The former included

families who were ultimately integrated socially into the Good Families: the Bertrands (Chapter VII), Rusiñols, and Fabras (Chapter VI). The latter group included brilliant ideologues like Enric Prat de la Riba and Francesc Cambó, who would act for the elite but never be connected to it through kin ties.

The Arnús network bridged both categories. The Arnús family amassed power and prestige in the nineteenth century under the leadership of the banker Evaristo Arnús Ferrer (San Pedro 1952). In the next generation Arnús passed his wealth to his son but left control of the operation of the bank with his nephew, Manuel. This arrangement collapsed, and the Arnús bank divided into two separate companies (Figure 17).

The Arnús-Garí Bank, that of the nephew, joined forces with another family of nineteenth-century brokers. They allied themselves by marriage to the López family. Moreover, they made important connections in Madrid. In 1909 Marta Arnús Gayón married Juan Gamazo Abarca, First Count Gamazo. He was the son of the government minister German Gamazo Calva (1840-1901) and nephew of Antonio Maura Montaner (1853-1925), who led the Spanish government four times between 1903 and 1925.

While this branch of the Arnús family followed the same basic strategy as the López group in overlaying economic ties with kin ties, the other line turned to a manager: Francesc Cambó. Cambó was active in the Lliga and would twice serve in Madrid as minister, once in the government of Maura. His political power meshed with his economic interests in international capitalization of Catalan firms.

In 1910 when the Arnús Bank split, Cambó was instrumental in the organization of Banca Arnus, S.A. Eighty-five percent of the original capital for this project came from Perière and Company of Paris, a family firm that had also been deeply involved in the Crédito Mobiliario of Madrid. Cambo's major coup, however, came after World War I, when he assembled non-Spanish investors into a major Spanish-based multinational, the Compañía Hispano-Americana de Electricidad, CHADE (Hispanic-American Electric Company; Pabón 1952-1969, 2:220-224).

CHADE was registered in Spain, although most of its investments were in Latin America, especially Argentina. Its capital was largely German. The financier Walter Rathenau wanted to extract his wealth from Germany before the Allies took it as war reparations. Rathenau knew Spain from earlier investments in electricity and also knew Cambó as a lawyer and politican. With Cambó he assembled an eminent Spanish board of directors for the company. Claudio López Bru was the first president. This post passed then to Cambó who retained it

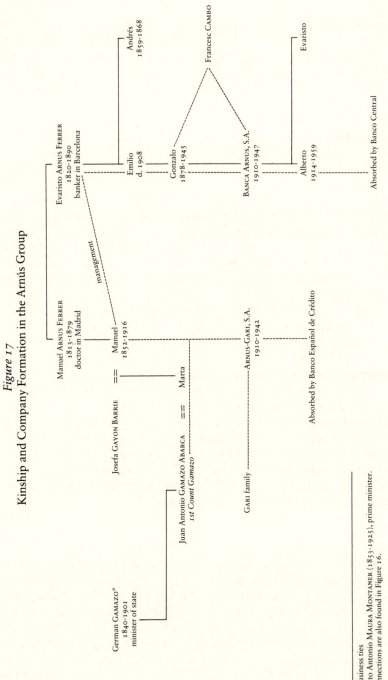

Figure 17
Kinship and Company Formation in the Arnús Group

NOTES: ———— business ties
* Brother-in-law to Antonio MAURA MONTANER (1853-1925), prime minister.
Arnús family connections are also found in Figure 16.

until his self-exile at the beginning of the Civil War after a dispute with Catalan leaders.

While Cambó acted as an agent for non-Catalan as well as Catalan capital, he was not unique among Catalan manager-politicians. Rómulo Bosch Alsina—shipping magnate, mayor of Barcelona, and officer of the Port Committee—was also repeatedly involved with an English consortium in coal and transport (RM 1914, 89:9,231; 1915, 93:9,349; 1916, 94:9,942; 1916, 95:10,117; 1917, 96:10,268). Management for non-Catalans has intensified since the Civil War, as the government openly encouraged foreign investment in Catalonia (Rubirola 1971:49-88).

The rise of the manager held implications not only for the organization of power groups within the Catalan economy, but also for the role of the Catalan economy within a world system. Schneider, Schneider, and Hansen (1972) have characterized the modern Catalan economy as a dependent one. I suggest that in these shifting styles of financial-industrial organization the effects of a shift from development to dependency are indeed evident.

This shift also has had social implications. Early investment management families like the Arnús, Garís, and Gamazos, or the Sala brothers of the last chapter, have been integrated by socialization and marriage into the Good Families. Cambó never established such ties, nor have subsequent members of the managerial elite. Perhaps, though, it is a question of time coupled with the resilience of social power even within shifting economic organization. That is, as the aristocracy once exchanged prestige for connection to a new economic order, so may these families appeal to a newly emergent power group. To this point, however, the new power elite has been a more marginal category in sociological, if not in economic, terms. In order to understand the separation of the Good Families as an elite, it is necessary to consider the social and cultural construction of an upper class.

CONCLUSIONS

This chapter has complemented the evolution of the industrial household studied in Chapters III and IV with the interpenetration of business and social ties in economic cohesion. Once again the family has been a central theme in the coalescence and reproduction of power.

The use of multiple case studies provides a rich perspective on dynamic processes of elite formation. Yet the historical development of each case, as well as the evolution of the family firm, are interdependent. The stages of the family firm, or of a family as a strategic unit, have been embedded in the development of the Catalan economy as a whole.

The experience of opportunity, expansion, and retrocession—the path from development to dependency—entails both individual choices and group values. Perhaps the culminating figure of all these processes is the modern businessman-politician like Carlos Güell Sentmenat, who combines an industrial and aristocratic heritage with managerial roles in both politics and industry.

Yet the choices involved in this development were not entirely economic. One of the repeated themes of this chapter is the relationship of the newly wealthy and the existing elite "establishment" of Barcelona. This drama was evident in the redefinition of control within the Caixa; perhaps it will be repeated in the confrontation of new technocrats with the aristocratic industrialists of the Good Families. The resultant synthesis, however, can only be understood within a wider comprehension of the meanings of power. The Good Families emerged as a synthetic elite on the basis of calculated interactions between a new economic power group and an older, more "cultured" and socially prestigious elite. The next two chapters will examine the process through which the industrialist became a gentleman.

CHAPTER VI

PIGS AND GENTLEMEN:
THE EDUCATION OF AN ELITE

The preceding chapters have concentrated on the economic structure and evolution of the household in the commercial-industrial lineages of nineteenth- and twentieth-century Barcelona. Yet, the values of the family intrinsic to Barcelona industrialization coexisted with other ideals among the aristocracy, who formed an important part of the social environment of the new bourgeoisie. Just as the *casa industrial* was shaped by its economic context, so this social establishment influenced patterns of socialization, conduct, and consumption. The coalescence of the Good Families entailed the ennoblement of new wealth, complemented by the economic renewal of old status.

Thus, from the eighteenth to the twentieth century there has been a striking continuity in prestige markers, behavior, and education among members of the dominant classes in Barcelona. Arno Mayer has observed a similar continuity and coalescence through much of northern Europe in the nineteenth century:

> Just as industrialization was grafted onto preestablished societal and political structures, so the feudal elements reconciled their rationalized bureaucratic and economic behavior with their pre-existent social and cultural praxis and mind-set. In other words, the old elites excelled at selectively ingesting, adapting, and assimilating new ideas and practice without seriously endangering their traditional status, temperament, and outlook. (1981:13)

As in Barcelona the aristocracy met a potential collaborator in the emergent bourgeoisie: "This prudential and circumscribed adjustment was facilitated by the bourgeoisie's rage for cooptation and ennoblement. Where the nobility was skilled at adaptation, the bourgeoisie excelled at emulation" (1981:13).

Yet coalescence was not without tension or price. A century ago a businessman in Narcís Oller's *Febre d'or* criticized the ongoing circulation of elites as well as the role of his own class within it:

> Barcelona is divided into two enemy camps: Old Commerce, the Established Bankers, the historical bank, we might say; and the modern bank, that of today, ours. . . . These gentlemen act to-

wards us the way the nobility treats today's aristocrats. They receive us well. They chat. . . . But they despise us, and if they can, they exploit us. They envy and mistrust us; we envy and mistrust them. . . . This cold war—who will lose it? I fear that it will be us. (Oller 1948:315-316)

The "cold war" between those who controlled social power and the emergent leaders of new wealth is the subject of this chapter. The next chapter, then, looks at the synthesis of old and new families: matrimony.

In particular this section examines how the bourgeoisie entered the core of the Good Families by mingling with the aristocracy and absorbing, while transforming, their values. The characteristics of an elite have been modified by new arbiters of status, by changes in access to prestige (inclusion of new groups or narrowing of access through financial barriers), and by new institutions. The contemporary social synthesis is the result of a long and tense process.

Two methodological and theoretical considerations predominate here. First, the mobility of any family, and the redefinition of the dominant class, took place over time and must be analyzed accordingly. For newly enriched industrialist social power inverted the law of three generations. The socialization of entrepreneurial children according to aristocratic norms diverted them from direct economic responsibility as it isolated them from the social milieu of their fathers. The economic movement from entrepreneur to rentier went hand in glove with a social transformation from rich man to gentle man. As a turn-of-the-century commentator noted: "The bourgeois is no longer an industrialist nor even a banker—he is a man who has style" (Marfany 1978:272). In later periods style has been retained even as the economic foundations for it have faded.

Second, in this transformation of the industrialists and aristocrats into a cohesive elite, multilevel development processes have interacted. Barcelona society in the nineteenth and twentieth centuries exemplifies a general process of elite circulation as described by social theorists like Pareto and Mosca. As Mayer's passage indicates the components, forms, and chronology of this process were also historically specific to the experience of nineteenth-century European society. Within these general frameworks Barcelona witnessed divergent familial and sectorial strategies as well. As in the study of economic organization and change, analysis must synthesize while recognizing variation.

In language use, for example, elite cohesion relied on common patterns of class differentiation on the basis of communicative codes. In nineteenth- and twentieth-century Catalonia this differentiation has been realized through the opposition of Castilian and Catalan, with an elite shift from their Catalan roots to Castilian and French as preferred tongues. This process was influenced by European trends, including the revitalization of minority languages and the internationalization of French as a cultured code. Spanish educational and legal policies have also shaped elite language use. Group evaluations, in turn, shaped the background of linguistic use and evaluation in any family or individual.

Discussion begins, then, with the most general considerations on the nature of social capital in modern Catalonia. The emergent bourgeois encountered an enduring ideology of refinement. This ideal has been associated with the public social status of nobility. At the same time it is embodied in the cultural ideal of the *senyor* and *senyora* (gentleman and lady).

After this general presentation I turn to specific aspects of the ethos of the elite and their evolution. Language behavior, education, and etiquette exemplify differentiating traits. Religious values are considered as a contrasting case of a unifying social institution used for elite distinctiveness.

The third section treats the fundamental mechanisms through which the ethos was shared, in the exchange of social knowledge and in economic expenditure. This discussion also considers the loss of status as part of ruling-class transformation. Ultimately, not only the ability to gain access to prestige codes but also the ability to maintain interaction and display must underpin elite status. This section, then, notes how individuals, families, and groups lose their position within the circulation of contending elites.

Noble and Gentleman: The Creation of Cultural Power

Throughout the nineteenth and twentieth centuries there has been a striking permanence in the ideals to which succeeding generations accede. On the one hand, these were epitomized by the aristocracy as a status category with concomitant patterns of seigneurial economic production, political control, and cultural hegemony. Within this categorization, however, there also arose a world view that condoned certain attributes and behaviors as indications of social status. Embodied in the figure of the gentleman, this code transcended the boundary of aristocrat and bourgeois to unify the Good Families.

Nobility in Spain demands public recognition by the king or a council of noble peers. While the word *aristocracy* can be applied metaphorically to such phrases as the "aristocracy of wealth" or that "of talent," informants of all social classes specified that the correct application was to those set apart by inheritance, by blood (*aristocracia de sang/de sangre*).

Prior to 1832 there were two systems for such recognition in Catalonia. The sequence of titles of the Principality of Catalonia—honored citizen, noble, and knight—had originated in the independent Catalonia of the Middle Ages. In the 1700s the membership of these categories was increased by ambitious men in politics, academics, and commerce. The newly enriched could essentially buy their titles: twenty-two patents were proposed in 1793 to raise 380,000 reales for work on the port of Tarragona (Amelang 1986; Morales Roca 1976). Political reforms after 1838 closed this pathway, although nobility continued to be inherited through the male line.

Catalans also held royal titles. The oldest titles in Catalonia were feudal privileges of the ninth century and creations of the independent monarchy. By the eighteenth century many of these had passed to the Spanish court through emigration or marriage.

The nobility that remained in Barcelona and its environs held more than social power, nonetheless. Three of the top ten taxpayers of 1852 held noble titles, while two others were nobles without titles (Solà 1977). Much of this wealth was in land, some in old mercantile houses. The nobility, as noted previously, rarely appeared in early factory investments. While data are as yet inadequate for elaboration of the economic contrast between aristocracy and bourgeoisie, a rentier/capitalist dichotomization is not unfair. The Catalan nobility also maintained its political aptitude, especially in urban life.

New power groups could imitate or overshadow economic and even political power. The unique attribute of the nobility is the social capital that Pierre Bourdieu has labelled *pouvoir social sur le temps*:

> [To] possess that which is old . . . those current things which come from the past, of history accumulated, treasured, crystallized, titles of nobility and noble names, castles or historic homes, paintings and collections, old wines and antique furniture, is to dominate time, . . . through all those items that have in common the fact that they are not acquired except with time, *with time*, against time. . . . (1979:78)

This social power became the capital in exchanges between old families and the new capitalists of industrial Barcelona.

In its extended time the aristocracy had undergone previous challenges and renewals. In the eighteenth century the minor nobility had absorbed merchant leaders. In the nineteenth, facing both liberal reforms and economic development, the aristocracy's potential for assimilation remained. This absorption was not without cost, though: in each generation some families and institutions would fade; others might adjust to new demands, as in the realm of education, in order to maintain their status.

Manufacturers themselves could seek titles as well. While few such honors went to wealthy Catalans before the 1860s, with the Restoration of Alfonso XII in 1872, titles proliferated. Between 1872 and 1932, 548 titles were added to the roster of the Spanish nobility, without counting the rehabilitation of previously lapsed privileges or new pontifical titles. The latter, granted by the Pope in reward for special services or donation, were not so highly esteemed: some modern families referred to them as "bought" titles. For the aristocracy this was "the first operation of integration of the elite from the upper bourgeoisie—as much as the financial group, already in progress, as the industrial" (Tuñón de Lara 1972:192). In this period 52 titles were granted to Catalans (Alonso et al. 1977).

Time and expense were necessary in this new quest for titles; one critic joked that "in order to amass so much nobility, Robert had to fight in the terrain of bureacracy as much as any medieval noble did on the battlefield" (Pla 1945:234). The recently ennobled industrialist risked becoming a comic figure (Pla 1945:234-236; see also Rusiñol 1968:159-187).

Nor did all Catalan families seek titles. In textiles, for example, the major families—Bertrand, Serra Feliu, or Sala—did not seek recognition of their wealth and power. Nor did bankers like Girona or Arnús. Nonetheless, some titles were later gained by marriage (the Gironas) or in reward for political service. Alfonso Sala rejected the title of Marquis in 1908, but after he had served as leader of the Mancommunitat he accepted the lesser distinction of Count of Egara (Joaquinet 1955: 320-321).

Even if an aspiring manufacturer obtained a title, his investment could not be realized until the second generation, when time and education accompanied the status marker. A Spanish commentator captured the essence of nobility as process: "Some people compare nobility to the zero of an arithmetical figure, which by itself has no value, but with another numeral makes the entire figure increase in value" (Delgado 1944:58). While various actions changed the membership of status categories like nobility and upper bourgeoisie, this code of conduct became a feature that unified both groups into the Good Families.

An old Catalan proverb states, *"De porc i de senyor s'en ve de mena"*—Good pigs and gentlemen only come from breeding. The word *senyor*, like the English "lord," encompasses training and power. The legal jurisdiction of *señorió* was curtailed in Spain in the early 1800s, although its connotations were not so easily erased. The complex of ideas associated with the education of the gentleman were scarcely altered.

The first etiquette book of modern Barcelona was printed in 1767 and reprinted verbatim thereafter until 1833. This book, the *Reglas de la buena crianza civil y cristiana*, extolled an ideal of courtesy appropriate to an elite:

> Courtesy is a way of acting and speaking: decent, sweet, and beautiful. It is a certain style in actions and words that ingratiates and manifests the attention we are paying. It is a mixture of discretion, condescension, and circumspection that allots to each that which rightfully belongs to him. Courtesy is a comeliness, and it is properly the science of honorable people. (*Reglas* 1767:1)

This courtesy was not necessarily an attribute of even the highest birth: "Be he a prince, be he the wisest man, be he powerful or rich—if he lacks education, if he is incivil, he will surely be despised." The book solemnly concludes: "Incivility is low and plebian; courtesy is always noble" (*Reglas* 1767:1).

One hundred fifty years later this ideal reappears in the biography of the first Count Güell, subtitled "Essay on the Aristocratic Sense in Catalonia" (D'Esplugues 1921). The author used Güell to personify the traits of the gentleman:

> That svelte, elegant and always correct silhouette of Eusebio Güell, who possessed in abundance the accoutrements of a gentleman and the manners of a prince. Were he to appear in any era, in the midst of any conglomerate, even if it were not his own class [*estament*], it would still have something remarkably "rich and full."
>
> A voice rich and sweet, romantic and optimistic in a melancholy manner, was the natural moral complement of a face which, in its own way (an elevated and pleasing way, as if he were some legendary hero of today) attracted and imposed itself at the same time. It produced a note of completion that is difficult to capture except in the words *distinction, elevation,* and *elegance*—which might be said to distill in its entirety the essential psychology of the first Count Güell. (1921: 82-83)

The 1978 obituary of still another industrialist, Domingo Valls Taberner, illustrates the endurance of such a code. Like Güell, he was the scion of a banking and textile family, known in addition for its Catalanism in politics and culture. His memorial in the leftist *Mundo Diario* enshrined the values of education, conduct, and elegance:

DOMINGO VALLS TABERNER HAS DIED!!

A gentleman has died. It is said that all men fail from an excess of passion or too little. This description is false for Domingo Valls Taberner. His human elegance—I still recall him in his overcoat with the vicuna collar, his careful gait, and his amiability at once warm and discreet—was echoed by the incongruous enchantment of a brilliant bourgeois. He did not rush: *j'anirem fent* [We do it as we go along]. Fertile in each step, constant in his goals.

He lived in the world of politics, of finance, of business, yet made culture his boon companion. . . .

May this gentleman rest in peace, this prudent politician, this industrialist, this exemplary being whom we have known. (S.A. in *Mundo Diario,* 20 October 1978)

In three centuries the ideals of the aristocracy have been absorbed by the industrialists and are reflected in speech, manners, education, and style. These ideals form part of the social capital of the elite—that set of knowledge, behavior, and networks that complement economic investment—and may even be exchanged for economic capital in such arenas as marriage. An understanding of social capital requires fuller examination of some of these traits and their development through time.

THE CULTURE OF AN ELITE

The attributes that dominated the coalescence of industrial families and the aristocratic establishment were embodied in values, institutions, and social interactions. This section discusses only selected features that highlight the pervasive code of the gentleman. Language has primacy not only because of its role in social and cultural life but also for its consistent position as a major issue in Catalan politics and national identity. Education raises the question of institutions through which elite mentalities were shaped and reproduced. By turning from the school to the content of the institutional process, particularly etiquette, one understands the reinforcement of elite values and obedience to them. In contrast, religion illustrates elite roles within an arena of apparently shared values. Until very recently Barcelona society was coterminous with Catholicism for all its members. Yet ideology and practice did not quite coincide in elite adhesion to the church nor in their claims to hegemony. Upper classes, while adopting patronal stances, were rarely especially devout, nor did they enter ecclesiastical service and dominate the hierarchy. Lower classes more openly rejected Catholic claims and participation in the church. Attempts at ideological manipulation were hardly received as the elite offered them.

Language

Language underlies all social interactions, uniting and dividing populations. Because of the political and economic context of Catalan industrial expansion, moreover, language use has synthesized a wide range of influences. Elite language shift recapitulates and comments upon the coalescence and changes of power groups in Barcelona.

Three general characteristics of elite language style are vital to the understanding of Barcelona language use and change. First, elite linguistic repertoires *condense* the networks intrinsic to a power group's status—regional, national, and international. Catalonia has shifted from a primarily monolingual Catalan-speaking society to a bilingual society with marked diglossia within the past two centuries. Catalan ruling classes, however, have been multilingual for centuries. These upper classes have learned languages whose importance was based on international business or prestige norms rather than the concerns of a local community. Elite use is also more immediately sensitive to many external policies such as those imposed upon Catalonia by the Spanish state. Modifications in the language of education, law, or publishing, for example, have a more dramatic effect on the usage of literate upper classes than on those denied access to schools in the first place.

Translocal factors are especially important in this process of condensation. Elite language use corresponds to a differentiation in the state and international cultural *evaluation* of language codes. For five centuries Castilian has influenced the social, political, and economic interests of Catalan leaders—a role intensified with increasing centralization. Those without access to power have not necessarily shared in elite evaluations of Castilian as useful, prestigious, or necessary. Thus attitudes and behavior of the Good Families have been ambiguous on occasions with regard to Catalan nationalist assertions.

The second characteristic of elite language style is that it supports the social cohesion of power groups. Small numbers and constant social intimacy favor a rapid flexibility in elite language shift. In addition, educational privilege has meant that elite children are *taught* new languages (such as English) when a perceived need arises. Language patterns nonetheless reflect role divisions within the upper class, such as gender expectations or the struggles of competing networks.

Finally, elite language use is a *reflexive* historical phenomenon. The upper-class domination over written media and public communication makes it possible for the student to analyze elite language patterns over an extremely long time period. Yet this same record and sense of history is also part of elite language consciousness itself. In discussions upper-class members were acutely conscious of language and language history. A power group manipulates language as well as using it.

With these general themes underscored it is possible to recapitulate language shift as an index of elite formation and change since the eighteenth century.

SPEECH AND POWER IN INDUSTRIAL CATALONIA

"Conversation is like the theater of civility and courtesy: it is a commerce in which each has to contribute with his own treasure to make it agreeable" (*Reglas* 1767:20). Early modern etiquette books published in Barcelona emphasized correct speech as an attribute of social class. Every citizen had a duty to speak as well as possible; nevertheless, performance inevitably revealed social background. As another eighteenth-century text noted, "Conversation is necessary, since without it we could not distinguish the noble from the plebian; even though, as they say, nowadays even cats want shoes—even charwomen try to imitate ladies" (Quijano 1785:3). The endurance and universality of such attitudes in social elites becomes evident in the repetition of the same theme in a basic handbook of American social behavior, Emily Post's *Etiquette*:

> To liken Best Society to a fraternity, with the avoidance of certain seemingly unimportant words as the sign of recognition, is not a fantastic simile. People of the fashionable world invariably use certain words and instinctively avoid others; therefore when a stranger uses an "avoided" one he proclaims that he "does not belong." (1922:58)

Eighteenth-century etiquette books also identified the prestige language for their social world. Although published in the Catalan capital, they almost invariably were written in Castilian, the language of the state and court. This pattern continued, with few exceptions in Catalan and French, in guides to behavior published in nineteenth- and twentieth-century Barcelona to socialize the parvenus of the Industrial Revolution. These interactions of code and class, however, must be situated within the broader social and political history of Catalonia.

In the Middle Ages and early modern period Castilian was rarely heard in Catalonia, especially outside the trading cities (Elliott 1963:43). Catalan was the language of politics, law, and literature, while Latin held a prestige role in the church. The failure of the Catalan revolt of the eighteenth century led to the transformation of Catalan nationhood and its linguistic expression (Elliott 1963). Catalan was discouraged from governmental life. Other decrees were directed towards the establishment of Castilian in education. These policies reduced the public domain of Catalan even in its homeland. Yet, the efforts of the central government were neither immediately nor entirely effective. The countryside, nobility and peasantry, clung to Catalan into the nineteenth century.

Residents in urban centers with frequent contacts with the new order were more sensitive to changes. Pierre Vilar has described the language patterns of a major merchant family of the late 1700s:

> Catalan and Castilian divide the correspondence. . . . University contacts, official or private, are made in Castilian. . . . By contrast, . . . the practical economic correspondence referring to cotton spinning is in Catalan—but in a Catalan so vacillating and mediocre that it calls into question the culture of those who use it. Since we are dealing here with the renowned merchant Joaquim Roca Batlle, must we not discern here the characteristics of a language still familiar but already in decline as a means of written expression? (Vilar 1973:61-62)

The leaders of Catalan mercantile society were increasingly bilingual. The inventory of the noble Joan Milà de la Roca (died 1825) included grammars and dictionaries in Castilian, French, Basque, and English (AHPB: Llobet 1825). Yet elite multilingualism also encompassed a growing division of domains. Catalan was used in the home and Castilian for academic or public situations. The language of technology, whose importance would increase with economic development, was Catalan—but marked by strong Castilian interference.

The shift in language evaluation in the urban mercantile elite of the eighteenth century reflected the difficult political and economic power of Catalonia vis-à-vis the Spanish state. While the masses remained as yet minimally influenced by state policies or opportunities with regard to Castilian, Catalan leaders of the period were caught by market interests and government demands that went beyond the communicative needs of the local speech community. These needs were met by the increased use of Castilian as a second language, augmented at times by French and Italian. Yet, Castilian was not *merely* utilitarian. As the etiquette books show, on the eve of the Industrial Revolution it also had acquired aristocratic associations that would shape the behavior of future generations.

Many founders of nineteenth-century industrial families came from Catalan-speaking homes in the countryside or urban lower-class neighborhoods. They invested in Catalan cultural projects and media. Yet, like the new aristocratized merchants, these industrialists were bound to markets and policy makers in a Castilian-speaking administration. Furthermore, the existing bilingual aristocracy (and visitors from the court) provided models of social success. Hence the new power group, like that with whom it competed, began to speak Castilian in addition to Catalan.

Economic expansion fueled a revitalization in political, social, and cultural life. Catalan also underwent a Renaissance (*Renaixença*) in literature, folklore, and linguistics. Since Catalan had remained the language of most of the people of the area, the Barcelona usage of "Renaissance" refers reflexively to those leaders who had drifted towards Castilian.

Even while Catalan was being reasserted as a cultivated language, other factors such as education, travel, and increased contact with other Spaniards favored the spread of Castilian. In nineteenth-century Barcelona newspapers and books were widely available in both tongues. An entire genre of comedies in which diglossia was copied and satirized (for an obviously bilingual audience) became popular (Fàbregas Surroca 1975:36-37). Elite language use, however, developed in a manner that emphasized distinction from general linguistic trends in Catalonia.

The oldest members of the Barcelona upper class with whom I spoke (those in their eighties in 1976 to 1979) recalled that their parents and other adults of that generation were fluent in Catalan as their first language. This turn-of-the-century competence was characterized as a "gentlemanly Catalan" (*un Catalán señorial*), of an elegance subsequently lost by other speakers. Catalan was used at home, in the work place, and in politics. Males also knew Castilian, while retaining at times a marked Catalan accent. Females knew Catalan, with some Castilian or French, depending upon how recently their family had risen into the upper class.

These scions, however, were themselves socialized according to values that differed from those that had formed their parents. Castilian was normally the language of their education, with a strong secondary emphasis on French. A woman in her mid-eighties, for instance, recalled using Catalan with servants, in shops, and in the countryside. To this day she prefers Castilian for conversation with family and friends and French and Castilian for travel abroad. Although her spoken Catalan is fluent, she is uncomfortable writing in it, in contrast to her mastery of other languages. Others of this generation concurred in evaluation and usage.

As industrial society developed at the end of the century, speech norms were shaped as well by gender expectations, with important consequences for elite language shift. The varied public roles of upper-class males at the turn of the century demanded knowledge of both Castilian and Catalan. After the 1890s, however, women of the Good Families were increasingly restricted in their linguistic competence to the languages of prestige and social/marital advancement—Castilian and French. As I will show in the next chapter, during this period, the dowries of the present finally tempted the titles of the past. According to the daughters of one eminent publishing family of the turn of the century, the father consistently spoke Castilian with them and Catalan with his sons. As Catalan/Castilian males married Castilian/French-speaking females, Castilian became the first language of new households of the next elite generation.

Educators and writers commented on the language changes of the early twentieth century. In 1918 the Jesuit Ignasi Casanovas found Catalan to be the primary language of the entire region, with the exception of the aristocracy. Among the latter, however, he included newly ennobled members of the manufacturing and banking communities, including vocal Catalan nationalists (Batllori 1979:339-348). Nonetheless he was alarmed by the spread of Castilian in elite education and in preaching, where it appealed to "feminine vanity" (Batllori 1979:339-348). Again, class and gender expectations are evident in language evaluation.

Meanwhile, the bilingual author Santiago Rusiñol (1861-1931) satirized language adaptation as a means of social advancement in the bourgeoisie. Rusiñol himself came from a prominent manufacturing family; his plays and novels enjoyed wide success. In *Gente Bien* (The Right People, 1917), he chronicles the efforts of a newly ennobled manufacturer to convert his Catalan household into overnight aristocrats. The Count insists on the shift from Catalan to Castilian whenever familiar intimacy gives way to polite public conversation—a distinction of domains quite humorously marked in the play itself. His mother, who speaks Castilian with difficulty, protests. He replies: "Of course we will suffer—and we will suffer greatly! When I speak Castilian for a few hours, my throat becomes as dry as toast. But it is the fashion, so we must speak it" (1968:162, first pub. 1917).

As the industrialists and the nobility interacted, Castilian slowly assumed the primacy that had formerly been held by Catalan. The latter became secondary and domestic. Other international prestige tongues also encroached on Catalan domains in business and society. The shift, however, was not apparent in the ideology of upper-class Catalanism between 1890 and 1920. Language was used by elite leaders as one of the most emotive symbols of Catalan national identity. In these political statements Catalan served a dual role, similar to that of the family. On the one hand, it unified the Catalans as a nationality with a common history and a distinguished literary and linguistic tradition. On the other hand, it emphasized the difference between Catalonia and the Castilian-speaking state. This duality was an effective device for an elite balancing local masses against a central state. Language ideology thus reinforced elite use of familial imagery. By the 1920s, however, the symbolic power of Catalan no longer corresponded to the usage patterns of the elite itself. Nor would elite usage adapt to the rapid political alterations of the decades to follow.

LANGUAGE POLICY AND COMPETING ELITES

In the Primo de Rivera period Castilian became more widespread in the general populace through its officially imposed dominance of education and mass media. Catalonia also received an influx of monolingual Castilian-speaking workers from poorer regions of Spain. This immigration continued to be encouraged under the Franco dictatorship, so that their descendants today constitute about one-third of the population of the area. As Catalan society as a whole became more bilingual, however, the elite itself became more restricted in the use of Catalan. By the end of the dictatorship Castilian was the dominant language of the "Good Families" of Barcelona. In effect, this produces two language patterns in Catalonia, with Castilian-speaking upper classes *and* workers. However, elite language use has been distinguished from workers both by their educated command of Castilian (often opposed by commentators to an Andalusian or Murcian accent) and their knowledge of nonpeninsular languages.

The reformist leadership of the Generalitat identified politics and language: Castilian was linked to the conservative and aristocratized capitalists, while Catalan was championed by the moderates and leftists who controlled the Generalitat. For the Good Families this was a period of active rejection of Catalan within their linguistic repertory. Many members of upper-class families raised in the 1930s are uncomfortable in both written and oral Catalan. One such adult was forbidden by her family to attempt to learn Catalan until she had mastered Castilian, French, and English. Although her parents both were fluent in Catalan, it was not spoken in her home. In effect, *multi*lingual upperclass speakers became *mono*lingual speakers with regard to *bi*lingualism of their home society.

The Catalan language was strongly identified with the leftist regional government of the Second Republic and the Civil War. The victory of General Franco in 1939 led to a reinstatement of Castilian as the official language of Barcelona. For nearly forty years Catalan was a target of Francoist repression. The language was barred from any public platform: books (until 1945), periodicals and newspapers, schools, public assembly, and official dealings. Only in the late 1960s did Catholic adoption of Catalan as a liturgical language provide a public forum for the language.

Through these decades two sociolinguistic processes coexisted. First, a strong cultural identification was forged between Catalan and opposition to the Franco regime. For some this became an equation of Catalan with the left and Castilian with the right. Second, Castilian was completely established throughout Catalonia. In fact, the only monolingual speakers in the area by the death of Franco were likely to be those who spoke only Castilian—a numerically significant group.

Since Franco's death Spain's democratization has focussed new attention on the relationship between national minorities, such as the Catalans and the Basques, and the Spanish state (Alba 1978; Di-Giacomo 1984; Woolard 1983). One symbol of change that inaugurated the reign of King Juan Carlos was the royal pronouncement of November 15, 1975, that regional languages "were national languages that should be protected as 'part of the national heritage' " (Alba 1978:247). Since then Catalans have gained language rights in public life under the guidance of the reestablished Generalitat. The Spanish constitution of 1978 has chartered a two-tier model for official languages that recognized Castilian as the language of the state and other languages as coofficial within their respective autonomous communities. (Preliminary title, article 3.)

Implementation of this ideal has been slow and difficult in a society as complex as Catalonia. It has entailed reforms in bureaucracy and education as well as shifting attitudes. Opposition has arisen both from within Catalonia and from outside. Some Castilian-speaking immigrants, for example, have been wary of proposals that appear to establish them in an inferior or foreign status (Jiménez Losantos 1979). Right-wing politicians throughout Spain have lamented the "dismemberment" of the nation into autonomous enclaves. Nevertheless, the Generalitat has dedicated major efforts towards a campaign for "normalization" of Catalan, with increasing results in administration, education, and cultural affairs, as well as everyday life.

Both Catalan and American sociolinguists have documented these changes (See Aracil 1982; Strubell Trueta 1981; Woolard 1983). In the midst of this reform elite language use has been influenced by the political and economic decline of the older industrial-commercial families. Despite a lingering claim to social prestige, evidenced in control of traditional clubs and some social institutions, the impact of this group on language patterns and policies is limited. In fact, the children of elite families today are likely to learn Catalan at schools and from their peers, in addition to the Castilian spoken in the home. Although some parents continue to express a preference that their children learn languages of international value, such as English, they have generally accepted these changes. Not only does this reverse the pattern of language use—but it also reverses the process that has differentiated elite language use from the rest of the society. Even adults are acceding to new norms of Catalan usage outside of the home. In many cases domestic usage remains Castilian-dominated.

Although language in Barcelona is intimately bound to power, Catalonia has entered a new stage in elite competition. The linguistic ideologies and practice of competing elites today are not clear-cut. Catalan, for example, is a nationalist language identified with the centrist middle class and leftist reaction to Franco. Castilian is both a symbol of past oppression and the language of many families of the lower class. Nor does this opposition take into account the shifting international values of language: Castilian has a special role in relationships with Latin America and perhaps with the Common Market, while the utility of English, French, and German as international languages undergoes constant reevaluation. Even if the immediacy of the situation precludes so clear a picture as that of the past, language and power continue to intertwine in changing patterns of Catalan life.

Education

Access to education is a stratified privilege in most industrial societies. As in Catalonia the turn-of the-century French bourgeoisie drew a basic class boundary between those who received only primary education and the upper classes who could afford an extended secondary specialization (Goblot 1967:77-78). Reviewing the French university system of the 1960s, Bourdieu and Passeron found inequality not only deeply ingrained but also reinforced and legitimated through education.

> In short, the potency of the social factors of inequality is such that even if the equalization of economic resources could be achieved, the university system would not cease to consecrate inequalities by transforming social privilege into individual gifts or merits. Rather, if formal equality of opportunity were achieved, the school system would be able to employ all the appearances of legitimacy in its work of legitimating privileges. (1976:27)

In nineteenth- and twentieth-century Barcelona the educational divisions among classes have been even sharper. Religious groups have privatized education; charitable and public schools have provided only limited opportunities for those who cannot afford the tuition and supplemental costs of an elite school. Educational institutions as well have shaped group cohesion and internal stratification: ousiders are not only denied knowledge but also acquaintances.

In fact, the epithet *educat/educado* applied to a lady or gentleman does not have strong academic associations. Elite families have produced distinguished historians and some major contributors in medicine, architecture, and law. Academic professions in general, however, are ill-paid and have little prestige for elite males. The goals of education for women, until recent generations, have been even more explicit:

> When I was ten (1901), my parents decided that I would complete my baccalaureate and asked how to do this through the director of my school, Donya Dolores. She resolutely opposed their project, alleging that with such studies—what a sin!—"the seal of her training would lose its innocence." (Bulbena Reig 1976:63)

Women learned social skills and basic knowledge of literature, music, and art. Yet to become academic was an aggressive pursuit of male public roles—and thus condemned as completely as woman's intervention into economic life.

Education, however, is still a unifying privilege of the elite: since the first "self-made" generation all men and many women have had at least some formal instruction. For elite males Jesuits have dominated schooling. The Society of Jesus had forged an alliance with European power groups during the Catholic counterreformation. In the seventeenth century they took over the Col.legi de Cordelles in Barcelona, which had been founded specifically for the education of the nobility (Galí Coll 1953:141-142). In 1767 the order was expelled from Spain, an edict repeated at several critical points in succeeding centuries. After the Revolution of 1868 the Jesuits returned to Restoration Barcelona with new patrons drawn from the leading industrial families rather than the aristocracy. Their Sacred Heart School was built with large contributions from Dorotea de Chopitea, wife of the banker José María Serra, and from the Marquis of Comillas. Through the Jesuits the new bourgeoisie guaranteed access to elite education not only by local standards but throughout the Catholic world.

The memoirs of Joaquín María de Nadal Ferrer, the scion of an older Barcelona family, portray the social connections of Jesuit schooling at the turn of the century. Nadal entered the Jesuit school in 1891 at seven-and-a-half, having begun his education at home with a private tutor. Apart from the classes, he noted that

> the hour of departure from the college was almost a social solemnity. Many of the children's fathers came to collect them and so-

cialized while they leaned against the walls of the waiting room. The Duke of Solferino, monumental and imposing; Manuel Girona, with a sad countenance presaging his later tragedy; Sanllehy, far removed from the political fickleness that would later make him a great mayor of Barcelona; Gallart, at the apogee of his fortune when he simultaneously built his house on the Rambla de Catalunya and his fantastic palace at Les Eures; Casanova, Baron of Puebla Tornesa, who came to fetch his only son. . . .

Years have passed, and those who waited have all disappeared. We who were once leaving school have gone to wait for our own children at the same time and the same place, and some are already preparing to meet their grandchildren. (1946a:48)

These memories of childhood are filtered through a prism of class. Eighty-five other students entered Sacred Heart with Nadal in 1891; over five hundred passed through the school in all its grades before he left in 1899. Of his class, however, only twenty-seven completed more than two years. The wealthy were thus distinguished from temporary scholarship students or members of the lower middle class whose family could scrape together only a few year's tuition. Those whom he mentions in this passage were sons of leading families who spent four to eight years with the Jesuits. Furthermore, they would have maintained ties after graduation; the Jesuits, indeed, have a strong alumni organization (Sagrado Corazón 1912, Nadal Ferrer 1946a).

Working-class scholarship students in upper-class schools confirmed rather than erased social distinctions. One exstudent, born in the late 1940s, noted that his school had a different uniform for scholarship students, in addition to a nickname, *fámulos*, sarcastically equating them with the servants of the college. An upper-class alumna of a prestigious women's academy complained that she was unable to associate with nonelite students in the alumnae association. Her own social class rejected the idea, while scholarship students put peer group pressure on each other to maintain boundaries. When one scholarship student became interested in the alumnae group, her classmates derided her as a *señorita*.

In contrast to Nadal's warm memories of school cohesion, middle-class students felt ambivalence towards the topmost circles coalescing before their eyes, as portrayed in a modern novel:

Her parents were rich; mine were not. They sent me to this school at the cost of enormous sacrifices. They did not do it for me alone, of course: it was their way of climbing the social ladder, unconsciously at least. Perhaps I shared their aristocratic dreams as well: I lived in the shadow of the wealthy, passed vacations with them, came and went in their cars, was given dresses and presents by them . . . the same old story. (Mendoza 1979:79)

This poignant recognition of social distance was reiterated by exstudents. (See also Salisachs 1975:13-77.)

More often, social boundaries were based on different institutions that catered to less wealthy families or to members of the managerial elite. In other cases private academies were associated with variation within the elite. The French academy was generally identified as liberal and agnostic. The German college was known as more conservative. The son of a Trasatlántica family in fact did not attend the Jesuit school but went to "a small school run by a former tutor of my father—just my brothers and I, my cousins and a few friends." Socialization established solidarity and distinctiveness within this tightly knit socioeconomic group.

Female education changed more than male schooling, which had accepted public standards and institutions. Aristocratic women of the preindustrial period had little access to schools despite the short-lived presence of a group of nuns who called themselves "Jesuitesses" (Amelang: personal communication). Azcárate (1968:177-192) concurred in the limited opportunities for women and also includes female comments on the problem. More schools emerged in the nineteenth century, but their subject matter was defined by cultural expectations for their gender. An 1824 prospectus, for example, listed as subjects: "Christian doctrine, embroidery, reading, writing, counting and Castilian grammar, learning the useful and wholesome rules for governance of the household, drawing, and music" (Soler and Espinós 1824:3). A later prospectus added French at extra cost (Soler and Espinós 1827: cover).

In the mid-nineteenth century the Madames of the Saced Heart were imported from France to found an advanced academy with social prestige for the daughters of the elite. The patroness of the order was again Dorotea de Chopitea; the actual foundress in Barcelona was her sister-in-law, sister to J. M. Serra. Like the Jesuits, the Madames of the Sacred Heart link students to international prestige. The order has served the daughters of wealthy Catholic families in Europe, Latin America, and the United States; its members are drawn from the same class background and teach behavior and expectations appropriate to the upper classes (Birmingham 1973:235-242).

Despite this development women's education has remained constrained at the secondary level. Although some females of the Good Families regretted not being allowed to continue in their education I found none who had received a college education before the Civil War.

Even in the 1940s and 1950s a year or two of "finishing" in Eire or Switzerland was considered suitable. Only since the 1950s have women come closer to equal educational opportunity in elite families.

The university was already normative for males by the beginning of the twentieth century. Law at the University of Barcelona has been the preferred career—although the considerations may have involved prestige as much as utility. Most have not practiced law since their careers have been shaped by the demands of the family patrimony: factory, land, or properties. Business school was not a socially accepted alternative (Pinilla de las Heras: personal communication). As one fictional aristocratic heir joked, elite males "studied to be a lawyer, in order to study something" (Sagarra de Castellarnau 1977:47). By contrast, a poorer student who struggled through law school around 1910 saw that

> to study a career . . . was a diversion permitted the sons of good families by mere reason of their existence. The effort necessary to earn the degree was insignificant, minimal. For wealthy families this system was trivial. For those who had less—as in my case— the situation was hardly edifying. (Pla 1956:215-216)

This student, of course, was not involved in the social network building that provided a significant value to shared elite education.

The institutionalization of education in Barcelona, then, has reinforced class boundaries. While the emergence of the bourgeoisie expanded the opportunities available for men, and to some extent women, of newly powerful families, it did not aim for democratization of knowledge. As in the rest of the continent educational institutions became further sites for the confluence of bourgeoisie and aristocracy and for separation of the powerful and the powerless. The content of education, especially social skills, affirmed solidarity and distinction.

Etiquette

Advice books have been published almost continuously in Barcelona since the appearance of the *Rules of Christian and Civil Life*, which was printed in multiple editions from 1767 to 1833. Many of these books, intended for the classroom, show simple choices between well-educated and ill-educated children. Knowledge and behavior are clearly linked to class as well. For example, in another book the proud girl "always tries to appear a little better than she actually is," while the proper girl has a secure economic and social position whence "she likes to be useful to those who are less rich" (*Cartilla* 1928). *Virtud y Patria*, ostensibly a reading primer, nonetheless included drawings of "luxury furniture appropriate to wealthy families" (Ruiz and Muncunill 1904?). It also taught such useful primary knowledge as the names of furs and how to fold calling cards to indicate the purpose of a visit.

These texts would have reinforced a sense of distinction for the children of those in power. Others imposed stratification on lower classes. In 1921, for example, the Mancomunitat published a Catalan primer entitled *The Treasure of the Poor and other Stories of Consolation, Stimulation and Dignity for Children of Humble Circumstances* (Suriñach Sentiés). The stories of this volume were chosen to reconcile workers to their place in the social order. Children of the upper class patronized the edition, thus being socialized into the paternalistic stance of their father-owners vis-à-vis the workers.

Some etiquette books were also published for adults. Their content changed little from 1767 to the present. Nor, in fact, has the relationship of the readership altered, even as these roles have been filled by new social groups. Readers come from groups emerging into the social establishment of Barcelona: the first generation of the industrial elite and families or marginal power elite groups who have arrived since.

In addition, authors are members of higher status categories, particularly the nobility. José de Manjarrés i de Bofarull, cited in Chapter III, was a member of the mercantile aristocracy. By the end of the nineteenth century a recently enriched industrialist showed that the new bourgeoisie could act as arbiters of taste and conduct. Camilo Fabra Fontanills, Marquis of Alella after 1889, produced the most famous etiquette book of the Restoration period, the *Código o deberes de buena sociedad*. Its fame was attested by Catalans of the period (Nadal Ferrer 1952:47) as well as by visitors to the city (Valero de Turnos 1888:209). Today's elite still knew of the book, although more current texts were generally to be found in their homes. A contemporary of Fabra noted its rationale:

> The Marquis of Alella was preoccupied by the infractions that many women made through their ignorance of the most elementary rules of proper society. Hence a treatise . . . which people baptized the *Código Fabra*. . . . The book caused a sensation; it was roundly criticized, but those who joked about it most were the ones who followed its advice. (Masriera 1926:170-172)

Etiquette books for adults, like special tutors for the newly enriched (Monserdà i Vidal de Macià 1929:80-82), indicate the barriers that social knowledge imposed on social mobility. The ability to live by an elaborated and arbitrary code of behavior became a condition of access to and movement in an upper class. As arbiters of conduct members of that group have power in exchanges insofar as others accept these codes and accede to them. This power was part of the social capital of the aristocracy but by the end of the nineteenth century was accessible to the industrialists-financiers as well. In the twentieth etiquette has been ruled by the Good Families (Soldevila Zubiburu 1927), although social changes have limited its scope since the Civil War. Furthermore, this power of social knowledge, as opposed to academic knowledge, lay with women—even if men consistently dominated publication of etiquette books.

As in the case of language and institutional education this reign of knowledge has been widespread in European industrial society. Comparative comments may highlight the cultural and political significance of etiquette for Barcelona society. Leonore Davidoff notes for England that

> the ever-changing rules of fashion often became an element of control by such groups, although as Weber rightly emphasized, lifestyles and fashions are almost invariably supported by the ownership of some property. Such groups, through social interaction (Weber's *connubium* and commensality) often bar aspiring others from the acquisition of privileged economic and political positions. . . . At the same time, participation in the group is a reward and badge of arrival. (1973:37)

This view was echoed for Goblot in France, who emphasized the intricate artificiality of bourgeois politeness. This intricacy included complex rules and the bending of rules:

> Therefore, it is not enough to be initiated, one must moreover be educated. Instructed in the rules, it is furthermore necessary to be able to appreciate how and when to apply them, when it is permissible and even preferable to violate them. . . . In France the boundary of classes falls between the "two middle classes," cutting in half the most numerous segment of the population. It is constantly menaced and difficult to defend. A politeness of pure forms, always easy to copy, would not be distinguished, that is, *distinguishing* enough. (1967:61-62)

In Barcelona etiquette books did not confront the pressing class struggles of industrialists and workers so much as they treated fine distinctions between old wealth and new. Yet even so, they were in themselves inadequate. Those in power were those who could break the rules as well as make them. Accepting a fixed code, then, excludes as much as it includes anyone within the calculus of social behavior.

All of these aspects of the elite world were profoundly bound to social and economic power and its reproduction. Other traits might be considered to "round out" the portrait of the gentleman: style of dress, decor, residence, or travel. A contrast, however, may prove more illustrative. A distinctive yet ultimately complementary process of elite differentiation is exemplified in the Good Families' participation in a universal institution of Spanish nationhood: the Roman Catholic Church.

Religion

In addition to academic studies most elite Barcelona schools also indoctrinated pupils in religion. Theoretically, Catholic theology could have promoted social unity as well as identification with the rest of Catholic Spain. Instead, as the educational system suggests, religion was pressed into the class and regionalist concerns of the Catalan upper class (see Torras Bages 1967; Batllori 1979).

The separation between the powerful and the disenfranchised grew with regard to religion through the nineteenth century. In 1909 this erupted in the Setmana Trágica when rioters destroyed churches and convents. In general these were not religious edifices especially identified with the upper class but belonged to those who reproduced class values through paternalism and charity (Ullman 1968; Romero Maura 1974).

Class divisions have continued since. Although Barcelona is now one of the areas of lowest religious observance in Spain, the interclass distinctions of practice and, even more, of attitudes towards the church remain sharper than interregional differences (Duocastella 1975:100-102). The working class has generally become secularized; the upper class, even if they do not attend church, think it is a good idea—for others.

One key to the relationship of church and elite in past times lies in those members of the upper class who have been promoted as paragons, either as saints or candidates for canonization. By the end of the century two other candidates were being promoted: Dorotea de Chopitea (Alegre 1926) and Claudio López Bru, Second Marquis Comillas (Regatill 1948). A memorial volume on the Seminary of Comillas, founded by Antonio López, and other lesser pious literature amplify this ideological portrait of the saintly gentleman (Abad 1928).

By the end of the century it became obvious that wealth was not inimicable to sanctity. Indeed, it was seen to facilitate a paternalistic stance. López and Chopitea, the latter as widow of José María Serra, were deeply involved in business. This kind of involvement was explained in another pious biography: "Don Manuel saw work not only as a means of gaining a livelihood but also as an expiation, as a law, and even as a noble entertainment and joy of the spirit" (Moreu Lacruz

1921:21). Work, of course, was not without return: of Antonio López, one priest wrote, "God wished to reward his love for work. . . . God wanted to crown his ideas of national restoration" (Abad 1928:20). Furthermore, the students of the seminary he endowed with 500,000 pesetas offered perpetual prayers and masses for the founder and his family.

The church and the class coincided in certain interests. Women were extolled as domestic and maternal figures. Despite her business life, Dorotea de Chopitea de Serra was extolled by her biographer, Father Alegre, for domestic and charitable activities. Yet, virtue was clearly tied to class. Alegre, for example, reviewed the list of "necessities" that Chopitea felt she might question as part of her spiritual exercises in the 1880s: the coach, the servants, and the house in the country. He applauded her scruples and self-abnegation but nonetheless lauded the dedication to the family that would force her to live in such material comfort. Through such interpretations of religious and ethical questions, elite women were encouraged to be charitable rather than critical of their role, or the role of women in general, within Catalan industrial society (Monserdà i Vidal de Macià 1907; 1916).

Men were expected to take their spiritual concerns into the work place as well as to act as patrons for religious causes. The charity of the Güells has already been noted. Later, under the Franco regime this train

Figure 18
Summer Home of the Serra-Chopitea Family
(now a school for the Sisters of the Sacred Heart)

of thought was exemplified in a treatise by Vicente Muntadas Rovira of La España Industrial. He began with a canon law justification for capitalist relations of production and then called upon his fellow businessmen to "treat the workers with the solicitude of a first-born brother, providing with largesse, insofar as the resources of the company permit it, the moral and material improvements that will elevate his spirit and make life more pleasant" (1950:109-111). Muntadas noted that such socioreligious action had defused the virulence of worker demands in countries such as England (1950:109-111). From the *colonia* to the modern factory charity confirms the position of both giver and receiver.

Most recently the religious interests of domination in Spain have been linked to Opus Dei, a Catholic lay association founded in 1928 by the Aragonese priest Escrivá de Balaguer. Under Franco Opus Dei was closely associated with government technocrats. In Barcelona it has had influence in the Harvard Business School affiliate. Members of families like the Salas, Bertrands, Güells, and Valls Taberner appear in Ynfante's 1970 listing of the organization's membership (I-LXXII), although several vehemently protested their inclusion. It may be possible that the Good Families no longer represent the kind of power group that Opus Dei has associated with in Spanish politics. Opus prefers the managerial technocrats of the new generation.

Right conduct, then, defined through both elaborated behavioral codes and the Christianization of the gentleman, has played a dual role within Catalan industrial society. On the one hand, it set standards for access to an elite. At the same time proper conduct, like proper education and language, sustained social stratification with both secular and spiritual authority. While Catholicism valued the life of poverty, it accommodated as well to the nobility and bourgeoisie.

CULTURE AND CAPITAL

The synthetic process that took place through bourgeois acceptance and transformation of aristocratic norms did not guarantee the transmission or reproduction of status over time. Once gained, such status must be reaffirmed in transaction. Shared values and heritage demanded interaction through which sharing recurs. This dynamic status demanded the acquisition of social capital through the expenditure of economic capital. While these transactions joined lineages to the Good Families or confirmed their position therein, such exchanges might also be involved in loss of social position.

Even if standards or language could be learned by someone entering an elite, other information is more central to the definition of the group.

To be a gentleman, one must know who the other gentlemen are, to have shared past experiences and style with them. This knowledge comes from constant interaction from childhood onward, providing the membership of an upper class with a shared history and historical consciousness inaccessible to any intruder.

Interaction and history were part of the solidarity of rural elites as well. Raventós Domenech focussed on social networks and knowledge in the training of the *hereu*, passed on by the grandmother (senior female of the *casa pairal*):

> And since this world of names and tales is entangled like a cherry orchard, she always ended up explaining the ancient kinship of the neighboring homesteads, the various entwinings of males and females with families of the Vallès or the Llobregat plain. . . . All this made me think that the most imposing ability in women is the analytic talent that is capable of following the thread of a family through five generations with all its derived branches, entwinings, and graftings, without hopelessly entangling her head, her memory, and her tongue. (1928:110-111)

Social knowledge of this sort is constantly reiterated in elite conversations. The speaker locates each person within a web of personalized associations that thus confirms shared group experience:

Figure 19
The *Rambles* of Turn-of-the-Century Barcelona

"I saw an exhibit of Tomasa's photos in a gallery on the Rambla de Catalunya the other day."

"Tomasa? Tomasa Montblanc? Whose family used to have that fantastic summer place at S'Agaró?"

"Not those Montblanc. They were the Bank Montblanc people, whose uncle got caught with the chorus girl at the Molino. Tomasa's father had a place in Sitges. Of course, they gave it up ages ago. Her brother married a Pi-Bet. She married the son of the Marquis de Fulano whose family has a huge estate near Seville. It all went to his brother, of course, but she got a nice chalet in the Vall d'Aran and an apartment on the Calle Bonanova."

"I remember her—she used to go to parties at Sant Pere, no?"

"I think so. Her brother went to the German college, so he knew Marc Capallet and that crowd. She's a tall blond girl, with a horsey face like her mother's folks."

This *constructed* conversation does not portray any one person in Barcelona, although all the characterizations are drawn from actual conversations. They indicate the markers used to situate people: kinship, family histories, residence(s), alliance, education, social interaction, and physical characteristics. All draw upon shared acquaintance and conversation. In my fieldwork, in fact, little of this information was actually available from research or study, so it was difficult for me to follow such conversations. Only after months did these families of the present become as real to me as the families of the past that I had been able to research and document.

Shared associations are encouraged by locales that bring the elite together, such as exclusive clubs or the opera (see Chapter VIII). They have been reinforced by the elite's ability to leave the city for summer colonies or travel outside Spain. Even the latter could entail meeting Catalans: "Ferrer i Vidal, like so many other Barcelonins of his era, went to Vichy. Vichy was, at that time, the supreme attraction and indispensable luxury" (Nadal Ferrer 1946:67). Such spas, of course, also affirmed contacts, or at least the possibility of contacts, with members of international power groups.

Interaction thus also defines a limited pool of information from which outsiders were again excluded. This flow of information is part of elite reproduction of control. Right connections are an indispensable part of business and finance: where a poor inventor might approach a banker for a loan, the upper-class industrialist deals with a friend in a shared investment. The control of information also has given special power to women, both in domestic affairs like the planning of marriage and in more public evaluations of conduct. It allowed women to police the boundaries of the elite in much the same manner as Davidoff noted for Victorian London society (1973).

Training and knowledge therefore tended to preclude smooth ascent for upwardly mobile males or females, especially as group coalescence became clearer at the turn of the century. A contemporary Catalan novelist captures the feelings of a woman stymied by such invisible barriers of class, trying to find the answers to her failure in the ways her parents had raised her:

> If only they had given her studies . . . languages . . . music. . . . In the end, you can never know what reading will profit you most, or how to memorize long passages to pull them out at the perfect moment. And yet those other ladies, instructed through their whole lives, know how to remain fine without becoming bluestockings, how to hold the cup with delicacy, and how to remember precisely the names of those they have just met. (Llor 1958:52-54)

The elite as a group can also limit or destroy prestige claims. "*Lo dir de la gent*," or "*el que-dirán*" (what people will say) is a powerful mechanism for social control: rumors or gossip can undercut both social and economic alliances. Socialization means a precise knowledge of what rules may be broken, as Goblot saw for France (1967:62); others will be punished. In recent Barcelona society the Muntadas-Prim case defined the limits of acceptable elite behavior—and the sanctions that follow.

The case, which broke into Barcelona newspapers in 1979, was one of the most imposing scandals of the upper class for decades. The protagonist, Juan Carlos Muntadas-Prim, is a descendant of both the industrialist founders of La España Industrial and General Joan Prim Prats (1814-1870), military politician and architect of the Liberal Revolution of 1868. Through Prim, this branch of the family currently holds six noble titles, most with grandeeship.

Juan Carlos Muntadas began his career managing his family's investments, property, and commercial activities. Eventually he expanded to more intricate financial operations that allegedly led to his downfall. He met early losses with short-term loans at impossible interest rates of up to 100 percent per annum. When the spiral of these loans collapsed, his debts were estimated as high as 1,400,000,000 pesetas ($20,000,000) (*TeleXpress* 6 February 1978). He owed much of this to his family and friends, but small investors and rural clients of the Muntadas had also been caught by his schemes.

Most members of the upper class reacted negatively. Muntadas-Prim was called dishonest, shameless (*sinvergüenza*), or a *cap verd* (a giddy or unstable person) (*TeleXpress* 6 February 1978). Misconduct shat-

Figure 20
José Antonio Muntadas of La España Industrial

tered his social prestige: as one businessman observed, financial mis-
dealing is a cardinal sin in Catalonia. Yet all this criticism did not
change his birthright. Muntadas-Prim is still a *senyor* by breeding and
education, although he failed to live up to his status.

The Muntadas-Prim family, his parents, and siblings suffered finan-
cially rather than socially once the immediate flurry of publicity ended.
The Duke Prim, Juan Carlos Muntadas' father, relinquished all his corporate posts and pledged the family patrimony towards full restitution
of his son's debts. Members of the elite viewed this as an honorable ges-
ture and felt sympathetic towards those involved.

Public reactions tended to follow class lines. The conservative *Diario
de Barcelona*, an elitist newspaper, refused to discuss the scandal. Leftist periodicals used the case as a critique of the family and the elite.
This, in turn, provoked upper-class defensive solidarity: the Count
Montseny replied to questioners that "I regret this type of unqualified
facts that do no more than disparage a class [*estamento*] that should
consider itself more subject to obligations than open to privilege" (*Por
Favor* 20 February 1978).

The Muntadas-Prim scandal was discussed widely by women and

men because the actions were part of the public realm of business. Other negative criticisms that seem to arise with frequency in Barcelona society concern presentation of self or sexual conduct, but these are dealt with more privately, limiting knowledge and networks. Women can also be sanctioned for violations of their role expectations. Yet what is especially important is their role as *sanctioners* in the crucial negotiations of matrimony.

Although Muntadas-Prim damaged his own social standing by his actions, the reputation of his family continues to be viewed favorably. Yet financial misdealings can have other unfortunate long-term effects on status if families cannot keep up economically with the exigencies of their social presentation. In the prologue to her novel *Buscant una ànima*, Dolors Monserdà contrasted the early entrepreneurs of Barcelona with their twentieth-century descendants on the basis of their social attitudes towards the value of money: "Between that Barcelona that knew how to make money and that which knows how to spend it lies a world of difference" (1929:9). In other words spending has not been a one-time purchase of status markers but rather a repeated and regular ability to invest correctly in socialization, accumulation of goods, and connections. This factor is crucial to both upward and downward mobility. A single large investment, whether jewelry or a large tomb, is often viewed as ridiculous or ostentatious. Nor does status decay imply *poverty* so much as the inability to meet normal demands of other families who claim the same rank.

On the basis of existing records it is difficult to say exactly how much it cost to belong to the Good Families in past times. Two suggestive fragments, however, are of interest. Masriera (1926:51) lists the excessive expenses of a young gentleman of 1859, including 2,300 pesetas to teachers of Italian and guitar; 2,300 for cigars and scents; 2,500 for carnival; and over 5,000 pesetas to the tailor, barber, and shoemaker. The total budget was 27,480 pesetas, over $5,000. This can be compared with the extremely detailed survey work collected by Ildefonso Cerdá in 1856 for the working class. Using data from 54,272 workers, he calculated the average daily wage was 8.55 reales, or 5.13 pesetas ($1.00). Given the average work year, this meant a salary of 1,380 pesetas, which rose to 2,496 pesetas for the most skilled workmen. Cerdá further calculated the minimum necessary expense of life as 1,380 pesetas for a bachelor and 2,505.5 for a family with two children. The expenses of a single upper-class male were twenty times that of a worker. This ratio is corroborated by the dowry ratios of the next chapter. Meanwhile, the salary of the average worker was not adequate to meet the minimal needs of his family (Cerdá 1968-1971, 2:221-312).

Masriera calculated that the equivalent budget for an elite male in

1926 would be 109,920 pesetas ($21,214). A detailed private account of a Barcelona elite woman in 1915 (still in a family archive) partially confirms this. Her total expenses were 49,332.55 pesetas ($9,521). Allowing for post-war inflation in Masriera's figures (Balcells 1974:88), all of these figures coincide. They suggest both the continued expenses of living as an elite member and the relative levels of spending that divide classes.

These two cases are only suggestive. They reiterate, however, the close correlation between the economic transformation of Barcelona society and the redefinition of social status categories. This was equally evident when a family could not afford to maintain its status through time.

The three-generation model of the family firm implies that descendants eventually will be isolated from, and uninterestd in, production. More time and effort are devoted to education and social interaction, and this does not sustain an expanding economic base. Even if not actually poorer, families may become poor *relative* to others as the economy develops in new ways. In other cases investments may actually decline, leaving the family in a difficult situation.

The aristocratic novelist Josep Maria de Sagarra de Castellarnau described this decadence of a noble family in his novel *Vida privada*. The work is such a thinly disguised portrait of people whom Sagarra dealt with that it was reported to have led to his ostracism in Catalan "Society" after its publication. Most characters are identifiable to elite readers today. Hence it provides an ideal pseudoethnographic case for analysis of elite decay.

Sagarra's Lloberola family was descended from the preindustrial landed nobility. By the early twentieth century its future was "important in appearance, but in reality impoverished by the Carlist wars and his father's follies, burdened with mortgages and forced to pay *llegítimes*, legacies, and pensions without end" (1977:27). Furthermore, the head of the family was ill-equipped to deal with the realities of his own situation:

> D. Thomas found himself at the age of twenty-eight to be head of his modest household. . . with a university degree that was good for nothing, with a fat but scrupulous wife who was likewise good for nothing, and with a total ignorance of any way to fight tooth and nail to take control of the situation or even save his own skin.
> . . .
> In compensation, D. Thomas had the consciousness of his magical superiority, because he sprang from thirty generations who

had never touched dirt. D. Thomas, using the only weapon remaining to him, fenced with his family pride. (1977:28)

At the beginning of the novel the Lloberola's position was already
tenuous. Individual and collective problems had forced their general retirement from public life. By avoiding social display, they forestalled
expenditure and the possibility of failure in their claims to social
power. The situation "of the Lloberola passed almost unnoticed. . . .
outside of their closest kin, they saw no one, were invited nowhere, and
were not seen at any major event" (1977:31). While not living up to the
behavior or interaction of the gentleman, they were not actively failing.

Other strategies were more direct. Wealthy relatives were cultivated
for the possibilities of inheritance. One son lived off his charm and his
friends. Another, whom Sagarra acidly portrayed as a success, became
involved in a sexual triangle through which he drove a wealthy businessman to suicide and married the widow.

Despite small gains the family soon passes into a more serious stage
when resources are not adequate for expenses and inherited possessions must be sold:

> The first alert in Barcelona society that the Lloberola's were tee-
> tering came out on Hortensia Portell's Nameday. In that salon
> many of the ladies who came to visit noticed the famous Gobelin
> tapestry that had formerly presided over the Lloberola's green
> room. . . . Everyone asked, in those theatrical whispers, and Hor-
> tensia, between embarassment and smiles, replied "Yes, the poor
> Lloberolas. . . . I have seen it coming for some time. I got the tap-
> estry at a good price." Later, in a more intimate manner and
> hushed dialogue, Hortensia abandoned this sentimental tone for
> one more reminiscent of the kitchen shears that would fillet a
> mackerel without any compassion.
>
> The scandal of the tapestry spread over fifty thousand spoonfuls
> of soup that night in the apartments of Barcelona, to be followed
> by the scandal of other sales, and finally the news that the Llobe-
> rolas were leaving their house. (1977:34)

By drawing on their inherited economic capital, the Lloberolas had
sacrificed their social capital: the elite accumulation of possessions, education, and prestige through time had been violated. Similarly, in the
recent recession sales of homes, jewelry, and art reverberated throughout information networks, causing second thoughts about proposed
marriages or investments. Yet social positions are still not lost: many
such families retain professional/managerial posts. They may also
maintain some contacts and family-historical consciousness. However,

these claims are less and less recognized by the successful members of the upper class or by replacements who lack "a sense of history."

In time even nobility "fades": titles are abandoned by the family as inheritance taxes become excessive. One folkloric case in Barcelona is that of an ancient noble family who have completely retired into the closed world of their palace, all children unmarried and without enough money to even keep the whole house habitable. Others have used their titles to renew their fortunes as in the past. To do so they must rely on synthesis of old and new power groups through marriage. But the elite that resulted from such a union in the past often finds itself anew in the position of the Lloberola, overwhelmed by structures outside the Catalan ambit. Yet this, too, was the appearance of the confrontation of feudal nobility and bourgeoisie a century ago.

CONCLUSIONS

This chapter has followed the synthesis of social and cultural values that underpinned the unity of a new Barcelona elite in the industrial period. This process entailed the renovation of established status claims and patterns of life in which both the older aristocracy and the emergent commercial-industrial power holders participated.

The cultural values of social power show a striking stability from the preindustrial period to the twentieth century. At the beginning of this period noble families clearly dominated these values, the social capital of Barcelona. With time, the children of the bourgeoisie were educated into the background, norms, and experience of the older establishment. Their social networks as well as their beliefs were indicative of a meshing of power-holding groups. In the twentieth century, then, the Good Families have been united by shared values, institutions, and history as gentlemen and ladies of breeding.

This elite is not simply an amalgam of aristocracy and bourgeoisie, however. The aristocracy of Catalonia was a complex and multilayered group whose ranks had been open to new members and institutions even before the industrial period (Amelang 1986). Some noble families proved unable to keep pace with the expansion and redefinition of power and fell out of active social intercourse as well. At the same time, some wealthy industrialists have lost their fortunes or failed to establish a social presence for their family. Elite reproduction has entailed both downward and upward mobility.

Thus the social transformation of the elite family has been more complex than an "industrialization of the aristocracy" or "an ennoblement of the bourgeoisie." Economic development stimulated a redefinition of social power. Social interaction and ideology were negotiated in the formation of the new power group. The family has been crucial to this reformulation, whether as producing household, as socializer, or as unit of interaction and history. Indeed, this became especially critical as families came together in the alliances and exchanges of matrimony that are examined in the next chapter.

CHAPTER VII

COMMERCIUM AND CONNUBIUM

Dolors Monserdà began her novel of the Barcelona industrial upper class, *La família Asparó*, with a wedding in the fashionable church of La Mercè. As the guests await the bride, they discuss the negotiations underlying the match:

> "But is it true what they say, that he is the one making the good catch?"
>
> "Certainly, my friend! How can the wealth of Casa Balcells compare with that of the Asparó's? Without taking into account that Rosita Asparó is an only child, while Pablito's family is over-run with six brothers!"
>
> Meanwhile Donya Catarineta, with the precision of a business agent, expostulated on her reliable information about both the bride's house and the groom's. (1900:9)

This vignette brings together three important aspects of elite marriage in Barcelona. First, matrimony, sanctioned by church and state, is necessary to the legal procreation of children in Catalonia. Therefore it has been basic to the reproduction of the economic and social power of the family. Second, marriage not only creates a new nuclear unit but links two lineages. It institutionalizes alliance and exchange between households. Finally, marriage arrangements entail both economic and social capital. Socialization instilled values through which industrialist scions became ladies and gentlemen; marriage was the seal through which this assimilation was approved and through which the social synthesis of the Good Families took place.

Anthropologists, social historians, and social theorists have concurred in emphasizing marriage patterns as a key for understanding status differentiation. Weber characterized a status group as one

> societalized through its specific style of life, its conventional and specific notions of honor, and the economic opportunities it legally monopolizes. A status group is always somehow societalized but it is not always organized into an association. *Commercium*, in the sense of "social intercourse," and *connubium* among groups are the typical characteristics of mutual esteem among status equals; their absence signifies status differences. (1946:300)

Vicens Vives characterized the Barcelona ruling class by "a phenomenon of social concentration which responds to the practice of class endogamy or at least the result of the accumulation of capital"
(1958:128-129). His analysis, however, meshed ideological values
with social theory. Both "endogamy" and "accumulation" are complex, even misleading terms, unless placed in a processual framework.
Marriage between aristocratic families and industrialists in the late
nineteenth century did not cross boundaries so much as they changed
them and redefined the limits of the elite marital pool.

This chapter begins with a general institutional view of the social,
economic, and psychological ramifications of matrimony in the Catalan elite. On this basis discussion focusses on generational patterns supplemented with case studies of representative families. These analyses
will illuminate the value of a dynamic interpretation of elite formation
and the limits of the Good Families.

The Meaning of Marriage in Catalonia

In Spain religious and state sanction of rites of passage generally coincide. Although civil marriage without religious approbation has, at
times, been an option, both middle and upper classes have disap-
proved. Despite the languishing interest otherwise accorded religious
ceremony in Catalonia (Duocastella 1975:137, 141-142, 160-162),
this opinion changes slowly. I found no cases of civil marriage in upper-
class family histories. As suggested in the previous chapter, the elite has
been socialized into public respect for religious norms.

According to Roman Catholic canon law and Spanish law, marriages
generally have been indissoluble. Catholic law has allowed an arduous
recourse to church tribunals for annulment. Spain permitted civil divorce during the Republican period and again legalized it in 1981 after
heated debate. In general, neither has been a socially acceptable option
for elite families.

Separation, however, has long existed in Spain. Catalan law stands
out in its safeguards of women's possessions in the marriage (Universidad de Barcelona 1973; Falguera 1889). The marriage contract lays
the groundwork for a legal division of rights within a marriage. While
not common, separations occurred in the past century as well as the
present. Glòria Bulbena Reig, the daughter of a commercial academic
family, has recorded her own experiences of marriage and separation:

> I was married at 22, on the 20th of April, 1914. At that time,
> courtship did not permit the bride and groom to know each other
> well, since they had no opportunity for acquaintance without the

presence of chaperones. Because of these false prejudices, my husband was a stranger to me until we were united by indissoluble bonds. Unfortunately, his manner of being and acting became clear in naked ugliness thereafter. . . .

We lived together twenty years, while I tried to hide or control his faults in front of our children, my parents, or society. I never wished for a divorce: I was driven to the separation by economic interests, which declined incessantly, to the detriment of my daughters. He was able to act with impunity since at that time the husband was administrator of the goods of the wife. (1976:119-120)

The expectations of Barcelona society not only led Glòria Bulbena into an unhappy marriage but kept her there until her children were raised. Only when her children's inheritance was threatened did she limit the marital bond, in the only legal manner available. Even so, the other social ramifications of the marriage could not be changed.

In the Catalan upper class matrimony is also the primary marker of the transition to full adulthood. Both partners are likely to leave their families of origin for the first time as they establish their new household. For males marriage is an economic shift, often signalling the passage from tutelage to executive action. For women matrimony is much more a social separation from the family to join a new unit. While a woman's economic dependence remains constant, her role changes with regard to her own lineage and her affines.

At his marriage a man has already been integrated into public social activities. Marriage confirms this status, revealing a psychological element underscored in the autobiography of one bourgeois novelist: "My father, a robust man who had never been ill, died in 1917 on the very eve of my wedding. It seems as if destiny pleased itself by giving my coming of age a much fuller significance than it normally would have had" (Soldevila Zubiburu 1954:287).

A woman's economic situation changes legally, but this has very few consequences in practice: administration of her goods simply passes from her father to her husband. Until recently she would remain effectively a minor in most cases. Her social transition, though, is much more rapid. In the nineteenth century, Manjarrés y de Bofarull contrasted the male's gradual entrance into upper-class society with that of a woman: "from the walls of her high school she passes to promenades and visits. . . . The transition from one state to another is so rapid that she has no time to study the situation" (1854:4). Women who made their debut as late as the 1950s were still expected to marry within a year. The "right match" became the goal and proof of a woman's socialization and identity:

> Girls were not educated for anything then—we didn't even finish high school. Everyone had her social charms and accomplishments [*culturita*]. Our triumphs were "I went to five dances this week" or "She went out with the Marquis of Something or Other." But my life changed, and what could I do? I had always thought little girls stayed pretty and married well.

This attitude has shifted with increased awareness of European and American norms in the 1970s.

The major change for a woman at marriage was her new social role within the networks of visits and information. Through such meetings a woman safeguards her family's reputation and prepares the way for marriage for her own children. This knowledge made mothers crucial in marriage choice, especially in the nineteenth century when the couple themselves had little impact on the family choice. In 1926 the historian Masriera Colomer recalled the entrepreneurial mother of his youth:

> . . . always demonstrating a fund of common sense and malicious insight in her social intercourse that her daughters, although educated in Paris, London, or Geneva, would never be able to surpass.
> . . . She knew the Calendar of Saints by heart, but she was also able to recite the amount of the dowry given to each marriageable girl in Barcelona by their fathers. (1926:53-54)

Although matches are no longer arranged, parental influence remained strong through the 1950s, with men and women recognizing the mother's knowledge and dominance. One woman recalled the *black border* that consistently surrounded the dance floor in the 1940s—an ironic equation of a funeral announcement with the widowed female chaperones who watched conduct and potential alliances. This woman recalled that parents were also the main clients of the photographers who circulated at such parties. They would buy photos to see who was dancing with whom and to praise or criticize the potential match.

This social control became vital to the cohesion of the elite as a whole in both its cohesion and its closure. As Davidoff has observed for Victorian England:

> Throughout the nineteenth century, arranged marriages were no longer acceptable so that individual choice had to be most carefully regulated to ensure the exclusion of undesirable partners and

maximum gain for both sides. Social exclusiveness insured the former. The latter was achieved by strenuous bargaining. . . .

Under such a system it was vital that only potentially suitable partners should mix. To meet these ends, balls and dances became the particular place for a girl to be introduced into Society. . . . Chaperones were necessary to overlook the social character of her dancing partners just as much as her sexual behavior. (1973:49-50)

The difference between male and female roles is indicated by their relative ages at marriage (see Table 8). Males in the Barcelona elite have tended to marry late, near thirty, when they take on company responsibilities. Women, on the average, were 6.4 years younger than their spouses in the years 1825 to 1950, indicative of their limited preparation and different responsibilities. The chart also shows changes through time. In the founding generation grooms were approximately nine years older than their brides: a man could not marry until he had established himself in business. The gap diminished over the next seventy-five years. Male age at marriage has varied more: in prosperity, when business offered more opportunities, age dropped; in a depression it rose. Social behavior was linked to forcees far beyond the family. Intermediate in this process, though, was the evaluation and selection that involved not only the couple themselves but the negotiations of their kindred.

The business of marriage could be vital to both families. In an elite family the dowry could be a large sum of cash and properties. This was visible in the guarantees against misuse or loss of the dowry enshrined in Catalan law (Falguera 1862). In the case of the inheriting female, for example, Catalan law provides for a male dowry, the *aixovar*, which specified all property the husband himself owned so that he might not appropriate his wife's goods (Maspons Anglasell 1907:65-66).

Table 8
Average Marriage Age of the Upper Class, 1825-1950

Generation	Male	Female	Difference
1825-1850	29.2 (11)	20.7 (10)	8.5
1851-1875	27.0 (22)	21.1 (19)	5.9
1876-1900	29.3 (18)	24.1 (12)	5.21
1900-1925	26.9 (14)	22.5 (4)	4.4
1926-1950	31.4 (12)	23.3 (4)	8.1

NOTE: Numbers in parentheses represent the total number of subjects on whom accurate information is available.

Just as the dowry was a potential assistance for the groom's family, it was a loss of capital for the bride's, who negotiated payment schedules or postponed settlement until the death of the parents. In this setting quarrels arose over nonpayment; in other cases useful property was tied up in mortgages to guarantee the marriage settlement (AHPB: Gibert 1864, 121; AHPB: Moreu 1875, 3:1,746).

Table 9 presents some figures on the actual size of dowries in the upper class, insofar as notarial archives are open. Even the contrast of classes here is incompete, for it fails to include wedding gifts and similar tokens that might be quite substantial. Elite wedding gifts included jewelry, coaches or cars, and other expensive items. At a Sedó-Peris Mencheta wedding in 1897 the *Noticiero Universal* devoted columns to the lavish presents received from other elite families, promoting solidarity while emphasizing the wealth of the couple. Not incidentally, the bride's father owned the newspaper: a wedding was an occasion for the display of wealth and power (20 February 1897).

The 1838 dowries show the confluence of social category and consumption. The dowry of a noble marriage that year was seventy times that of the average peasant—even apart from those peasants who married without contracts. Urban artisans and urban professionals were intermediate groups. Merchants and nonaristocratic landowners, while lavish, did not reach aristocratic heights. Early industrialists had not yet amassed capital, while their display was limited by the role of the mobility as social and political arbiters.

In 1858 peasants and artisans remained at the bottom of the scale, but the gap between those groups and the upper classes had widened.

Table 9
Average Dowry According to Occupational Group, 1838-1878

Occupational Group[a]	1838	1858	1878
Peasants	522.4 (14)	667.5 (3)	2,072.2 (6)
Urban artisans and guild members	1,794.2 (17)	2,767.5 (13)	4,860.7 (13)
Urban professionals	3,371.0 (3)	19,310.0 (6)	51,000.0 (2)
Industrialists and merchants	11,913.0 (5)	49,420.6 (7)	40,173.0 (10)
Landowners	16,020.0 (1)[b]	10,401.6 (4)	85,000.0 (3)
Nobles	37,380.0 (1)	34,710.0 (3)	—

SOURCE: AHPB.

NOTES: Numbers in parentheses represent the total number of subjects on whom accurate information is available.

[a] This survey examined 10 percent of all established notaries in Barcelona for each year.

[b] The husband's profession is not specified. The wife's father is listed as a landowner.

Meanwhile, the average dowry for industrialists and merchants exceeded that of the only noble marriage in my sampling.

In 1878 this trajectory of differentiation is clear. Peasants and urban artisans remain in the same position. The gulf between lower classes and upper groups has grown. Yet professionals, industrialists and landowners overlap in the range of their dowries. The categories themselves have become confused: by the late nineteenth century an industrialist could be a landowner or even a noble.

By the end of the century finances were bound to transactions between money and status. In the play *El dinero y la nobleza* (Money and Nobility), which premiered at the Liceu in 1873, this theme was made explicit. The protagonist is a ruined Marquis who contracted marriage with an industrial heiress. Commenting on his father-in-law, he says:

> Señor Manzano wished to invest his funds, and I was looking for a loan. . . . We met by chance, but . . . we met. I was afraid that I would lack sufficient guarantees, but he saw enough in my title to fulfill all his aspirations and decided to accept me as a son-in-law. I investigated his morality and found that his fortune had been honorably acquired and did not hesitate to take his only daughter's hand. (García Parreño 1873:10)

In the drama a crisis arises over the Marquis' style of living, which is ruining his father-in-law. The wedded pair, though, are reconciled by true love and the Marquis' commitment to cultivate his estates. As the play ends the bourgeois father considers agriculture himself—looking along this path to his own acquisition of a noble title.

While the story of the impoverished nobleman wed to a business heiress has been a cliché in Catalan literature for a century, as it has been in other industrial societies like France or England, it is not a misrepresentation of the values of either the bourgeoisie or the aristocracy in this century. One modern woman remembered that her grandmother had always told her to marry a nobleman "because it was easier to get into heaven." Although she laughed at the advice, both she and her sister had followed it. Arno Mayer's observations on northern Europe echo the process evident in Barcelona society:

> The nobilities, especially the magnates among them, bolstered their failing economic fortunes by securing government support, by investing in the nonagrarian sector, and by adopting clever marriage strategies. . . . Doubting their own legitimacy and in no position to subvert or conquer the old ruling classes, the new big businessmen and professionals decided to imitate, cajole and join them. (1981:127)

This synthesis will become clearer in the history of generations and individual families.

MARRIAGE AS A HISTORICAL STRATEGY: GENERATIONS

An overview of power-holding families in the past century shows that within the institutional continuity of marriage, economic and social conditions have constrained some potential marriages while suggesting valuable strategies to be followed. This approach highlights the chronology of bourgeois and elite synthesis suggested in the last chapter's study of elite values.

In general, Barcelona marriages have been less a vehicle for social mobility than a confirmation of status claims. For early entreprenuers a wedding often preceded the capture of economic power. It was an alliance with a woman of the same or a slightly higher social class as the founder. It was by no means an alliance with the social class with whom the founders would interact by the end of a successful life. Such claims might occur in his own lifetime through the marriages of his children.

This pattern characterized the founders discussed in past chapters. Antonio López wedded into a Catalan commercial family in Cuba—one possibly in financial straits. Even so, his in-laws were loud in their disapproval. Juan Güell was forty-five when he married his first wife, the daughter of a modest banker. José Ferrer Vidal married a woman whose family history echoed his own—the daughter of a self-made *indiano* for whose family he provided managerial skills. Gradual mobility was more evident in the Girona marriages. Ignasi Girona Targa married a woman from his native village; his son, Manuel, married the daughter of an *indiano*. These limitations in marital mobility were echoed by later entrepreneurs. Salvador Andreu Grau, who achieved success in the early 1900s, married Carmen Miralles, daughter of a minor banker and sister of the well-known painter Francesc Miralles. His children and grandchildren have married into major families of the city.

In the nineteenth century elite endogamous castes already existed in Catalonia such as the landed nobility. Ennobled merchants from the eighteenth century also seem to have interacted primarily with each other—leading later to a social marginalization. The Sentmenat and de Gònima-de Janer families will illustrate both of these patterns in later discussion.

For the first generation of industrialists and bankers marital mobility was not equivalent to economic mobility. When the children of the founders reached marriage age, between 1860 and 1890, they had acquired the background and connections that their parents lacked. The children of the bourgeoisie—and some nobles—had been brought up with common values, shared histories, and constant interaction. Their economic foundation was secure, and the aims of families—and group—were clearer.

This second generation was characterized by intensive alliances among the main industrialist families. Most established at least one bond with another power-holding family; large families had even greater potential. Equally important was the avoidance of bad matches or problematic marriage settlements. The Güells, for example, were only two in the second generation. Yet their marriages—to a López and a Ferrer-Vidal—were extremely important. The Villavecchias established a more imposing network through the marriages of seven children. The will of Ignacio Villavecchia Viani, however, noted that four of the dowries were unpaid at his death; his sons faced these additional obligations (AHPB: Moreu 1875, 1:2,059; 3:1,746). The ideal was a balance, represented by the Gironas, who each moved into a different sector and married well (see Figure 41, Appendix).

Differentiation by economic sector characterized the second generation as well. Children in family firms, especially in textiles, tended to marry into other such firms. Those from larger, "associative" corporations married with their fellow board member's families or other members of the grand bourgeoisie.

Aristocratic matrimonies remained exclusive and endogamous. The economic situation of the nobility was changing in important ways, though. Some of the aristocracy held both prestige and rents. Others saw their income decrease, not only relative to the new standards of the bourgeoisie but also in absolute terms. The foundation for new solutions were laid.

In 1889 Isabel Villavecchia Milà de la Roca married Luis de Dalmases de Olivart, grandson of the Marquis of Vilallonga. At almost the same time Rosa Ricart Cordova, the daughter of ennobled industrialists, married Ignacio de Despujol de Chaves, Sixth Marquis Palmerola and Count of Fonollar. A decade later Isabel Güell López, daughter of the First Count Güell, married Carlos de Sentmenat de Sentmenat, Eighth Marquis of Castelldosríus and Twenty-Fifth Baron of Santa Pau, Grandee of Spain. These three marriages indicate a major shift in upper-class marriages: in the third generation the daughters of the bourgeoisie became wives to the aristocracy.

Gender roles were important in these marriages, which represented a balanced exchange of economic and social capital. Titles pass through the male line; while aristocratic daughters are noble, their offspring rarely have the chance to claim a title. Women of the bourgeoisie were not primary heirs, either, but they carried liquid capital in the form of dowries. The opposite alliance, of a noble female and a bour-

geois male, was of less interest to both noble and industrialist and only
came to pass a generation later. In the first such marriage I recorded, in
1922, the female bore the title, thus equalizing her social capital with
the economic strength of the male.

Men of the third industrial generation wed daughters of other industrialists, including those ennobled by Restoration monarchs. Others
continued to build networks with the bourgeoisie, although perhaps including some distant noble affines.

A finer stratification was evident within the marriages with which
this section began. Luis de Dalmases was a direct descendant of the
First Marquis of Vilallonga (title awarded 1710), but the title had
passed through another line. The Villavecchias also lacked a title. In the
other cases the women belonged to families who already had noble
connections. The Ricarts were Marquises of Santa Isabel by affinal inheritance; the maternal grandfather of Isabel Güell had been made a
grandee in 1881. These matches mingled the most prestigious of the
new families with the magnates of the old.

Some other boundaries remained intact. Both the families of the
eighteenth-century mercantile aristocracy and those of single-family
enterprises continued their patterns of endogamy. The meaning of
these marriages, however, was transformed by their context—by the
connubial upper class from which they were, in effect, isolated.

In speaking of industrial organization a generation refers to those
who hold power and relinquish it at death or retirement. Marital
succession involves more condensed generations. The Good Families
have passed into their fourth and fifth generations of marriages. The
fourth generation, who married prior to the Civil War, was the generation of consolidation. At this time marriage boundaries between industrialist and aristocrat were eliminated, although prestige differences
may be evoked in some social contexts.

Postwar generations have faced new situations of contact and courtship. While marriages among elite families continue to the present, children have also had a wider range of acquaintances from schools and
university. At the same time parental power over decision making has
decreased. Furthermore, the economic and social capital involved are
likely to be less significant and less differentiated from middle-class or
professional families. Despite indications of continued intermarriage,
then, there is potential for both adaptation and fragmentation in contemporary marriage patterns.

FAMILIES AND NETWORKS

Having set forth the general patterns of marriage and class formation
that characterized the Good Families over time, it is important to reex-

amine these from the standpoint of groups and sectors who embodied Barcelona *connubium*. Four families exemplify these different patterns over time: the Güells, representing a core family of industrialization; the Sentmenats, from the old landed aristocracy; the Bertrands, a textile family; and the de Gònimas-de Janers, a key family of the eighteenth-century mercantile aristocracy.

The Güells

Figure 21 presents the marital history of the Güell family. From generation to generation Güell alliances manifest the expanding range of the upper class into which the family has been incorporated.

Juan Güell, the founder, did not make an upper-class marriage despite his economic and political success. Güell married Camila Bacigalupi Dulcet in 1846, but she died in childbirth the next year. The Bacigalupis and Dulcets were small-scale banker-merchants. Güell married Camila's sister, Francisca, who also died shortly thereafter. He did not remarry.

The two children of the next generation permitted only two weddings to establish an affinal network. These were, however, matches of quality. Eusebio Güell married Isabel López Bru, daughter of the wealthiest man in the city. Josefina married the major industrialist José Ferrer-Vidal.

The expansion of matrimonial horizons was clearer in the third generation. The males married daughters of Restoration nobility like themselves. The heir, Juan Antonio, wed Virginia Churruca, from a distinguished Basque naval family, resident in Barcelona. The bride's brother would become Count Churruca in 1910. The Marquis of Gélida, whose heiress daughter married Eusebio Güell López, was a financier and shipper who received his title in 1896. The Ricarts, whose daughter Adela married Santiago Güell, were recent affines to the Despujols. Each of these Güell lines would also receive a title through creation or inheritance, thus accentuating their status as ennobled industrialists.

The women of this generation married into older aristocratic families. In addition to the eldest sister, who married the Marquis Castelldosríus, another sister married the heir-apparent to the Marquises of Sant Morí, a cadet branch of the Sentmenats. A third sister married the bourgeois politician Bertrán Musitu. While the Bertráns had held jurisdictional seigneuries as early as the eighteenth century, this match was more significant in binding the Güells to Catalanist politics.

Distinctions of status categories slowly blended into a Güell kindred. When Juan Güell López wrote his memoirs, he saw his family, and

Figure 21
Genealogy of the Güell Family

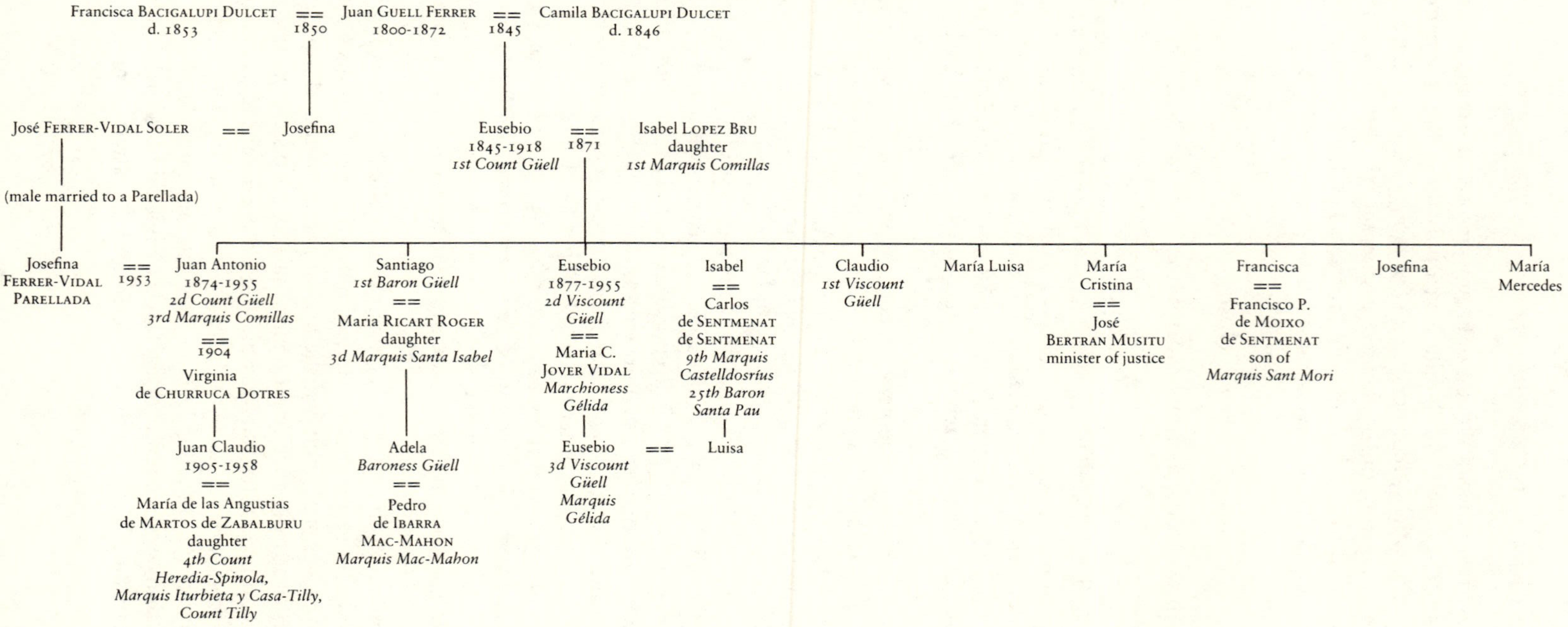

SOURCES: Fluvià 1970 and various sources.
NOTES: Siblings in this genealogy and those that follow are not necessarily arranged in birth order.
Living members of the Güell family are allied by marriage with the Merry del Val Melgarejos, the López de Satrústeguis, the Moixó Montolíus, the Ampuero Urruellas, and the Malets de Tracy. See Appendix for more information.

others such as the Ferrer-Vidals, the Sentmenats, and the Ricarts, as representatives of a universal process of selection that defined

a very small group at the top—sometimes less than one hundred persons in a population of millions. It is a group that constitutes itself as the center of fashion and elegance and which is so recognized by the rest. (1932:96)

The Good Families perceived themselves as an endogamous elite.

The fourth generation continued to expand the marital network built by the third. The Viscount Güell married his first cousin, Luisa Sentmenat Güell, reversing the noble-bourgeois exchange roles of their parents. Two other Güell lines left Catalonia. The Count Güell, in Madrid, married María Angustias de Martos y de Zabalburu, daughter of a military family with interests in Navarre and the capital. His son and heir married into another *madrileña* family, the Merry del Vals. One member of that family was considered a strong candidate for the papacy in the early 1900s.

For a century, from the 1840s to the 1950s, the Güells have steadily expanded their connections in economics, society, and kinship. Yet in records of the family and in their own consciousness this has not been perceived as a breakthrough in social categories. If the Güells have been endogamous, as Armand de Fluvià (1970) has characterized them, this is meaningful only within a dynamic sense of the Barcelona elite as an expanding and adapting social group. This interpretation can be clarified by a related family who had reached a stable caste endogamy before the industrial period: the Sentmenats.

The Sentmenats

The Sentmenat family is one of the oldest noble lines in Catalonia. It traces its foundation to Pere, warden of the castle of Sentmenat and knight in the reconquest of Tortosa (1148). Today there are two main lines: the Marquis Sentmenat and the cadet line of the Marquis of Castelldosríus. The latter acquired their family castles in 1453. Their main line was extinguished in 1842; it passed to the line whose genealogy is presented in Figure 22, drawn from a genealogical essay on the family by Armand de Fluvià (1967).

The landed aristocracy of the preindustrial period had been unified through affinal ties as well as the shared exercise of power. In the case of the Sentmenats the solidification of social and economic status was present in two related processes: the exchange of marital partners with other noble families and the consolidation of the main masculine line through lineage endogamy.

Figure 22

Genealogy of the Sentmenat Family, 1740-1967

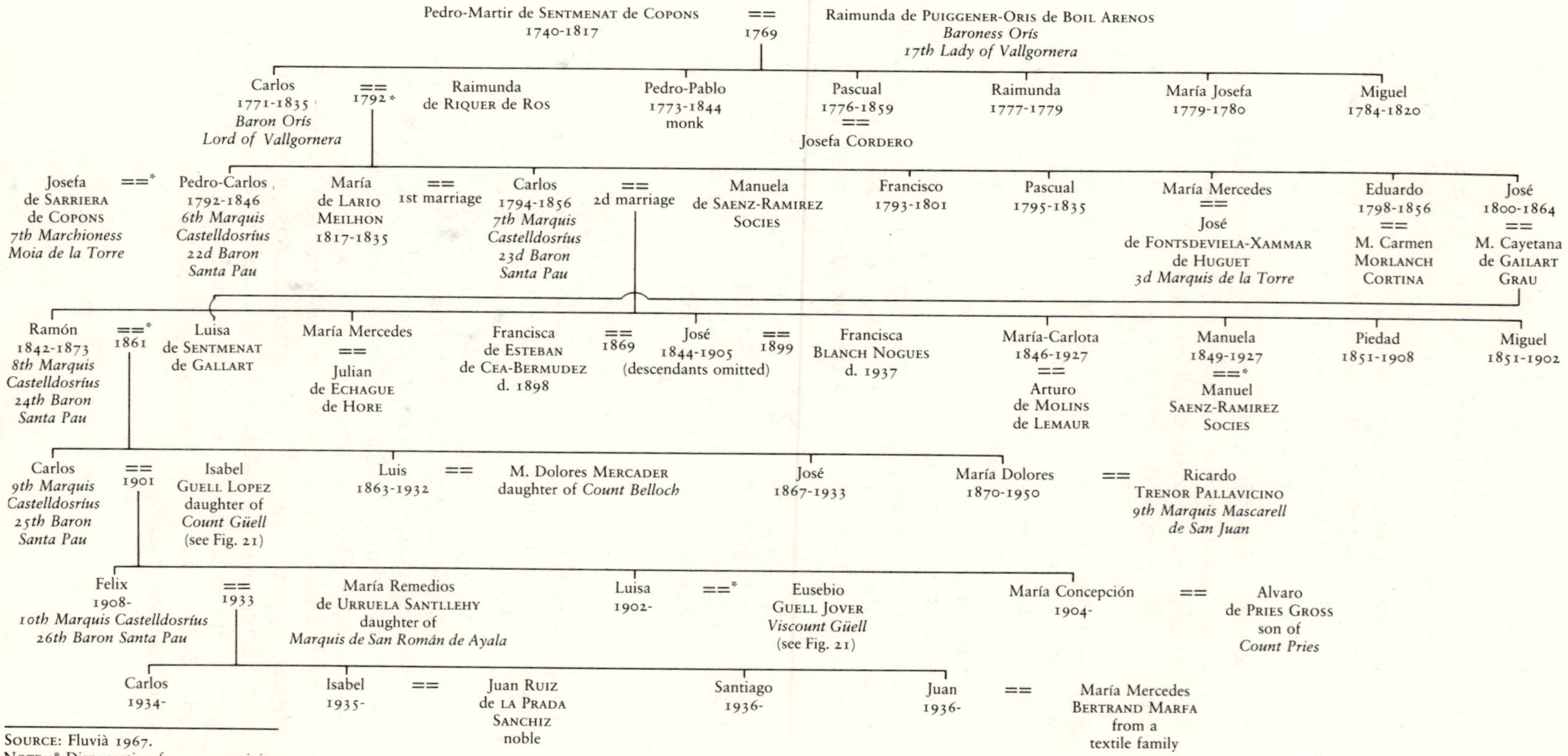

Pedro-Martir de SENTMENAT de COPONS
1740-1817
== 1769
Raimunda de PUIGGENER-ORIS de BOIL ARENOS
Baroness Oris
17th Lady of Vallgornera

Carlos
1771-1835
Baron Oris
Lord of Vallgornera
== Raimunda de RIQUER de Ros

Pedro-Pablo
1773-1844
monk

Pascual
1776-1859
== Josefa CORDERO

Raimunda
1777-1779

María Josefa
1779-1780

Miguel
1784-1820

Maria de LARIO MEILHON
1817-1835
== 1st marriage

Carlos
1794-1856
7th Marquis
Castelldosrius
23d Baron
Santa Pau
== 2d marriage
Manuela de SAENZ-RAMIREZ SOCIES

Francisco
1793-1801

Pascual
1795-1835

María Mercedes
José
de FONTSDEVIELA-XAMMAR
de HUGUET
3d Marquis de la Torre

Eduardo
1798-1856
==
M. Carmen
MORLANCH
CORTINA

José
1800-1864
==
M. Cayetana
de GAILART
GRAU

Pedro-Carlos
1792-1846
6th Marquis
Castelldosrius
22d Baron
Santa Pau

Luisa
de SENTMENAT
de GALLART

María Mercedes
Julian
de ECHAGUE
de HORE

José
1844-1905
== 1869
(descendants omitted)

Francisca
de ESTEBAN
de CEA-BERMUDEZ
d. 1898

Francisca
BLANCH NOGUES
d. 1937
== 1899

María-Carlota
1846-1927
Arturo
de MOLINS
de LEMAUR

Manuela
1849-1927
==*
Manuel
SAENZ-RAMIREZ
SOCIES

Piedad
1851-1908

Miguel
1851-1902

Josefa
de SARRIERA
de COPONS
7th Marchioness
Moia de la Torre
==* 1792

Ramón
1842-1873
8th Marquis
Castelldosrius
24th Baron
Santa Pau
==* 1861

Luis
1863-1932
==

José
1867-1933
==

María Dolores
1870-1950

Ricardo
TRENOR PALLAVICINO
9th Marquis Mascarell
de San Juan

Isabel
GUELL LOPEZ
daughter of
Count Güell
(see Fig. 21)

M. Dolores MERCADER
daughter of Count Belloch

M. Remedios
de URRUELA SANTLLEHY
daughter of
Marquis de San Román de Ayala

Carlos
9th Marquis
Castelldosrius
25th Baron
Santa Pau
== 1901

Luisa
1902-
==
Eusebio
GUELL JOVER
Viscount Güell
(see Fig. 21)

María Concepción
1904-
==
Alvaro
de PRIES GROSS
son of
Count Pries

Felix
1908-
10th Marquis Castelldosrius
26th Baron Santa Pau
== 1933

Isabel
1935-
==
Juan RUIZ
de LA PRADA
SANCHIZ
noble

Santiago
1936-

Juan
1936-
==
María Mercedes
BERTRAND MARFA
from a
textile family

Carlos
1934-

SOURCE: Fluvià 1967.
NOTE: * Dispensation for consanguinity.

In the first centuries of the Castelldosríus the Sentmenat marriages formed an intricate network of exchange with other houses of the Catalan nobility. This was particularly evident in the case of women: females of the Sentmenat patrilineage had the option of a good marriage or none at all. Matches were negotiated with the Baron of Santa Pau (title established 1587), the Count of the Castillo de Centelles (1651), the Count of Cedillo (17??), the Marquis of Baños (1757), and a member of the French aristocracy (1757). Other daughters remained at home or in a convent.

Males concentrated on territorial resources. Through heiress brides, the Sentmenats acquired the Barony of Santa Pau as well as the jurisdictional rights of Vallgornera. The strategy of consolidation was most evident in the main line, where marriages tended to stay within the lineage even more than the caste or class. In six generations of this line between the sixteenth and the nineteenth century half the marriages of the barons of Dosríus required papal dispensations on account of proximity of kinship. Generally the brides seem to have been cousins through the maternal line; in the two specified cases, they were maternal first cousins. Further investigation of the property records in marriage settlements might clarify the exact economic implications of this prescriptive pattern. Did it regain land or capital otherwise lost in dowries? Or was it a manifestation of the concern for values of breeding and culture as found in many closing elites?

In modern times all marriages of Sentmenat women have continued to be with other Catalan nobles. In two of the three twentieth-century cases, however, these have been ennobled industrialists, like the Güells. Male patterns also continued: three of the four title holders between 1792 and 1900 required dispensations for consanguinity at their marriage. Since the first Sentmenat wedding with an industrial family, however, no such dispensation has been necessary. Subsequent weddings have taken place within an expanded pool of potential partners and with rather different stakes in exchange. Rather than being based on a landed strategy, these indicate the perceived value of extensive connections to industrial and commercial wealth.

The careers of the Güells and the Sentmenats have been complementary. Whereas for the Güells weddings have indicated a steadily expanding range of social power, for the Sentmenats they show the reaffirmation of power and position. From both perspectives, though, the concept of the breakdown of marital boundaries between groups would appear to be a misleading image for a more subtle process of strategic coalescence. This becomes clearer when contrasted with two more classically endogamous lineages of the Barcelona upper classes.

The Bertrands

As the genealogy in Figure 23 shows, the Bertrands trace their corporate and familiar lineage to the factory of Lorenzo Clarós, who died in 1831. For six generations the family has been involved in textiles, though this is no longer their exclusive interest. Males have entered the firm; females are rigidly excluded. Yet male selection has been balanced by constant intermarriage with other textile families in a sectorial endogamy.

Clarós's heiress, Mariana, began this tradition with her marriage to Domingo Serra Armada, head of the textile printers' guild and alderman of Barcelona (Aliberch 1952:24). As *pubilla* she relied on her husband to continue the firm. By Serra's death in 1853 the company was worth over 1,000,000 pesetas. It was organized in a family partnership with his sons, although he held four-fifths of the capital. Domingo Serra was "a patriarch surrounded by his seven sons whom he associated . . . in an enterprise that united two great names—his own surname of Serra and that of Clarós" (Aliberch 1952:25).

The company eventually stabilized in the hands of two sons, Lorenzo and Eusebio. The latter married Inés Casanova; the premature death of their son left the firm once again with a female heir. Flora Serra Casanova, in turn, married Manuel Bertrand Salsas, eldest son of a wealthy French immigrant family. At her wedding in 1878 Bertrand's sister brought a dowry of 300,000 pesetas—three times higher than any other settlement in my sampling for that year (AHPB: Tramullas 1878, 373). As *pubill* Manuel Bertrand separated himself entirely from his own lineage to devote himself to Serra interests. Other Bertrand descendants, although prominent in Barcelona, are not even mentioned in the official biography of Eusebio Bertrand. Family was defined less by lineage than by common participation in a unit of production.

Eusebio Bertrand Serra was the only child of this marriage. He combined the undivided economic power that he inherited with social and political activities. A constant participant in exclusive clubs and a fan of the opera who once hired the whole Barcelona opera house for a private performance of *Othello* with his friends, he was also a Catalanist of the Lliga who represented the mountain (resort) district of Puigcerdà. In marriage he chose Mercedes Mata Juliá, daughter of another textile family.

Three of Bertrand's children and heirs have married children of other textile houses: Batllós, Marfás, and Rosal Catarineus. Most of the marriages in this generation, therefore, and almost all of those of the previous generations are explicable on the basis of a single rule of en-

Figure 23
Genealogy of the Bertrand Family

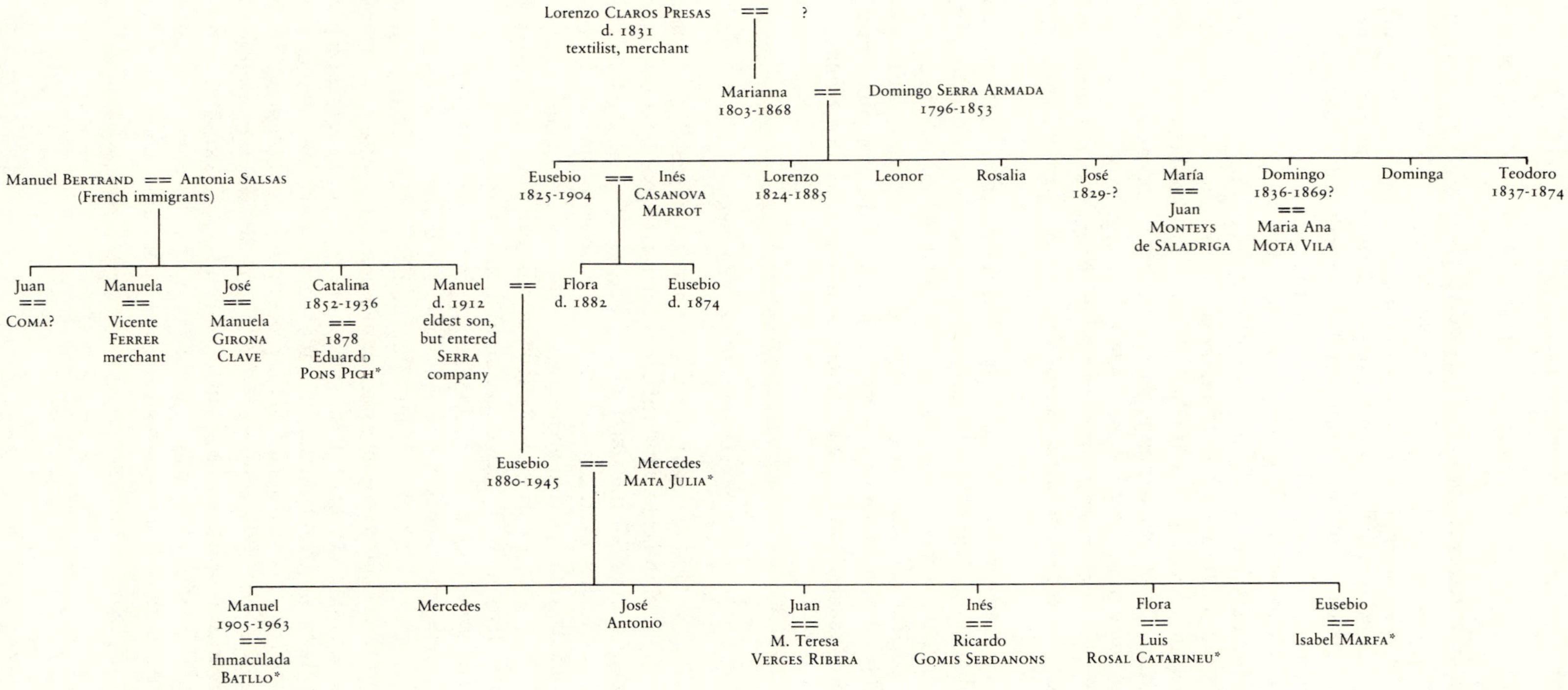

Lorenzo CLAROS PRESAS
d. 1831
textilist, merchant
==
?

Marianna
1803-1868
==
Domingo SERRA ARMADA
1796-1853

Eusebio 1825-1904 == Inés CASANOVA MARROT

Lorenzo 1824-1885   Leonor   Rosalia   José 1829-?   María == Juan MONTEYS de SALADRIGA   Domingo 1836-1869? == María Ana MOTA VILA   Dominga   Teodoro 1837-1874

Flora d. 1882   Eusebio d. 1874

Eusebio 1880-1945 == Mercedes MATA JULIA*

Manuel BERTRAND == Antonia SALSAS
(French immigrants)

Juan == COMA?   Manuela == Vicente FERRER merchant   José == Manuela GIRONA CLAVE   Catalina 1852-1936 == 1878 Eduardo PONS PICH*   Manuel d. 1912 eldest son, but entered SERRA company

Manuel 1905-1963 == Inmaculada BATLLO*   Mercedes   José Antonio   Juan == M. Teresa VERGES RIBERA   Inés == Ricardo GOMIS SERDANONS   Flora == Luis ROSAL CATARINEU*   Eusebio == Isabel MARFA*

SOURCE: Aliberch 1952.
NOTE: * From textile families.

dogamy: the Bertrands have married within their own sector and style of capital organization, the traditional family textile firm.

Nor are the Bertrands unique. Among other textile families the Araños showed even tighter endogamy, with three cousin marriages and a triple marriage of three Araño brothers with three Pratmarsó daughters (Figure 42, Appendix). The same pattern recurs in the Serra Felius (Terradas Saborit 1979) and the Rosals (Moreu Rey 1967).

The explanation of this pattern is more problematic. While these weddings appear to join common economic interests, this sector has been precisely the area in which the male line has been most carefully guarded from affinal interference. Women have been excluded from inheritance in the family business lest the integrity of that firm be jeopardized. In corporate terms marital exchange has not influenced the independence of business enterprises in a sector known for its fragmentation.

Yet I suggest that it is precisely this fragmentation on the basis of familiarism-individualism that accounts for recurrent endogamy. The exchange of women produces a private social cohesion that balances the competitive division of the male public domain. In this case social capital is not traded with economic capital, as in the other lineages examined. Instead, it acts as a complement in a distinctive articulation of a power group.

The de Gònima/de Janer

Erasme de Gònima exemplified the rapid social mobility possible for late eighteenth-century industrialists and merchants in Barcelona. Born a weaver in provincial Catalonia, by his death he was a noble. His descendants, however, did not enter the economic and social world of either the older landed aristocracy or the new bourgeoisie. The result was an endogamous group "between" the other two categories. Elite social marginality reflected economic change within a new milieu.

The genealogy of the de Gònima/de Janer (Figure 24) shows a remarkable consistency in marriage choices over four generations. Wives are given to *and* taken from other families of ennobled merchants. Erasme de Gònima's only daughter married too early to profit from her father's rapid rise. In the third generation, though, weddings bound the family to the great commercial leaders of the day. The eldest daughter, Maria, first married a scion of the older nobility, although the Baron de Maldà reported the protests of the groom. She was widowed soon afterwards. A year later Maria married Pau Felix Gassó. Although not a noble, Gassó's family was extremely powerful; his father was secretary of the Junta de Comerç, which acted as a political-economic center and lobby for mercantile leaders (Molas Ribalta 1975:273, 298). Pau Felix followed him as secretary in the declining years of the junta. The eldest son of this marriage, Erasme, appeared in 1852 tax records as one of the wealthiest men of the city (Solà 1977, 2:244). He married a Nadal, daughter of another mercantile family.

The second daughter married Ramón de Bacardí Cuyàs, heir to another commercial fortune of the eighteenth century. This money had later been invested in property, including a productive inn. The family continued to reside on the Passeig Bacardí until this century. Ramón de Bacardí was also active in the Caixa.

The direct heir of Erasme de Gònima, Erasme de Janer de Gònima married Josefa de Gironella Ayguals (marriage contract AHPB: Torrents Sayrols 1817). The bride's grandfather, Cristóbal de Gironella Pujols (1727-1790), had been a member of the register of commerce, a director of the junta, and a ciutadà honrat after 1780. Josefa's father and brothers were also members of the junta and aldermen in Barcelona.

The social network formed in this generation had multiple connections. Cristóbal de Gironella was brother-in-law to Baltasar de Bacardí, grandfather of Ramón. Erasme Gassó's wife, Rosa de Nadal de Dodero, was the daughter of Virginia de Dodero Montobbio, who later married Antoni de Gironella. She was thus an affine to both Erasme de Janer and his wife.

In the nineteenth century this extremely tight kindred moved their wealth into land and other status markers. They held political power through the Junta de Comerç and the municipal administration. Yet in the next generations their situation and circumstances changed radically.

Josep Erasme de Janer de Gironella, heir in the fourth generation, took a reactionary political stance diametrically opposed to the liberalism of the new Catalan industrialists. He ruined his fortune with the Carlist cause, leading to the closure of his great-grandfather's factory. In 1862 he married Dolors Milà de la Roca Vilaseca. The Milàs de la Roca, although ennobled as merchants, had also become landowners rather than becoming involved in risky but potentially productive ventures. De Janer served in the Caixa until his death in 1911, the last of his line to do so. In general the family retired from public activities.

De Janer's heir, Erasme, entered the Jesuits, where he died at age twenty (1887). The next son, Ignasi, married Soledad de Duràn de Brichfeus, descendant of two lines of the minor nobility. Her father, although mayor of Barcelona, had sold off much of the family property. Ignasi's sister, Mercè, was the only other sibling to marry. Her husband was a Carlist leader for rural Catalonia—indicating the continued

Figure 24
Genealogy of the de Gònima/de Janer Family

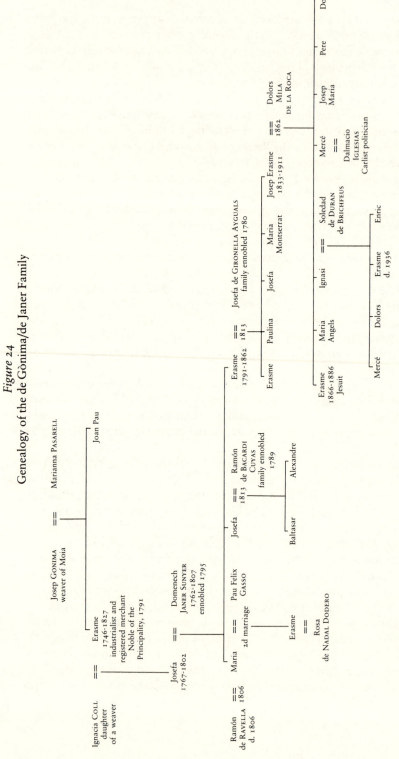

SOURCES: De Imbert 1952 and various sources.

conservatism of the family, separated from the political activities of the Lliga.

Endogamy here suggests the peculiar position of the mercantile elite caused by the appearance of new capital and power. These houses held status markers that were valuable in an earlier situation but whose very process of creation had been eliminated. Furthermore, there were new exigencies of consumption and display: clubs, the opera, promenades in carriages, and then autos. One strategy to maintain their position without entering new exchanges was intermarriage. Social cohesion became associated as well with conservative Catalanism and intense religious feelings. Although the Lloberola portrayed by Sagarra in the last chapter do not refer to specific real families, their story is relevant to the process of marginalization that these families have undergone. In the words of one contemporary descendant of another minor noble the families have been *destronades*—"dethroned."

In the most recent generations such exclusion has broken down. The marriage pool has diminished through the disappearance of families such as the Gironella and the Bacardís. Some families have intermarried with the Good Families—a descendant of the Bacardís is Count-Consort of Almodóvar, a Castilian grandee. Other lineages have faded into the professional middle class, although they still evoke their noble heritage and status claims in private conversations.

These four family histories have illustrated diverse trajectories in the formation of the Barcelona elite. The exchange of social and economic power by the beginning of this century resulted in a new elite network, exemplified by the Güells and the Sentmenats. Other families followed different patterns, based on their distinctive economic and social interests. Currently, these divisions seem to have disappeared, as the Good Families themselves are marginalized by new internal and external decision makers in Barcelona.

In 150 years of elite formation some constant boundaries have remained within which all elite families have married. A brief examination of these proscriptions situates this elite once more within a broader framework of class and region.

THE LIMITS OF MATRIMONY: CLASS AND COMMUNITY

Weddings between upper and lower classes rarely appear in the families for whom I have complete genealogies. These marriages are often hidden; in one case it was only after repeated interviews that the lower-class origins of the wife of one cousin were clarified. In total I found four cases of extreme class disparity in over eight hundred documented marriages. In all cases these were marriages of upper-class males with

female servants or tradeswomen. In one case an heir was stripped of all
privileges in his company on account of this liason, although he maintained affective bonds and even access to the family homestead. In another, the heir received his inheritance and a title, but his children were
socially disdained. All of these cases occurred in the late nineteenth century. Older cases might have been effectively eliminated from the historical consciousness of the lineage involved, although this is less likely
for the memory of other families. All were individual reactions to the
family: confirming the general class barrier in alliance.

"Borderline" marriages have also occurred, in which there is some
disparity of background or prospects but not enough for social sanction. Indeed, these echo the sentiments that might have been evoked by
earlier "redefinitional unions" between aristocrats and industrialists.
Men and women agreed that it would be more difficult for a woman to
marry up the social scale at present than for a man to do so. Their rea-
soning differed, however. One man told me, for example, such a
woman would be unsuitable as the bearer of family honor: a classic
Mediterranean view. Women judged the matter in terms of competition. In a group discussion several elite women agreed that if a woman
married into their circle "we will never let her forget it . . . because she
has taken away one of our possibilities." Hypergamy means a limitation on the marriage pool for these women, in an ever-decreasing number of families who maintain their status. Their position is parallel not
to their middle-class ancestresses but to the women of the preindustrial
noble caste, as in the Sentmenat family. This is even clearer when the
possibilities of interaction with national and international power
groups are considered.

Men who marry into the elite face different restrictions. Their public
power has often brought them into contact with females of higher status, as in the Sala brothers who guided the company in the absence of
inheriting males. Fifty years ago the upper-class historian Masriera
Colomer wrote on marriage rules in shipping families: "If on some occasion the daughter of a shipping family married a young boat captain
or the firm's clerk it had to be for the extraordinary qualities of the
spouse, or as an exception that confirms the rule" (1926:54). Such
cases occur in many families, particularly in those stages where family
and firm are closely connected.

Yet such men are in an ambiguous position. Despite their executive
control they lack resources to pass on. No matter how talented, women
may see them as fortune hunters. Indeed, for rentier families a new in-
fusion of capital may be much more important than effective management of decreasing resources.

In recent years marriages continue to set families and groups apart.

The Cambós, for example, who were introduced in Chapter V, have not yet established kin ties with lineages who shared in their projects. The same is true of other executive and technocratic families (Ynfante 1974). On the whole, interaction affirms the division between a "power elite" and the cohesive inheriting power group constituted by the Good Families. While trained managers and politicians may fill positions of vital importance within a national system, they lack the social connections that would bind them to a reproducing dominant class.

One of the most striking characteristics of the Barcelona marriage patterns has been the regionalization of the marriage pool. Over four-fifths of the matrimonies I examined involved two Catalan families. Only a handful involved Castilians; even fewer, non-Spaniards.

Marriages with non-Catalans confirm a priority for residence in the choice of partners. Generally, when members of the Good Families married outsiders, either the former lived outside the city or the latter resided in Barcelona. Thus, in the Güells it is the Madrid and Basque branches who have married non-Catalans. These marriages in turn facilitated interconnections with other Güells. The pattern of the Trasatlánticos continues.

In other cases non-Catalan aristocrats who have maintained an extended residence in the city have also established marital connections. This has happened with those who arrived as administrators under Primo de Rivera and Franco: the Forondas, the Mesas de Asta, or the Olanos. These marriages tended to be foreign males with Catalan females.

Connections between the Barcelona elite and international power holders are rare. Does this indicate the relative status of the group vis-à-vis multinational leaders? The synthesis of American industrialists with the British nobility of the nineteenth century comes to mind as a contrast. In that case, though, there was a definite exchange of wealth and prestige to be negotiated. Certainly the Good Families do not have the same resources or renown to offer the Fords, Onassises, or Rockefellers, even were status markers generally agreed upon.

It is not necessarily clear that an international orbit is characteristic of elites in core countries. While economic ties can be built on complex bonds, matrimonial negotiations require social and economic information gleaned from continuous and intimate contact. Even the common methods of control of social settings mentioned in the last chapter would act to exclude strangers without an adequate introduction. These filtering mechanisms and the role of women as arbiters, whether in Spain, France, or England, did not arise to deal with geographic mobility but with social change. Yet their exclusionary function may also have contributed to the apparent parochialism of Catalan upper-class alliances.

CONCLUSIONS

The observations on the historical evolution of social connections and group cohesion of this chapter complement the economic analysis of the fourth and fifth chapters. Yet social capital was not a separate arena of power. Instead, marriages entailed a balance—and negotiation—among different claims to power.

Although intermarriage has been an indication of group cohesion, the data have shown that this heuristic device demands several qualifications. First, endogamy, in the sense of a class-linked marriage pool, is not the classic lineal model of anthropology. There are no rules designating preferred partners by family or lineage; there seem to be few, if any, explicit rules concerning marriage at all. Instead, various considerations—availability, wealth, social claims, and potential networks—have been weighed within the strategies of each lineage.

Endogamy has not been static, either. There have been closed groups within Barcelona society, as embodied in the preindustrial nobility or the mercantile aristocracy. Yet, rather than seeing these groups as bounded entities, we must look at choices through time. In this perspective it is evident that power-holding families are re-creating closure by their openness to selective absorption of challengers through marriage insofar as there are gains to be made. Each marriage, whether or not accepted, tests and refines the boundary of the elite group for the next generation—or the next marriage.

In a parallel process diversity appeared even within an intermarrying group. Such strategies were apparent on economic grounds, as the Bertrands or Trasatlánticos, or for social reasons. Again, the dynamics of an elite demand attention to both individual and familial strategies and their overall articulation into a sense of community.

Within this articulation the cultural imagery or mentality of the family again plays a central role. The next chapter returns to the study of the ideological manipulation of the family. In Chapter III, we saw that the family was situated within the politics of elite hegemony, local and national. In Barcelona the elite also used the household as a building block in visible models of the social order they sought to establish and control.

CHAPTER VIII

THE FAMILY AND THE CITY: POWER AND THE CREATION OF CULTURAL IMAGERY

Beyond its value as an economic and social institution the Catalan family has also been the basis for cultural imagery. As a metaphor for Catalan society the family became the cornerstone of cultural legitimization and domination by the upper class. As Bourdieu has noted, "The dominant fractions, whose power is based on economic and political capital, seek to impose the legitimacy of their domination whether through their own symbolic production or through the intermediary of conservative ideologists . . ." (1979:80). In Chapter III the cultural presentation of the family was examined in terms of political strategies that situated a Catalan polity between state politics and local class conflicts. In this chapter the family will be analyzed with regard to specifically urbanistic themes, including the control, and even the construction, of modern Barcelona.

As I have already shown, the family was a key symbol in the political strategies of the Catalan bourgeoisie of the late nineteenth and early twentieth centuries, through which they sought to establish and unify a national movement. It was both an emotive image and an ambiguous one. In contrasting Catalonia and the rest of Spain the Catalan Civil Code was a symbol of unity, of a distinctive socioeconomic heritage, and of the right to political hegemony. At the same time, when challenged by internal conflicts, the elite and its ideologues interpreted the family in terms of hierarchy, authority, and order. It was the complexity of the image that made it uniquely valuable to one elite in its epoch and to a particular embodiment of Catalan nationalism.

Within everyday interaction in the Catalan capital, however, family was evoked as the basis for a new understanding of the changing social order. In this regard it became an element in an elite sociology of classes and rights. To understand this cultural manipulation of the family, it is necessary to analyze more complex representations of urban society and their impact upon urban planning and urban life.

This chapter focusses on two institutions that embodied an elite "sociology" of industrial society: the Cementiri Vell (Old Cemetery) and the Gran Teatre del Liceu (the Barcelona Opera House). Both were built in the nineteenth century under the aegis of the emergent elite. Both have been dynamic constructions whose physical structure and interpretation have been sensitive to shifting power relations. Both continue to stand in modern Barcelona as historical monuments to class differentiation and the cohesion of the Good Families. Thus, these edifices are keys to past and present world views of the power groups that dominated Catalan industrial society.

The cemetery, however, is a walled and ordered world. When built, it lay outside the physical limits of the city. Today it has been marginalized from the social life of modern Barcelona. Yet it may be situated within a succession of burial sites and patterns in Barcelona that reflect changing ideas about family and city. Furthermore, the isolation of the graveyard gave it a special integrity as a laboratory for urbanistic planning. Necropolitan patterns do not simply reflect metropolitan development: the Old Cemetery actually modelled the architectonics of a later Barcelona as envisaged within the ideology of the industrial-financial elite.

The Liceu stands on the Rambles, the main artery of downtown Barcelona. It is central to the social and cultural life, even the mythology, of all Catalonia. For Barcelona this theater is the paragon of loci in which power groups interact for social, economic, *and* cultural ends. The building in which this interaction occurs—housing the theater and an exclusive social club—derives its basic form from international usage of the opera as a prestige marker. At the same time it has entered the heritage of every member of the elite through family and life cycles. As in the cemetery class membership and boundaries are clearly demarcated. In contrast to the former, however, the interaction of *living* Barcelonins at the opera has also made it an arena in which boundaries are crossed by acts of violence that spring from social and economic inequality.

THE CEMETERY AS URBAN IMAGERY

Since the early 1970s the French historian-demographer Philippe Ariès has explored the changing ideas of death within Western society (1977). This analysis, even though concentrated on individual and familial mentalities, provides a chronology for comparison with the social historical development of death in Barcelona (García Cárcel 1985; Domingo 1985). At the same time the holistic study of family and elite suggests new questions on the imagery of death and burial as expressions of social change. In particular, the cemetery has been more than the vehicle for reproduction of ideologies and power; it has also been a construction through which power groups experimented with models for the city that was developing under their control.

Three perspectives must be balanced in the analysis of the bonds of necropolis and society in Barcelona. The first is the long-term historical interaction of death and social life in Catalonia, within which any particular representation must be fixed. The second is a detailed interpretation of the architectural and social expression within the Old Cemetery itself. Finally, this representation must be reinserted into urban history as an influence upon the formation of subsequent patterns of urban life.

The History of Death in Barcelona

Citizenship, religion, and rights to burial have generally been coextensive in Catalonia. The identification of church and community from the Middle Ages onward was such that those who were not good members of the church or state were prohibited membership in the community of the dead. Heretics, the unbaptized, suicides, and robbers dying in the act of their crime were denied burial in consecrated ground by Roman Catholic canon law. With the increasing role of the state in the nineteenth century more domains of social definition intersected. Thus

the decision for lay burial, ultimate consequence of a religious or philosophical option which is "not Catholic" and foreign to the *Gens Hispanica*, has been both a political and an anti-Spanish decision. It is equally true that the decision of the church to deny burial in holy ground to anyone has meant a sociopolitical sanction. (Jiménez Lozano 1978:21)

After the divisions of the Spanish Civil War, burial outside the state, especially in protest of the Franco regime, continued to be an emotional issue. Since the death of Franco the return of the remains of such leaders to Spanish and Catalan soil has been a continuous reminder of past divisions and modern politics.

Within this broad framework, however, burial reflected urban society and its segmentation. Indeed, until the eighteenth century death and burial in Barcelona were phenomena of individual neighborhoods rather than indications of any concept of the city as a whole. Each parish church was the district center for guild activities, for seasonal celebrations, and for the major rites of passage for neighborhood "citizens." At death, the kindred, the professional group, and the residential community of the decedent assembled in the parish for a final sanctification of the transition. The corpse then was interred, either within the church and its cloister, or in a consecrated graveyard that flanked the building.

Neighborhood burial also tended to level most distinctions within the local community. As Ariès notes, apart from antisocial actions, burial practices seemed to ignore any individual memorial. The vision of each person was directed to an afterlife that eclipsed concerns with his or her mortal identity in the community. Burial sites, pious or impious, were rarely marked or even clearly recalled by later generations (1977).

Exceptions to this practice in preindustrial Europe tended to be power groups who preserved individual or lineal identity after death. In France these groups included clerical, learned, and noble strata. Much the same situation is apparent in the Gothic chapels and memorials that remain in Barcelona.

By the late eighteenth century, though, new groups were crossing from anonymity to history in Catalonia as well as other European societies. Among these the merchant capitalists were prominent. Erasme de Gònima, for example, buried both his son-in-law and his daughter in monastic cloisters—behavior suited to his claims to noble status. Yet by the time he himself died in 1821 the social order of the city and the graveyard had altered. Ultimately, he was memorialized in a chapel in the elite section of the new urban cemetery.

The reasons for such a change were complex. Industrial and commercial expansion were linked to population growth: cities like Paris and Barcelona were hard-pressed to exploit intramural urban space to its maximum efficiency for the needs of the living. Ariès also notes the change in European cultural attitudes. The Roman Catholic Church had attempted to stop the practice of burial in churches for centuries. During the Enlightenment, additional support for the Vatican's campaign came from new scientific theories on hygiene and disease: cemeteries were perceived as places of pollution. In Paris all the urban burial grounds were moved beyond the walls to distant and "safer" locations (1977:145-153).

Finally, population pressure and new values were cemented by new attitudes towards the family and the memory of the dead:

> Interment in a crypt reserved to a particular family is the opposite of communal inhumation, solitary and anonymous. The need to unite in perpetuity, in a closed and preserved space, all the dead of a family corresponds to a new sentiment that is later extended to all social classes in the nineteenth century. The affection that binds the living members of the family is extended to the dead. Thus the family crypt is perhaps the only spot that corresponds to a patriar-

chal concept of the family where several generations and households are united under the same roof. (Ariès 1977:142)

These themes converged in a new and human-centered vision of death
that was complemented by new practices for the ordering and domination of life as discussed by Foucault (1965; 1972) or Ginzburg
(1980). The prerogatives formerly limited to nobility and clergy had
spread to new elites and thence diffused to the middle and lower
classes.

In Barcelona as in France, the first steps in the changes of burial space
and attitudes towards death took place in the late eighteenth century.
In 1775 Bishop Josep Climent of Barcelona had inaugurated a new urban burial plot on the outskirts of the city. His speech dramatically
evoked the overcrowding, unhealthiness, and abuse of individual remains in parish graveyards that had spread as complaints throughout
Europe:

> Hence I derive the feeling, my brothers, or, more accurately, the
> horror that grips me when I see the bones of your grandfathers
> evicted from their sepulchers in the churches and left, even
> thrown, on profane and unclean sites, exposed in rags, and
> gnawed by animals. (Climent 1775)

In 1787 King Charles III abolished all parish cemeteries in Spain. He
was castigated as a liberal and a Freemason on account of this decree
(Curet 1952:237).

Economic recession and wars in the late eighteenth century reduced
population pressure in Barcelona while precluding major public works.
In 1819 Bishop Pau de Sitjar augmented the site that had been granted
to Climent and inaugurated the Cementiri de l'est. This move was re-
sented by clergy and laity who held to the values of the parish graveyard. Ultimately, however, the cemetery won acceptance not only as a
burial place but also as a site for meditations and promenades. The
cemetery grounds, like those of other European burial gardens, became
a park for artists, philosophers, and lovers. By the end of the century
the Old Cemetery became an urban landmark. "Barcelonins were so
proud of it that they showed it to all foreigners who came. For the visits
of royalty or distinguished persons, it was an obligatory stop" (Curet
1952:262).

As the city of Barcelona continued to grow, this burial space became
overcrowded. In 1883 a new cemetery was opened on the slopes of
Montjuich, a rocky pinnacle on the western edge of the city. This was
a project begun at the apogee of the grand bourgeoisie, reflecting its
power and its taste. The contemporary Barcelona novelist Juan Goyti-

solo has described the new cemetery in just such terms. In *Señas de identidad* (Signs of Identity) a bourgeois character muses on the necropolis as a product of his social experience:

> The cemetery had been conceived at its origin as a peaceful and somnolent provincial city, with its gardens and avenues, squares and promenades, its niches for the middle and lower class, and its pantheons for the bourgeoisie and aristocracy. Inaugurated in the era of Barcelona's development and expansion, when the grounds of the old cemetery had revealed themselves to be completely insufficient, the diverse architectural currents of the period coexisted in it in profuse and overblown aggression . . . like a synthesis and prolongation of the political economic adventure of their owners.
> . . .
>
> The spirit that had animated the development of the city was clear there, . . . with a coherence foreign and immune to death. It was as if the deceased leaders of cotton, silk, and fine cloth had wished to perpetuate in the unreality of nothingness the norms and principles (common sense, pragmatism) that had oriented their lives. Those pompous mausolea responded perfectly to the rustic and uncultivated tastes of their proprietors, just like a chalet or summer house in Lloret or Sitges (work, perhaps, of the same ar-

Figure 25
The "New" Cemetery of Barcelona on Montjuich

chitect). Both were offspring of the same system of paternal enterprise, silently undermined with time not only by the struggles and
demands of the workers (silenced with a quick thrust) but also by
the imperatives of modern State capitalism. (1966:66-67)

This municipal cemetery highlighted the prerogatives of earlier elites.
During the riots of the Tragic Week of 1909, the discovery of bodies of
nuns who had been buried within their convent walls excited popular
horror and indignation. Graves were opened to reveal bound corpses,
and in one case "a handsome, dirty, simple-minded coalman did an ob-
scene dance as he carried a corpse" (Ullman 1968:247). Others proposed dumping the bodies in front of the Güell's and Lopez' palaces. At
the same time: "The women now organized an expedition to city hall;
the corpses would be taken in their caskets to the authorities who must
be forced to end the cruel practice of cloistered orders, or at least the
unhygienic custom of cloistered orders burying their dead within their
convent walls" (Ullman 1968:246-247). Privilege in death was an emotional question for the unified city of the living.

By the 1970s the Cementiri Nou of Montjuich was also inadequate
for urban needs. The mountain is honeycombed with niches, and much
of the original order of the park has been obscured by the need for more
space for new tombs. Still another cemetery has been initiated outside
the heavily urbanized area of Barcelona. Once again it is a product of
contemporary urban society:

The cemetery of Moncada, with its isolated housing blocks set
amidst green belts, will be the cemetery of the Barcelona of hous-

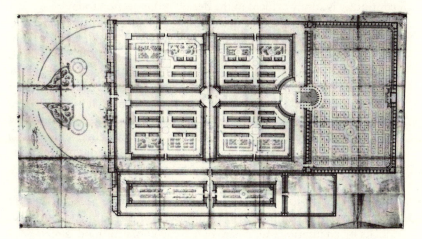

Figure 26
Official Map of the Old Cemetery of Barcelona

ing projects, of highways, of parking lots and of frustrated attempts by the municipal council for urban reform. Even the niches
seem to respond to an architecture of consumption in its most
acritical form. (Bohigas 1973:53)

There is, then, a clear succession in the burial patterns of the city of
Barcelona from anonymity in the parish to a new and secular uniformity in Moncada. Each of these stages, furthermore, corresponds to a
particular conjuncture in urban social and cultural values. Yet the Cementiri Vell stands apart as a transitional project that emerged contem-
poraneously with the financial-industrial elite and shaped their urban
view thereafter—even in the Cementiri Nou.

The Old Cemetery and the Transformation of Industrial Society

Even in its most obvious limitations the Old Cemetery of Barcelona is
shaped by the physical and social characteristics of the nineteenth-century city in which it took form. Its walls, for example, recall those walls
that constricted Barcelona for most of the nineteenth century. A city,
whether living or dead, was clearly separated from the land around it.
Social barriers are equally present. Those who have died in Barcelona
without sharing all defining characteristics of nineteenth-century society—the Protestants or the unbaptized—were interred in a separate
space, within the cemetery but set apart by internal walls, and, indeed,
in lower ground than contiguous sections. Those buried here were
often visitors or foreigners who lacked continuity in the city. This dis-
continuity is sorely evident in the decay of this section today.

The main unit of the cemetery thus coincided with the perceived
boundaries of Catalan urban society. It was also a template for map-
ping the internal divisions of the city. This space was subdivided into
three parts: a common ditch, a large main burial space, and a cloistered area farthest from the entrance (Figure 28). The first section, a
semicircle in front of the main facade, was for paupers. It has since been
paved over as a reception patio. The main section is constituted by
blocks of niches, arranged in rows of fifty to one hundred and piled as
high as seven layers. It is a large-scale version of the columbarium for
crematory remains more familiar to Americans. These blocks of niches
are divided by avenues and enclose planted gardens with cloisterlike
tombs on the inside and a few isolated monuments. Some early elite
burials took place in this area. A third section is separated from these
blocks by an interior wall where two arched porticos flank a memorial
chapel. This portion is devoted to cloisterlike tombs and mausolea, the

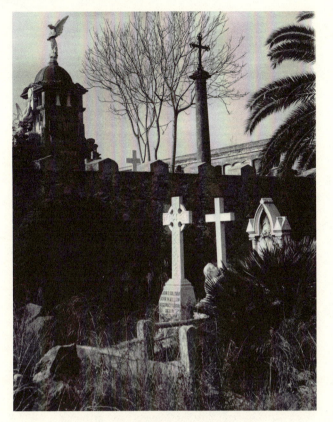

Figure 27
The Protestant Section of the Old Cemetery
Photograph by the author

planning and construction of which was dominated by the Catalan elite.

Nineteenth-century planners saw this three-part structure as a representation of the social classes of the city. An 1858 commission of inquiry that reformed the cemetery observed that "just as the social scale is divided into three levels—lowest, middle, and superior [*ínfimo, medio*, and *superior*]—so should the mortuarial scale be divided into three gradations of site" (Cil 1858:43). These sections were graded by cost, aesthetics, and rights to family unity and historical memory.

Curet records the earliest price range (apart from charitable burial in the pauper's ditch) as 20 pesetas for a niche to 60 pesetas for a site within the cloisters. By 1877 the range extended from 50 pesetas for a minimal brick niche to 600 pesetas for a choice site with ossuary (*Reg-*

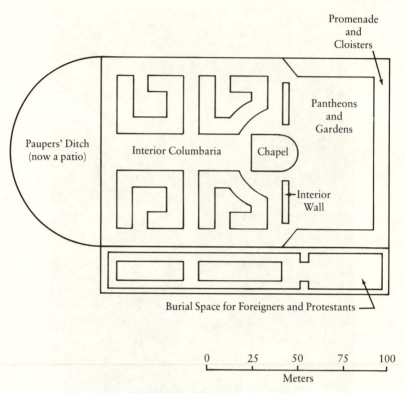

Figure 28
Guide to the Old Cemetery of Barcelona

lamento 1877). In actuality the cost differential was much greater. The ossuary price covered only the lot and was increased by substantial expenditures for design, construction, and upkeep of a mausoleum.

These divisions also embodied differential aesthetic valuations. The pauper's ditch allowed for no ornamentation. In contrast, the main portion inside the walls (Figure 28) was described by the 1858 commission as "monotonous and poor—Yet wait, for this, too, is certain— neither this poverty nor this monotony lack sublimity, given that there is nothing so poor and monotonous as death" (Cil 1858:43). This main section is reminiscent of a cityscape, with regular buildings and broad avenues. Its geometrical precision recalls the Barceloneta, the major urbanistic expansion of eighteenth-century Barcelona. More significantly, it prefigured the uniformity of the design proposed for urban expansion in the last half of the century, where octagonal blocks alternated with arteries of transport (Cerdá 1968-1971). Only the interior of the blocks and, finally, the third, elite section was planned as a park in its plantings and diversity.

Finally, each section determined different rights to history. The pauper's ditch allowed no memorialization, no continuity of individual or family. This anonymity was not a continuation of the attitudes of the early modern period, however. In the context of the Cementiri de l'est anonymity indicated the alienation of the urban poor from the claims to humanity exhibited by other groups. The poor were excluded from a new social history in the making.

The middle section preserved memory and sense of family:

> Nor would it be possible, without these modest and uniform sections, flat and plain, filled with tombs in the range of the smallest fortunes and the most humble aspirations, for families with less pretensions to be able to bury their dead with minimal expense. A large portion of the lower classes [*clases populares*]—the majority undoubtedly—would thus have no other recourse than to place the remains in a common ditch, reserved for indigents. (Cil 1858:43)

While this intermediary zone fostered ownership and continuity, it also limited the sense of family for the lower middle classes. The most common family practice in the columbaria has been to reuse the same niche, pushing aside former remains with each new burial. Hence a bereaved family may face the unpleasant spectacle of clearing remains at a new burial. Even so, a niche rarely holds more than a nuclear unit. And it would be unlikely that any descendants could locate a contiguous space not already in use by others. This limitation on the burial of the family thus reified social nuclearization in the proletariat.

Just as these two divisions affirmed the social changes and the new position of lower and middle classes within industrial society, so did the elite pantheons of the third section. In elite economic and social cohesion family became a triumphant motif, even in death.

Power and Burial: Elite Patterns

In 1858 the upper-class area had not yet developed. Members of the commercial-industrial families who died earlier were buried amid the columbaria—often in mausolea set apart from the blocks of niches by architecture or plantings. The early cloisters recall the monastic burials and parish cemeteries that they replaced. Yet the commission of inquiry looked forward to this section in its report:

Figure 29
Gustave Doré's 1879 Etching of a Burial in a Niche in the Old
Cemetery

This new department will be without a doubt the most magnificent
section within a few years. . . .

In addition to the noble yet severe face offered by its apertures,
open in the manner of vaulted cloisters and barred with grilles . . .
and in addition to the magnificent structure of the funeral chamber, reserved for burial with distinction of the remains of men, this
department also offers ample space for the erection of individual
pantheons (of which there are already several) girded by their
small fenced gardens. There, the families of middling fortunes, as
well as the most opulent, can visit and offer prayers and memories
in honor of their ancestors, separated from the mob [*vulgo*] of the
visitors. (Cil 1858:41)

This zone was also perceived as the best expression of the necropolis and of the city as a whole in urbanistic competition with other cemetery showplaces. The ruling classes became leaders in both the social and aesthetic order, who championed Barcelona's artistic claims against other European capitals:

> Once the work of this magnificent precinct is concluded, our suburban cemetery will be able to sustain an honorable competition, with more advantage every day, not only with the best cemeteries of Spain but also with the most famous and widely admired of all Europe. (Cil 1858:41)

This competitive intent was apparently defeated by poor soil and overcrowding, although the modern-day neglect of the cloister area makes any aesthetic evaluation difficult. Nonetheless, it is still possible to identify the primary characteristics in construction and use of the cloister precinct that parallel those critical to the reproduction of the living elite: the sense of class cohesion, the role of the extended family in promoting cohesion through time, and the significance of display both within the group and to differentiate the elite from those beyond the walls.

The unity of the section was constituted by basic architectural planning. More than the other two parts, this precinct is oriented inwards. Arched tombs form a cloister on four walls that encircle the individual mausolea and gardens. Unity is underscored by a raised promenade along these walls. In the center space tombs are placed along avenues in parklike settings. A chapel unifies and dominates the entire precinct.

Architectural unity affirms social homogeneity. Although as an expansion this section encloses some more modest burials, it is clearly dominated by the urban elite. The promenade chapels and the mausolea shelter those who were prominent in industry, finance, and society in nineteenth-century Barcelona. Roughly half were members of the Círculo del Liceo or held boxes at the opera. Even those exceptions who were not members of the elite per se confirm the wider cultural evaluation of this elitist area. Josep Anselm Clavé, a major figure in the revival of Catalan music, was thus accorded a prominent monument. Other tombs belonged to wealthy provincial citizens or *indianos* attracted by the prestige of the cemetery.

The individual pantheons, owned by each family, vary in their design and ostentation. They range from simple markers to complete Gothic chapels with stained-glass windows, marble altars, prie-dieus, and gilt candlesticks. Some were designed by the most prominent architects of Barcelona and proudly display the names of architects, sculptors, and builders.

Figure 30
Pantheons in the Elite Section of the Old Cemetery
Photograph by the author

These tombs are differentiated from the niches in the main section by the ossuary they enclose. Generally, a family mausoleum or chapel would hold ten to twelve coffins without disturbing any previous remains. Two and even three generations of a family might be successively entombed within a single monument. At this point the most common elite practice has been to abandon further burials and close the tomb. The family then constructs a new mausoleum, even if in a different cemetery. Figures 32 and 33 show two sets of familial relationships typical of this section. In the mausoleum of Figure 32 a family has continued to use the same tomb through five generations. In each generation, however, only the line of the eldest male is followed. Collateral relatives are included only when they failed to establish independent households. In the case of the Espalter/Rull family, Figure 33, where the large sibling group buried together seems to violate this principle, all the *fadristerns* were unmarried. The married sisters are buried elsewhere with their husbands. Eusebio Coronas, however, who married two Espalter sisters in succession, acquired an adjoining tomb. The most striking anomaly is the absence of the heir's wife in the second

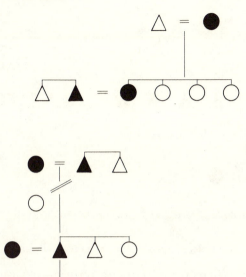

■ Members of the family actually buried in the mausoleum.

Figure 31
Burials in an Elite Pantheon of the Old Cemetery

generation. Evidence from the notarial archives, however, indicates that the families of the bride and groom, although closely related, fought over the marriage contract and marital expenses (AHPB: Prats 1827, 1:307). Social as well as economic unity characterized the burial unit.

Both cases affirm the emphasis on family that underpinned elite unity and reproduction. The pattern of succession, however, follows the classic succession model of the rural homestead rather than the generalized inheritance of the nineteenth-century industrial elite. While this may be a survival associated particularly with sacred burial rights, it is more likely that this pattern confirms a fundamental motivation previously suggested for the extension of capital inheritance. That is, when a patrimony is finite and difficult to divide efficiently, as in the case of the land—or a tomb—inheritance follows the stem-family pattern. When resources are apparently in continuous expansion, or at least more easily divided through shares, a partible strategy is followed.

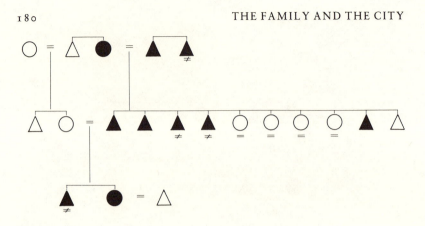

■ Members of the family actually buried in the main pantheon.

Figure 32
Mausoleum Burials of the Espalter/Rull Family

Display and differentiation introduce further complications. While it might seem incongruous to associate display with the cemetery, by mid-century it was a fashionable promenade. Furthermore, Spanish Catholicism maintains a strong tradition of ritual obligations to visit the tombs on the Feasts of All Souls (Día dels Morts, 2 November). As late as the 1920s, Society Notes in the *Diario de Barcelona* reviewed the mausolea for visitors in terms more reminiscent of plays or salons than of burial sites. Even during my fieldwork, the old and new cemeteries filled on these feasts with visitors strolling the grounds—and commenting on the ornament and display of the most prominent tombs. Graveyard display had a wide audience among the living.

It also had a more narrow audience within the elite. In understanding the Old Cemetery and its elite section it is important to ask who was not buried there, and why. Some members of the older nobility were buried at their rural estates or in parishes outside the city. Others chose more modest niches in the main section, such as the Baron de Maldà. Such choices could have been a shrewd accommodation of a secure social position to a reduced economic power: the viewpoint of the older establishment would suggest that more expensive or elaborate projects were parvenu or vulgar. The aristocracy, in turn, set a style for a renewed elite. This idea finds suggestive affirmation in the Montjuich cemetery, where more securely ensconced generations of the financial industrial elite built unadorned tombs that contrast sharply with the neo-Egyptian fantasies criticized by Goytisolo. It also reappears as a theme in class competition at the early opera.

Key families within the industrial-commercial power group also manipulated the sense of unity represented in the cloistered upper-class preserve. Although the Marquis of Comillas owned a prominent corner tomb in the elite section of the cemetery, he was entombed in a private pantheon near his summer palace complex at Comillas. The Jesuit seminary that he patronized there made this into a major display of the solidarity of Church and power groups (Abad 1928:254-265). His descendants are also buried there: replicating the pattern of the seigneurial household. Manuel Girona claimed the prerogatives of an early modern aristocrat as well. For his financial aid to the completion of the facade of the Barcelona cathedral, he was rewarded with a chapel and tomb in the cloister. Both founders thus claimed an elite status within the Good Families.

Josep Xifré Casas adopted a different patronal stance and was buried in a chapel of the hospital that he constructed for his native village of Arenys de Mar. His descendants are not buried with him, however, once again marking Xifré's failure to establish a social lineage in the city.

While elite burial patterns have been analyzed at greater length than those of other sections, they should not be seen as independent so much as contrastive alternatives. Even within the affirmation of rights to family, display, and history evinced in the elite section, this area drew its significance from a system of burial in which these prerogatives were the dominant form, accessible only to a power-holding elite (in contact with cosmopolitan ideas and models). This becomes more apparent when the cemetery is resituated within the unity and division of the city that this elite controlled.

Necropolis and Metropolis: The Cemetery as Urban Image

The neoclassic *Cementiri Vell* coincided in design and patronage with the major architectural thrust of Catalan urbanism in the early 1800s. Both responded to a renovation, even a "revolutionary impulse," in urban society that was shaped by a new understanding of man, society, and power:

> The formal austerity, the ethical demands, the enlightened rationalism and humanism, the evocation of "real antiquity" coupled with the sentimental aspects introduced by Romanticism make it one of the symbolic foundations of our cities. If the neoclassic city is the unity of the mercantile bourgeoisie based on social and economic status combined with a new faith in human reason, then the neoclassic cemetery reveals in itself the same attitudes and the same forms. (Bohigas 1973:60)

In fact, the cemetery was a more controlled exercise in urban planning than the city itself could ever be. Even as a tract like the Old Cemetery grew from the Romantic era to the Victorian, it synthesized the major principles of the neoclassic city as both a social and an architectural order.

> The neoclassic cemetery is not simply an individual parcelling like the eclectic and modernist ones, built when the bourgeoisie had already encountered its expressive terminology. It is always an *ideal city*, geometrically traced, where the niches and tombs are ordered according to a monumentality whose formal bases are to be encountered in the tremendous range of urban renewals that links the Rome of Sixtus V with the Paris of Haussman. (Bohigas 1973:57)

As an ideal city, how did this construction project the future development, physical and social, of Barcelona itself?

In 1819, when formal construction began on the Old Cemetery, residential and activity patterns in the city were only beginning to experience the changes conditioned by new industrial groups—elites and laborers. Various areas of the city were already identified as high-status residential zones. The Carrer de Montcada retained a medieval prestige and association with the palaces of the older nobility (Amelang 1986). The Carrer Ample was the center of mercantile, banking, and port activities. Other palaces were scattered along the Rambles. Yet all these nuclei of elite residence were dispersed through the city in a mixture of classes characteristic of many Mediterranean cities of the period.

As industry began to consolidate in mid-century, so did the social geography of the city. In 1860 construction began on the *Eixample*, the northern exansion of Barcelona beyond its walls. Even wealthy families of the Carrer Ample found the new distances difficult: one brother complained that he would now never see his industrialist sibling who had moved only three kilometers away. A contemporary satirist criticized another extramural palace, the Casa Gibert:

> The house in question is the most faithful representation of our era. If in architectural order it represents the synthesis of the fortress and factory, of the feudal castle and the train station, in the social order it represents the confusion of classes caused by speculation. That is, it symbolizes taste overruled by money, the transaction of the past with the present. (Curet 1952:98)

This critic clearly saw that this new taste was the product of a new elite who would shape a cultural capital that would dominate Barcelona's expansion. The Casa Gibert opened the Passeig de Gràcia, a tree-lined boulevard that joined Barcelona to the formerly exurban village of Gràcia. This street soon became a center for promenades. With its

parallel artery, the Rambla de Catalunya, the Passeig defined a residential strip northward from the congested urban core around which the
new elite concentrated:

> Houses, in reality palaces, were built there by aristocrats who had
> the money to do so, by industrialists, by shipowners, by bankers,
> and especially by wealthy families who had grown rich in America
> and returned to find, in our city, a comfortable and regal repose.
> (Curet 1952:100)

Like other nineteenth-century metropoles with financial-industrial
power groups, the needs and values of an emergent elite reshaped urban space as well as urban design.

The general plan for urbanization of the new city of Barcelona had
been proposed by Ildefonso Cerdá, whose use of geometric blocks has
already been compared to the design of the cemetery. Side streets accommodated the middle classes in much the same way as these niches,
although with considerably more variation. Economic speculation,
however, converted Cerdá's mixture of geometric apartments and
parkland into an unceasing uniformity of overbuilt blocks. The lower
classes, meanwhile, were confined to the decaying older city, or clus-

Figure 33
Map of Barcelona in 1891: The Plan Cerdá

tered outside the city into mill towns and suburbs huddled around the factories. The physical and social separation traced out in the idealized city of the dead was emerging as a set of divisions in the city of the living.

This trend has continued in the subsequent expansion of Barcelona. Major arteries like the Diagonal divide the city into class-based districts as much as neighborhoods. The Parc Güell, northeast of the urban core, was originally planned as an upper-class garden suburb isolated from the urban core by both distance and walls. It failed because of this perceived inaccessibility. With the introduction of the automobile, however, distance has become a social wall of tremendous importance. The elite were first able to remove their domiciles from the lowland plain to one-time resort hillsides like Avinguda Tibidabo or Sarrìa. More recently, some have moved their domicile from the city entirely to outlying villages. Such enclaves, often renovations of abandoned rural communities, were once vacation dwellings. Yet, as noted in Chapter III, several elite members suggested that these country houses are being viewed at present more as a primary residence, converting the urban apartment into a *pied-à-terre*. Classes are thus divided in residence

Figure 34
Aerial View of Barcelona Showing Realization of the Plan
Cerdá

and interaction more effectively than nineteenth-century urban analysts might have imagined.

Nonetheless, the structural clarity of the cemetery as an urban model far surpasses that of the city itself. The cemetery is a limited space, where order could be imposed according to a uniform plan; the city encompasses historical residues, as well as crazy-quilts of individual ownership and direction that have consistently distorted urban planning in Barcelona. The cemetery has also been a space apart, undisturbed except for ritualized visits; the city encompasses more complex social and economic interactions that I have not touched upon in the impressionistic overview just offered. The Old Cemetery must be seen as an ideal model, a socioarchitectural exercise rather than a microcosm. It is precisely in its order, coherence, and division that it still reveals the mentality of an emergent power group.

THE THEATER OF THE CITY

In his introduction to Loewenberg's standard *Annals of Opera* Edward Dent situates opera as a cultural product within its social milieu,

> beginning with what we might call academic opera in Florence, produced before a small audience of excessively cultivated people. And because the only people in that period who were in a position to become excessively cultivated were princes and cardinals and courtiers attendant upon them, opera struck root as an eminently aristocratic and court entertainment, becoming gradually more sumptuous and spectacular as the seventeenth century progressed. In spite of simultaneous currents in different directions, what we might call "dynastic" opera survived indeed right up to the end of the eighteenth century, even after the French Revolution had begun to change the the face of European society. (Dent 1978:xxvii)

While everyone dies and faces the prospect of some burial/disposal, opera has consistently been defined within Western culture as a domain of High Culture and of wealthy, learned, and powerful patrons. Beyond this distinction, though, there are similarities in its development to the pattern already illustrated for elite representation in cemeteries, even after the genre was established as a commercial form.

In seventeenth-century Venice the opera house was as familial as the pantheon; commercial houses "were known by the names of noble families which erected and supported them" (Dent 1978:xviii). By the next century the opera house became a public work, under the aegis of new forms of domination rather than a single patron. Thus, the Theater of San Carlo in Naples became "not only in size but also in position a symbol of the new state" (Robinson 1972:8). San Carlo represented the social and political order of the Neapolitan monarchy for which it was constructed in 1737. It was built adjacent to the palace and was dominated by the presence of the king, whose central box was flanked by the stalls of the nobility. This social pattern was so fixed that no aristocrat could even relinquish his box without express royal approval. The king was also arbiter of behavior for the theater: "No person other than the king or his official deputy . . . could order an encore" (Robinson 1972:111).

In the nineteenth century the opera found patrons in new elites. These drew upon the history of opera houses, while modifying these associations to accommodate social differences. Such modifications were often minimalized. Thus in 1849, when the new rich of New York were rebuffed in their attempts to enter Knickerbocker society at the Academy of Music, they decided to build an alternative institution. In designing the Metropolitan Opera patrons and architects turned to European aristocratic models:

> To invoke such non-American influence was, of course, absurd: the nineteenth-century European houses were built to suit the hierarchy that supported them. Imperial boxes, and others arranged at reasonable distances from the throne, were appropriate enough in theaters that endured through the bounty of one class. It could be contended that the Vanderbilts and Morgans regarded themselves in somewhat the same light, but it is apparent that only the display appealed to them, not the attendant responsibilities. (Kolodin 1966:51)

In the later 1800s, however, the opera became the nexus for the synthesis of old and new elites. Both its symbolic value and its social patterns facilitated exchange in business, courtship, and politics. In Paris, Vienna, and Barcelona, aristocracy and bourgeoisie coalesced in the halls and boxes of the theater.

In the changing social climate of the twentieth century opera has tended to gradually follow the fading of older elites before the bureacrats and managers of new state formations. London's Covent Garden was built in 1858 with three full tiers of boxes for the nobility in addition to the Central Royal Box. After World War I this number was nearly halved to fifty-seven boxes, mainly concentrated in a single Grand Tier. Since World War II further social change has been evidenced in the conversion of boxes to ordinary seats and stalls. Only twenty-two boxes remain, huddled around the Royal Box (Rosenthal 1958:118-119).

Obviously, the sheer visual and acoustic properties of the opera house limit democratization: there is always potential for the representation of stratification, even if only on the basis of the ticket market. If a royal hierarchy is absent, other leadership may substitute. Yet these uses are in reaction to, more than as a continuation of, the national and international traditions within which the Barcelona opera house took on meaning as an arena for the expression of—and contestation to—class divisions and elite coherence.

Three themes from this general overview are particularly important to the examination of the Liceu. All coincide with the analysis of the cemetery, while elaborating upon distinct aspects of social and cultural life. First, the opera house was constructed under the tutelage of a power group to which it gave special prominence. As a corollary the opera also has embodied the succession of elite groups through time, either in structural changes in a single building or in the competition between theaters. The opera has also served as a locus for the coalescence of competing elites.

Second, the opera house is a microcosm of society as a whole. That is, as in the cemetery the hierarchical position of the elite was meaningful in relation to other classes. Again, as in the cemetery, class differentiation extended to the expression of fundamental social units and values: the family, property, and social cohesion.

Figure 35
Drawing of the Gran Teatre del Liceu, 1847 (by F. Parcerissa)

Finally, the opera has been a scene of social drama. As a key symbol of power and privilege within Western society it is also the focus of dispute within class conflicts. As will be evident in Barcelona, this drama could become violent even off the stage.

These themes to some extent presuppose another significant point: namely, that communication among international elites which led to a universalization of symbols of power in the nineteenth century. Opera houses implied prestige as much to the entrepreneurs of a rubber capital in Brazil and the newly enriched miners of the American West as to bankers and industrialists in European capitals. As in the cemetery or in the values of gentlemanliness the formation of the Good Families of Barcelona rested on both adaptations of Catalan traditions of status and the adoption of foreign prestige paradigms. The Liceu has been, historically, a place where internationalized claims have meshed with local elite formation—and with counterevents from other classes.

The Liceu and the Rise of Opera in Barcelona

The upper-class memoirist Joaquín María de Nadal Ferrer distilled the image of the Liceu that was constantly reiterated in my conversations with contemporary Barcelonins:

> The Liceu that I knew in my childhood was not a theater—it was an institution. Even today, when many of its characteristics have disappeared, one goes to the Liceu with a spirit different from that with which one attends any other theater: one goes there as someone fulfilling a ritual. (1952:103-104)

Nadal's introduction of the term *ritual* is particularly apt. Although secular by comparison to the cemetery, the Liceu gradually has come to enshrine widely accepted symbols and behaviors through which membership in the ruling class and the conflict between urban classes are both reenacted. Even so, the Liceu is only one representation within a history of spectacle and celebration in Barcelona (Fàbregas Surroca 1979; Amelang 1986). The use of theatrical spectacles in aristocratic consciousness is a telling prelude to the emergence of a new nineteenth-century elite.

Opera antedated the Liceu in Barcelona. Early representations took place in private noble homes, using aristocratic amateurs as well as professional singers (Curet 1935:60). In 1587 the Theater of the Holy Cross (Santa Creu) was established by a royal privilege granted to the Hospital of the Holy Cross. This theater survived wars, invasions, and fires to become the chosen theater of the eighteenth-century elite. Urban nobles patronized its reconstruction after a fire in the late 1700s, and families transmitted their boxes from father to son through generations. The old urban power structure, including the canons of the hospital and various aldermen, also supported the Santa Creu (Alier 1979:11-88).

The Liceu was founded in 1837 as a money-raising project for a company of national militia. After using an expropriated convent for its first performances, the group made plans for a permanent building on the Ramblas. The building was begun in 1844 and finished in 1847. This triennium also witnessed such economic milestones as the foundation of the Bank of Barcelona (1844), the Barcelona Savings and Loan (1844), and the giant textile firm La España Industrial (1845).

Like these institutions, the Liceu was founded as a joint-stock corporation—drawing on much the same membership as the other ventures. Manuel Girona Agrafel was a key figure in the construction of the building. Others had more aristocratic connections. Joaquín de Gispert Angli, first president of the Society, was a Noble of the Principality (like the stratum who founded the Savings and Loan). His family was also linked by marriage to the industrialist-banker José María Serra. Manuel Gibert Sans, the third key figure in the theater's construction, was a former military man who devoted his wealth to the improvement of Barcelona. His house, as noted, was a symbol of the new bourgeois city.

In order to finance the construction boxes were sold rather than rented. The cheapest ticket price was one-third of a peseta. Ownership of a box ran as high as 15,000 pesetas in addition to a yearly service fee (Aurelia Capmany Farrés 1943:82). While the cheap tickets permitted a wide audience, power rested only with the box *owners*. Until the last few years they formed a commission who leased responsibilities each season to an impresario. Since the death of Franco this system has given way to partial control and financing by the Generalitat de Catalunya, further exemplifying the decline of the Good Families and the role of government in replacing their power and patronage.

In 1847 the addition of the Círculo del Liceo amplified the interactional dimensions of the opera house. The Círculo has been an extremely important and elegant male social club that became a ready meeting place for urban leaders. It is physicially incorporated into the opera house: in the present building there is an entrance from the street and from the main or "noble" floor (*planta noble*) on which the boxes of the upper class are concentrated. Its hours and functions have been more diverse: beyond the short opera and ballet season the club hosts elite meetings to discuss politics, business, and social matters. Furthermore, it is a specially defined space. While the lower classes were expected to observe the display of the boxes, the club was separated as a class prerogative. Its membership also encompasses only the males of the primary families of the city. Women are allowed to enter as guests but not as members. The box, as an extension of the household, is the female domain for social networking and knowledge. The Círculo, by contrast, becomes a more sociable extension of the male office. Yet both club and box are parts of the Liceu as institution.

By mid-century the Liceu was in active competition with the Santa Creu. A theatrical interpretation of this conflict was recorded by the Catalan playwright Serafí Pitarra. Pitarra saw the competition as one of classes as much as theaters. In his play the partisans of the Holy Cross are introduced as "bald, ancient, and bewigged": stereotypes of a declining aristocracy bound by eighteenth-century fashions. The Liceists are "young, elegant, and rich," even though a Cruzado reviles them as "mere manufacturers" (Soler Humbert 1855, see Fabregas Surroca 1975:103).

Competition was not the only difficulty of the Liceu. The building was destroyed by fire in 1861. Yet a new edifice was financed and built within a year. The rapidity of this process manifests the importance that opera had assumed within the social life of the city. Meanwhile, the decline of the Holy Cross became more apparent. Those eighteenth-century families who could afford a box there also attended the Liceu. The Santa Creu, renamed the Teatre Principal, did produce the Catalan premier of Wagner in 1883. But it, too, was hard hit by a late nineteenth-century fire. Unlike the Liceu, it has never regained its status and now functions as a movie house and entertainment center.

Other amusements also competed for elite patronage. The Hippodrome was memorialized in satirical couplets about elite families. Other members of elite families regularly attended *zarzuelas*, as well as more popular theatrical performances.

There were also individual statements of class and imagery. The Teatre dels Camps Elisis, for example, was built as a commercial opera house in the new and fashionable Eixample. The patrician banker Evaristo Arnús Ferrer converted it into the Teatre Líric, which he patronized almost like a family opera house. After his death the sixteen-hundred-seat theater proved economically burdensome, and it was torn down in 1902. The Liceu flourished.

In the twentieth century the career of the Liceu has been susceptible to the political and economic fluctuations of its patrons. Many informants recalled a Golden Age in the early decades of the century, including the Primo de Rivera dictatorship. This ended with the social reforms of the Second Republic and with expropriation during the Civil War, when the Liceu was rebaptized the National Theater of Catalonia. In the 1940s and 1950s efforts were made to revive the Liceu. The Francoist bureaucracy and military joined the Catalan upper bourgeoisie. A magazine, *Liceo*, was even founded to carry musical and social news.

Changes continued with the end of the Franco regime and the increasing collapse of the older factory elite. In 1978, for example, a news magazine ran the headline "Is the Liceu Dying?" (*Destino* 9-15 March 1978:20-24). In an interview the theater's manager blamed the crisis on anachronistic structures: "It lives with those of one hundred years ago, when the current situation is very different" (Moya-Angeler 1978a:21). Both anachronisms and decline are facets of the same problem: the Liceu as an institution is a product and reproducer of a historically particular elite formation and has followed the trajectory of this elite. Recognition by the Generalitat de Catalunya of the theater as part of the cultural and historical patrimony of Catalonia has led to support in exchange for control. Political leaders of the socialist and nationalist parties mingle with the older aristocracy there—and programs are printed in both Catalan and Castilian.

Like the cemetery, the Liceu has had a rich and changing participation in the cultural meanings of the elite in Barcelona and an even greater participation in day-to-day social interaction. The "meanings" of the Liceu, however, must be elucidated by reference to architectural design, social interpretation, and elite usage as a marker of upper-class life cycles and cohesion.

The Structure and Meaning of the Liceu

The Liceu is built in a horseshoe design common to many opera houses. Its thirty-five hundred seats fill an orchestra level overhung by five balconies. Three of the balconies, as well as the orchestral floor, have boxes as well as individual seats. The top two tiers contain only individual seats.

The differentiation of balconies is reinforced by other features of ornament and access. Only the lower four floors can be reached from the main entrance. A triumphal marble staircase leads from the lobby to the second floor (*planta noble*, or *principal*). There it divides into smaller and less decorated staircases to the third and fourth floor. The topmost balconies, from whose cheaper seats the opera itself may be invisible, are entered through an undistinguished entrance on a side street. Today an elevator takes patrons directly to these seats, without any possible connection to the lower balconies.

The *planta noble* was designed with special care to emphasize its high prestige. In addition to the focal ceremonial staircase it has a large salon for conversation and the entrance to the bar and dining rooms of the Círculo del Liceu. It shares with other floors a wide passageway that

Figure 36
Interior of the Gran Teatre del Liceu

girds the seating area, onto which the boxes open. This is the scene of a constant promenade between the acts; the passageway is five meters wide to accommodate considerable movement.

The floors with boxes have another special feature: the anterooms. Doors open from the passage onto an elegant room that holds four to six people, a private space between the corridor and the seats. The box is semipublic, enclosed by walls roughly one meter in height. It has seats and benches on each side, with a raised seat at the back. Boxes on the main floor hold six to ten guests.

This distinction among floors permeated nineteenth-century architecture in Barcelona. The second floor of the palaces of the Rambla de Catalunya or the Passeig de Gràcia was the desirable floor for residence, indicated by a separate and formal entrance staircase, larger and ornamented bay windows or balconies, and more spacious rooms. The ground floor would hold businesses, a concierge, and space for carriages. Upper floors repeated the pattern of the *planta noble* with decreasing ornamentation and size. In some palaces these were allocated to the children of the owners who occupied the *planta noble*. The topmost floors, containing servants quarters, were cramped and dark, with small windows or none at all (Figure 38). Only in the construction boom after the 1950s has the penthouse emerged as a new symbol of social prestige.

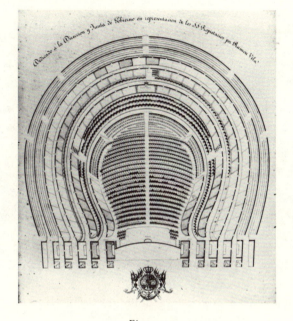

Figure 37
Interior Plan of the Gran Teatre del Liceu

The six floors of the opera house, however, were distinguished by more than design features. The seats of best visibility were also those of highest prestige: the *planta noble* and, to a somewhat lesser extent, the orchestra and third floor. The fourth and fifth floors (third and fourth balconies) were less valued. Boxes were owned by less important families, by groups of friends (*peñas*), or by younger couples whose parents held boxes on lower floors. Individual seats were also owned by modest families. The uppermost balconies have been associated with those of limited resources, who might otherwise not hear any opera: students, artisans, or workers. One Catalan author interpreted these levels of meaning by contrast to another nonelite institution:

> Although conceived and constructed by the wealthy and aristocratic, it has never been a theater of class. Every social category fits: in the orchestra, second, and third floor, the *aristocracy*, on the fourth and fifth floors, the *mesocracy*, and on the sixth and seventh, the *democracy*. . . . the confusion and mingling of all these classes took place in the celebration of the splendid dances of Carnival. (Puig Alfonso 1943:25-26)

While the Liceu juxtaposed classes, it did so within a controlled differentiation. It was a theater of one class in active distinction from

Figure 38
Residential Architecture in Turn-of-the-Century Barcelona

others. The opposite of this was Carnival, a traditional festival of disguise and critique of social roles. Even within the Liceu, Carnival was an image of the world in reverse. Thus its mingling was in direct opposition to the clear demarcation of categories in the Liceu itself. While there was a nineteenth-century custom of Carnival balls in the theater, this was increasingly frowned upon. For the elite Carnival was limited to private and single-class parties. Under Franco the Barcelona Carnival was completely banned as a threat to public order. Under the new Generalitat it has been revived as part of Catalonia's national public heritage.

In the Liceu social groups existed in relationship to each other rather than in isolation. The upper floors were linked to the lower by their observation of the social activities below. Those in the aristocracy displayed not only to other families of the elite but to a popular audience above. The contrasting yet interwoven perspectives can be regained from two authors born at the turn of the century in different social backgrounds. Josep Pla attended the Liceu as a poor student in the *galliner* ("chicken roost": a nickname for the uppermost balconies) and later recorded his impressions:

> The spectacle of the Liceu on a good night is magnificent when viewed from the top floor. . . . the view is literally fabulous—an ocean of bourgeoisie, dripping with jewels and diamonds. What a

spectacle, by God! On the fifth floor . . . a group of people carefully positioned, with the faces of train mechanics. . . . In addition,
there were the music fanatics, with or without score in hand, for
whom nothing but the music of the drama was important. These
fans had an Olympian disdain for the bourgeois sea below them.
(1956:40)

Meanwhile, Joaquín María de Nadal Ferrer described the thoughts
of a member of the aristocracy looking upward—or at least conscious
of those looking down:

> The public of the Liceu was formed by all classes, but not all went
> for the same reason. If they were not all friends, at least all were
> acquainted. . . . the inhabitants of boxes and choice seats knew the
> preferences of the denizens of the upper floors, and those were
> aware of the engagements and the loves that were important on
> the principal floors. They knew perfectly well that X had broken
> with Y, or who had made the dresses of Mrs. Z or Countess A, and
> what the emerald of this or that woman would cost. . . . the most
> humble seamstress of the *galliner* could have named without error
> the owners of the boxes on the principal floor, and even those of
> many individual seats. (1950:133-134)

These two commentators suggest the dialogue within which the social meaning of the Liceu took shape. Nadal, the elitist, imputes a mu-
sic-hall ambience to the social dramas of the Liceu, with benign interest
on the part of those above. Pla's memories are more charged with hostility. Nadal could not impute to the upper floors, for that hostility had
already scarred the security of the elite within its ordered domain. Neither account of itself expressed the complete perception of the Liceu.
Instead, they illustrate the clash of the generally hegemonic expression
of the elite with the less than complete acquiescence of those over
whom this control was to be exercised.

To speak of elite appropriation of the Liceu it is necessary to go beyond the static framework of urban society embodied in the edifice. For
the elite, by contrast to other groups, the Liceu was a fundamental locus of social and cultural identity. This is apparent in the way in which
the theater enshrined the concept of family and ownership, in its use in
the upper-class life-cycle, and in its value for the integration of the upper class as a whole.

Boxes in the Liceu are property. Families are identified with the
boxes that they have owned for generations. At least one family displays the original bill of sale from 1844 in the anteroom of its box. In

the testament of Juan Güell (Appendix) the box is specifically included in the distribution of resources as going to his son and primary heir.

Since the box has a capacity of ten to twelve an extended sense of family or network can be cultivated for any performance; distant relatives and others can be accommodated on the second and third performance of the opera. On the other hand, since this is not an expandable or divisible resource, the box, like the family pantheon, tends to follow the main male line. Other lines may buy new boxes. Middle-class owners, by contrast, might have only a pair of tickets or a single seat.

Because of this confluence of family, box, and status, lack of a box raises serious questions. Retirement from the Liceu is a withdrawal from assertions of prestige and from connections of friendship and potential marriage. In the recent economic crisis some older families with declining revenues sold their rights, relinquishing this display. Their private protestations of disinterest did not always coincide with public evaluation of their actions.

For those who have owned boxes over generations the "theater became a complement of family life and an extension of the house. Its boxes enjoyed a certain privilege of extraterritoriality: people went to them without leaving their home" (Nadal Ferrer 1952:105). Nowhere was this connection more evident than in the elaborate etiquette that surrounded rites of passage. This began in earliest childhood:

> The juridical condition of the boxes as private property had repercussions on the audience. Children invaded them on Saturday with governesses and retainers, and even wetnurses. Is there anything more extraordinary than a wetnurse at the opera? (Nadal Ferrer 1952:105)

The transition to adulthood was also marked at the opera house, especially for women. As late as the 1950s women made their social debut by appearing in a formal dress at an evening performance. This was followed by visits and courtship, according to the strict rules already discussed. One woman who made her debut in the 1920s noted that male visitors were only permitted to pay their respects to her in the public box, in the presence of her parents and chaperone (as well as the view of the rest of the group). Only after her 1929 marriage did she receive guests in the privacy of the anteroom. Nonetheless, the Liceu was central to both the contacts and the flow of information that made marriage the foundation of social cohesion.

Death was also ritualized in the Liceu. Any family who lost a member was expected to close its box and cancel its social calendar for the season. The failure of one family to do so was memorialized in a turn-of-the-century satirical couplet:

Figure 39
Ticket to a Private Masked Ball at the Gran Teatre del Liceu,
1860

En memoria de un ser querido
Los Fabra han venido
In memory of a loved one
The Fabras have come.

Finally, the Liceu was a meeting ground for the cohesion of the elite
as a group. Well-placed individuals at the Liceu's apogee had rights to
several boxes according to their different roles. One woman recalled
her father had a family box on the second floor that was owned by his
parents, a box on the third floor with his wife and children, and a third
floor tontine of male friends. Boxes on the upper floors were also ru-
mored to be used for mistresses or assignations. This information is difficult to verify but emphasizes the subtle decrease in status in the mid-
dle-upper floors.

Elite spectators circulate during the evening. Between the acts males
talk in the passageways or visit the ladies in their boxes. More extensive
discussions take place in the Círculo, over drinks or a meal. Conversation includes the exchange of social, political, and business information
as well as musical criticism. Before the Civil War nonmusical displays

of solidarity were even more frequent, including political rallies and social events.

The Liceu was familiar in another sense, in the comfort of constant interactions. In 1985 an octogenarian described to me the theater in her youth: "It was like a get-together (*reunión*) of the families of Barcelona. It was not Fulano goes one day and some other stranger the next. Instead, you looked around and asked 'Who isn't here today?' "

In all these characteristics the Liceu is a living cognate of the stratificational projections and usages of the cemetery. But, as noted in the Introduction, the opera house was never outside of the city in a spatial, ritual, or social sense. Hence it has been less an urbanistic projection than an arena for urban social confrontation.

Social Drama at the Liceu

On the opening night of the 1976 season spectators leaving the Liceu were confronted by protestors who reportedly pelted them with fruit or vandalized their cars. This was also reported for the next season. Such occurrences were seized upon by those who wished to withdraw for other reasons, including economic difficulties. They insisted that the Liceu was dead, that "no one goes anymore." These rumors were also used to criticize the destabilization of the post-Franco era. It was not, however, the first time that class violence had erupted in the opera.

The Catalan folklorist Joan Amades cites an anecdote about the fire that destroyed the first Liceu:

> It is said that the associates were people of position who felt disdain and lack of consideration for the common people to such an extent that, in building the theater . . . they were deeply concerned that those who sat in the upper floors could not descend to the orchestra or lower floors where the builders had their seats or boxes. Because of this, the first theater had no communication between upper and lower floors. If someone in the house wanted to go from a higher floor to a lower, or vice versa, he had to exit to the street. Popular opinion said that the blaze had been set by theater workers or members of the lower class who met the disdain of the owners with fire. (1947:71)

Amades gives no context or reference for this story. While it may be suggestive of the class tensions of mid-nineteenth century Barcelona, it may also have been influenced by the more decisive action that followed at the end of the century. On the opening night of the 1893 season, during the first intermission of William Tell, two bombs were thrown from the top floor of the theater into the seats below. One exploded in the first floor between rows thirteen and fourteen. Twenty people were killed.

The turn of the century was a period of extremely violent class confrontation in Barcelona. In retrospect, the Liceu incident fits into a dialectic of terrorism and repression between owners and workers that included the bombing of the Corpus Christi procession of 1896; the Tragic Week and its aftermath in 1909, and the pistol gangs that roamed the streets following World War I. Yet the reaction of the upper class both in its repression and in its transformation of the Liceu bombing in historical consciousness provides important insights into their sense of order and control.

The bombing of the Liceu was an excuse for a widespread crackdown on anarchists and dissidents. Over four hundred were arrested and seven executed. The bomber himself, Santiago Salvador Franch, was arrested in February and executed in July. Later historians have suggested that since he had no previous background as a militant this action might have been a personal reaction to the execution of the anarchist Pallas. The elite judgment, even fifty years later, is more sweeping: "His intent was to destroy society" (Bertrán 1931:217).

The Liceu bombing has tended to eclipse later and more destructive confrontations, like the Tragic Week, in elite historical consciousness. It is commemorated by a relief on Barcelona's Temple of the Holy Family and has also been enshrined in popular novels, such as Ignacio Agustí's *Mariona Rebull*, which was serialized on Spanish television in 1976 and 1977. Agustí's depiction, widely known among elite families during my stay in Barcelona, focusses on the mythic carnage of the upper class rather than on the actual events that transpired:

> From one of the front boxes they carried a young girl, screaming like a demon, trailing blood on the rug—as the last drops of her life escaped. On the main staircase men and women sat, their faces glazed by pain and shock, shirt fronts and collars disarrayed, the most intimate flesh revealed as tragedy overcame shame. . . . He was horrified and turned away in the other direction, but the macabre display continued. That was Jacinto Miralles, who said that he never went anywhere. And this, Carolina Millet, who had played Schumann on the day of her debut. (1969, first pub. 1945:196-197)

Agustí uses the bombing as a climactic intervention to eliminate the heroine and her lover, struck down behind the closed door of the anteroom of a box. His account is clearly fictionalized: casualties were limited to middle-class or foreign patrons in the orchestra seats. Yet Agustí was appealing more to the *consciousness* of the event among elite families than to the facts. While contemporary members of the Good Fam-

ilies dismissed Agustí's exaggeration, the tale of the Liceu bombing—
and a more genealogical link through "someone" in the family who
was there that night—was a common feature of interviews.

Once again, Nadal summarizes the impact of the Liceu bombing on
elite historical memory:

> A long time passed before the seats and boxes recovered their life,
> and a group of orchestra seats remained deserted forever, as a si-
> lent memorial to that great catastrophe. People involuntarily
> raised their eyes to the roof as if they feared to discover the same
> criminal act from another hand, repeating the tragic gesture, sow-
> ing that seed of death in the midst of life. (1952:111)

Why did this event, this one bombing among so many incidents of its
epoch, take on such a mythic power in the historical consciousness of
the Good Families of Barcelona? The answer lies in the ideological
meaning of the Liceu as a projection of the social order of Catalonia
and the stability of control that the new elite sought to hold in that society. The bombing of the Liceu was a direct challenge to the Good
Families' image of power and society, on its presentation of its own
identity. By attacking within the Liceu, the confrontation assumed even
greater meaning—and left greater uncertainty. As Nadal notes, even
brutal repression could not restore the integrity of that model of the city
and its classes that the Liceu and the cemetery had been built to display.

The further comments of a bourgeois writer who actually attended
the Liceu that night may further illuminate the depths of the connection
of the Liceu, the social order, and the family. Joan Maragall added the
subtitle "returning home from the Liceu" to his poem "Paternal." In it
he mixes images of chaos with a sinister vision of the family as nexus of
violence:

> Furious, the hatred explodes across the land
> The contorted heads rain blood,
>   and one must go to the *fetes*
> With heart well-fortified, as if to war.
> ....
> Watching the child who suckles—the mother
> sighs, the father wrinkles his brow.
> But the innocent infant,
> Who, satisfied, leaves the empty breast
>   looks at him,—looks at her,
>   and laughs, barbarously.

> (1929, 1:47)

In the work place and the voting booth this same bourgeoisie sought
to use the family as a metaphor by which to control the proletariat as if

children. The sanctity of the family was further ritualized in the Liceu. Hence, any attack on the social order of the Liceu betrayed a lie at the heart of not only the symbol but of the family as the ideological projection of the whole class.

CONCLUSIONS

Both the Liceu and the Cementiri Vell share an ideological model of social structure, class cohesion, and control. The necropolis reveals the urbanistic mentality of the nineteenth-century elite in a way that the city of Barcelona itself and its documents can do no longer. The opera house has been more actively intertwined with urban life. Thus, it has been the subject of more visible challenges to the elite image of an ideal society.

In both of these social projections the family is a central motif. It is the basic unit of the well-ordered society. Tombs and theater seats delineate the boundaries of households, while patterning the interaction among them. Rights to tomb and loge are established in familial succession. Both become an "extension of the house," a cultural manipulation of the structure that was so effectively used in the economic and social life of the emergent elite.

Yet in both of these models the symbolism of the family has been subsumed by the projection of an ordered inequality among classes. Hence, elite models abandon the uniform traditional values of the family evident in political rhetoric to condone differences in rights of property, size of the household, and continuity through time. Was there no contradiction in imagery?

In fact, this variation in the use of the family as metaphor tends to reaffirm a point made in the earlier analysis. The family has obviously been important to the Barcelona upper class for its practical values in economic and social life, for its historical associations, and for its deep emotive appeal. Yet other images might have met the same conditions or have been adapted to the ends of the group in different ways. The special value of the family as metaphor also lay in its multiplicity of meanings and the consequent ambiguity or indeterminacy it allowed in cultural projections. In political rhetoric the family was emphasized in its dual capacities as unifying and hierarchical. In modelling the ideal urban society it was depicted as fundamental to membership in that society but fundamentally differentiated according to the segmentation of rights and privileges within that society. Ambiguity rather than contradiction was the key to the value and usage of the family as a cultural image to legitimize the elite's claim to domination.

CHAPTER IX

FAMILY, AGENCY, AND NETWORKS OF POWER: TOWARDS A COMPARATIVE UNDERSTANDING OF ELITES

Most analyses of elite formation and reproduction have rested on abstract theories of society and power. The methods and concerns of ethnology, however, propel the analyst and reader into immediate contact with individuals, values, and strategies within actual power groups. To construct an anthropology of power, a bridge must be built between abstraction and data, between theory and action. In addition, this effort must go beyond specific case studies to allow generalizations to be made concerning elite groups and processes of domination within distinct societies and histories.

The family has emerged in this study as a complex agent within the social history of inequality. Three themes summarize the work as a foundation for future comparison:

1) As an agent for the distribution of rights and privileges within a society, the family is shaped by access to and control of power within that society. Catalan industrialists have been characterized by their intensive use of kinship in business organization as well as social interaction. This usage, however, has been embedded in a particular evolution of organizational possibilities responding to local practice, national laws, and international markets. The confluence of these processes has, at the same time, differentiated elite groups from other social groups within Catalonia, whether rural producers or urban lower classes.

2) As the basic unit through which power is held and distributed, the family is also the structure through which competing interests can be mediated and reconciled. The emerging bourgeoisie of nineteenth-century Barcelona confronted an aristocratic establishment in firm control of prestige as well as some privileged aspects of political and economic life. The coalescence of the Good Families as an elite resulted from a "transaction between the past and the present" (Curet 1952:98). It was an exchange of economic for social capital, embedded in relationships of alliance and inheritance that cemented a ruling class.

3) Finally, the family has had a potent symbolic role within processes of domination. The traditional Catalan household was a multivalent image through which ruling classes attempted to identify Catalonia as a separate national domain. On the one hand, their ideology of the typical Catalan family signalled regional distinctiveness vis-à-vis the rest of Spain. On the other, the household stratification offered a persuasive parallel through which to counter the class tensions of Catalan industrial society. Other symbolic manipulations occurred in the genealogization of history or the statements of unity made in the cemetery and opera.

In these realms the family has not been simply a metaphor for the Good Families of Barcelona. Nor has it been a mere social device shaped by the capitalist system: family has been a crucial structural element in the formation of the elite. As a component in a process of domination, as well as a key symbol shared and manipulated within Catalan society, the family has been a critical unit of action in relation to structure and process.

As such, the family also should be a basic structure of comparative elite theory. A review of the still incomplete literature on social organization of primary elites within capitalist societies continually encounters marriage, kinship, networks, and reproduction as foundations of group action. Many comparisons already have been developed in this study: others, in turn, suggested by the Catalan data may become the foundation for future comparative research.

This orientation towards an ethnography of elites via the close examination of family, in its broadest sense, emphasizes two themes of interest within contemporary anthropology. First, the study of the elite family emphasizes agency in the sense of a personal localization of responsible and effective actors within a social system. As social science looks at power, the reader often senses no one person or group acts so much as he/she/they participate in movements or represent consciousness. In the study of elites, however, it is possible to clearly identify a locus of social action and reaction. By dealing with elites as human agents who are extremely visible and influential within social structures, we begin to unite macrotheory with the human actors one knows in the field. This does not, as I have frequently pointed out since the preface, imply consistent consciousness or even agreement of all members of an elite. It does, however, identify a set of actors and interests from which to understand the mechanisms of power.

Second, the family synthesizes divergent levels of social and economic organization. It reflects the impact of changes at many levels upon the power groups of a local society, while it encapsulates reaction to such changes. As such, the elite family is an ideal vehicle for complex comparisons in modern societies.

This final chapter speaks to both points with reference to materials from this discussion and relevant comparisons from other ethnological studies, especially those of Cohen (1981) and Marcus (1980, MS). Discussion begins with the individual in relation to the family and the corollary theme of enduring identity of families over time. From there analysis moves to the question of families as interlocking collectivities. Here my concern will be less on the mechanisms of coalescence and control already discussed than on the structural meaning of such coalescence: families as agents in opposition to the state or as representations of the interaction of local economies with world political economics. Finally, I return to the meanings of family as metaphor and the analysis of ideology, domination, and criticism within complex societies.

The Family as Unity

Anthropologists long have been interested in the individual as participant in, and representative of, divergent cultures. Catalan biographers assume a familiarity of custom and structure in their reader, within which an individual life is set; anthropologists look for this framework through the lives of their subjects. Yet both outside observers and Catalan chroniclers concur in the extent to which upper-class Catalan individuals are culturally situated in the stream of family history. In an extreme case one meets the imposing image of the "sons as second existence" cited for bourgeoise families in Chapter III. The elaborate genealogical tomes cherished by the older noble families also stamp history onto the individual consciousness of their scions. Elite individuals are socialized into responsibilities to live up to their family and to act in its interests according to its positional claims. Even rebellion against the family is phrased in terms of household and lineal dynamics.

This is not to say that the individual is not himself or herself an active agent. Yet apart from philosophical questions that this discussion might evoke, one might suggest that the individual is not the most appropriate unit through which to understand power. There are dynamics of power among individuals within the family, especially in the relationship of men and women, but the family remains the domestic theater in which such conflicts must be played out. And men and women in the Catalan elite, as in other power groups to which I have made reference, have been shown to hold complementary roles, where the absence of strong female participation may be a vital weakness in a family's social and economic success. Similarly, individuals may oppose or reject parental domination, but they remain *hijos de buena familia* in their upbringing, networks, and social categorization. Such a theme might well be pursued by a comparison with studies of self-realization and individual-family bonds in other classes, exemplified in the work of Oscar Lewis (1959, 1961) among the poor of Mexico City or Unni Wikan with the poor of Cairo (1980).

The importance of the family as agent becomes most apparent in questions of economic or social mobility. Here the lifespan of an individual is not regarded culturally by Catalans as a suitable period on which to base analysis of socioeconomic status. Families rise and fall through generations, while still uniting the generations in the choices of any individual. One does not disgrace oneself so much as bring dishonor on the family. Nor does one enrich oneself so much as accumulate wealth to be passed on to the next generation, thereby fomenting a whole series of controls on distribution.

This processual vision of the individual within a stream of family consciousness is by no means limited to Catalonia. Indeed, it characterizes aristocracies from the non-Western world as much as those of European industrial society: here the chants of the *griot* have much in common in both function and manipulation with the writings of genealogists or family eulogists in London, New York, or Barcelona. In an ideologically nonaristocratic society like the United States, this sense of family sagas, real or fictional, pervades our view of the upper class, from televised nighttime serials to the lives of the Rockefellers or the first families of Virginia.

The lives of individuals in the upper class may be a useful focus for future study if framed within this broader perspective. The tensions of individual and family, in fact, account for the often oppressive constraints on the hero in upper-class novels—or the similar concerns echoed by later generations in family histories such as the Collier and Horowitz collective biography of the Rockefellers. Materials for such analysis—biographies, autobiographies, and fictional memoirs—certainly exist. Yet this examination of the individual has rarely been brought into play in anthropological writing, which has turned to the individual only to exemplify oppressed or exotic groups. A rare exception, George Marcus's analysis of the Hunt family's attempt to corner the silver market, uses these popular published materials to explore anthropological questions of exchange and power and suggests the fruitfulness of reviving the question of the individual within this perspective. Marcus, too, points to the dynastic family as the overriding determinant of behavior and response (MS). Janik and Toulmin's analysis of Wittgenstein and his context also might be a good model for such anthropological research (1973). There the authors link rich individual philosophical materials to family history and interactions within a wide milieu of science, arts, and letters that made this interaction meaningful. In both cases individuals are presented within the constructed realities of larger social and cultural units. For elites, as I have shown, the family is such a primary social and cultural reality.

THE FAMILY AND THE NETWORK

The family differs crucially from other units of analysis in the study of power—whether companies, political interest groups, or social classes. While the household may appear to be only one kind of organization among many in economics or culture, the unique position of the family lies in its "natural" synthesis of such domains. A Catalan businessman, as much as an American businessman of an earlier period or the wife of a modern industrialist in many nations, accepts the coalescence of associations and acquaintances from all spheres of life as normal. That males of an ascending generation dominate in domestic life, for example, was hardly challenged as an assumption in industrial society until recent decades. That older males should exercise equivalent control in the workplace or in political life has seemed equally true. For centuries, in Barcelona as in much of the Western world, the strength of male domination has been the "naturalness" of this pattern in all realms rather than one, reaffirmed by the pervasiveness of the family.

All these patterns of control are linked together in a natural order reified in the bourgeois "Holy Family." Thus Marx observed in the *Theses on Feuerbach*: "After the earthly family is discovered to be the secret of the holy family, the former must then itself be criticised in theory and revolutionized in practice" (1972:108, first pub. 1888). Even today as the assumptions of patriarchy are challenged in Catalonia as in other areas, the interlocking patterns of familylike roles hinders clear analysis or reformulation.

The multivalent values of elite households increase as they interact with other units. In Barcelona, as in other Western capitalist societies, the strength of the Good Families as an elite has rested in the continual intermeshing of many strands of contact: two businessmen are also cousins; a politician marries the sister of another industrialist; a banker was schoolmate to the merchant who needs a loan, while his wife attends church with the wife of the merchant. To speak of neat divisions of economics, social life, politics, and culture belies the fundamental strength of the elite as a densely connected network. Hence those who achieve success in one realm may remain marginalized from the elite as a whole, at least until their heirs can be more fully socialized into the next generation.

This pattern recurs with striking frequency in elite groups. In Sierra

Leone, Abner Cohen has documented it among the Freetown Creole elite who have acted as power brokers in the colony and state (1981). Dennis Gilbert has charted it for leading families in Lima (1981), as George Marcus has in Texas (personal communication). In the European tradition the intermarriages of royalty and nobility long antedated the machinations of industrial elites—and perhaps did so on grander continental scales. Even in a society like the Soviet Union that ideologically abhors such interconnections, observers note the confluence of education, privilege, and marriage in the political elite (Smith 1977:60-65).

The accessory connections that unite the Good Families while excluding others are repeated in power groups throughout the world as well. Where the Jesuits and the Madames of the Sacred Heart helped the Catalan elite cohere, Andover, Harvard, and Radcliffe have performed similar roles in Boston. Public schools, followed by Oxford or Cambridge, did so in Britain. Similarly, the Bohemian Grove celebrates masculine solidarity among men identified with disparate interests of economics and politics in the United States as much as the Círculo del Liceo has done in Catalonia. In a complementary fashion, parties, weddings, and gossip control social information and economic life in London, Paris, or Freetown as much as in Barcelona.

The synthetic role of the family does not preclude other manners of coalescence: economic interest group, political party, or positional linkages. All of these have coexisted in Barcelona. The Foment del Treball was organized as a representation of the Good Families and smaller manufacturers, as was the Lliga. Yet each was ultimately linked to a familiar continuity.

However, economic lobbies for workers, competing political parties, and the bureaucracy of the central state have long been part of Catalan life. In some real sense familial elites must be compared to alternative agents and strategies. The strengths and weaknesses of kin-based power groups become especially apparent in opposition to other interests. In Barcelona the regional elite took on a pattern of organization that opposed it to and yet isolated it from the interests and bureaucracies of the central Castilian government. It is important to compare the elites' structure and fate with divergent courses such as that of Basque industrialists who married into Madrid political families, moved headquarters to the capital, and in other ways adapted the family program to the demands of a centralizing state. A contemporary journalist has described the contrast:

> The Catalan families that appear amid the fifty big families in Catalonia are in many cases relatives of those who dominated the Lliga in the time of the Republic. The Bertrands, the Güells, the

Ventosas, the Bultós, and the Escalas are names of the Lliga elite. The conservation of this historical tradition may derive from the maintenance of the family structure in large sectors of the Catalan economy. This does not mean families like the Basques who control a diversified business group from a strong banking position. Instead, they are families grouped in a single sector—generally textiles—with weak economic positions rarely based in finance. . . . The whole problem of Catalan industry appears, then, at the family level—the need to seek capital from banks based outside of Catalonia. (Claret Serra 1973:17)

All forms of power group organization are not equivalent. The Catalan socioeconomic elite promoted cohesion at the expense of isolating itself from political power in the state. In the era of the Lliga this cohesion was used as the foundation for an excursion into government. Yet, as the events of the 1920s and 1930s showed, the Good Families were vulnerable to actions of the central state. Other national elites have survived shifts in the structure of power more successfully than the Catalans because of their multiple bases, including access to political power or international capital. As I also suggested, familial organization may tend towards stabilization rather than rapid change or flexibility, again isolating the Catalans from the more malleable strategies of other power groups.

Perhaps the most striking claim for the power of a family model of elite formation is that which links this case study to the work of Mosca, Pareto, and Gramsci, as well as the historical reconstruction of Mayer: the survival of aristocracy in nineteenth- and twentieth-century Europe. The rise and fall of an industrial elite in Barcelona was played out against the backdrop of an aristocratic group that has endured for centuries, absorbing and surviving challenges to its control. Mayer has claimed this to be a much more significant feature for European society as a whole. It demands further investigation by both ethnographers and historians. The concept of marginal groups in social capital used to categorize the eighteenth-century mercantile aristocracy in Barcelona, drawn out in parallel to E. O. Wright's formulation of class consciousness, may prove useful in structuring such analysis.

FAMILY, IDEOLOGY, AND DOMINATION

The key question arising from these general considerations of elites as a form of organization based in familial syntheses of multiple powers is that of hegemony. Who has access to control within the state, and how are they most effectively organized? Who has the information and control to make decisions concerning participation in or adaptation to international marketing changes? The crucial separation of power groups from the state, discussed in the introduction to this book, is now clearer as a framework for future research, for example, on socioeconomic foundations of the Lliga or comparable nationalist revivals in capitalist states. Divisions within elites can also be discussed within this framework as steps towards an effective attempt at control. The use of the familial elite as a foundation, furthermore, allows a much clearer look outward at the intermeshing of local power with national and international changes.

The question of hegemony is linked to that of ideology. The meaning of the family within the Catalan elite is not only social and economic but also cultural. It is both a symbol to be manipulated and a way of organizing the world into emotionally meaningful categories on the basis of family membership. In this realm Abner Cohen's work on Sierra Leone provides not only dramatic parallels but also a sense of how to organize further study on elites.

The forms of domination in both Barcelona and Freetown can be approached through Cohen's sense of culture as "manifest in symbolic performances that are objective and collective" (1981:30). Shared kinship, style, and associations provide forms through which unity and domination are displayed. In England, France, Austria, and the United States the same enactment of differences recurs within the same theaters. The ubiquity of opera houses as representations of stratification in the Western world, for example, points to the universalization of a cultural vocabulary of stratification, with conscious actions to adopt and adapt such a vocabulary to each historical context. In all cases men *and* women of the upper classes are united quite literally as actors in their rehearsal and enactment of symbolic dramas that constitute their power.

The Barcelona case makes clear that ideological statements may have value to the ideology-producing groups without necessarily being fully instrumental or effective with regard to dominated groups. The emphasis on the family as social unity and as the basis for society affirmed the continuing power of certain aspects of an existing sociocultural establishment and the boundaries of an emerging elite. This valuation of the family was imposed upon urban society through the models cited in the text. It permeated education, religion, and recreation as well as formal institutions. Yet the model represented in the Liceu was not necessarily an ideology accepted or internalized by other classes, particularly those who found themselves in political and economic opposition to the elite. The working class violently confronted the elite in precisely those areas where familiarity had been championed: in the *colonia*, the schools and churches, and the opera house. Where the elite erected statues to Güells or Lopez's, others tore them down in the time of the Republic. Spectators have had active and critical roles in dramas of power.

Family and family history may serve nonetheless as more subtle instruments of metaphorical domination. In Barcelona history often has been converted to genealogy, in the inverse of a process long familiar to anthropologists. While the family as a model for society might have been rejected directly, in the guise of history it has become another part of the elite claim to urban power (see Sahlins 1981; Jameson 1981; Lukacs 1985). The anthropologist, therefore, must not only critically examine this history but situate it as an active component of urban conflict and cohesion through time.

In the study of culture, as in social and economic roles, the meaning of the family within power groups affirms the need to see and study ideology as a process. Whether discussing institutions and particular values, as exemplified by schools and language use, or symbolic models, as in burial, cultural statements made by the elite have changed through time in response to their own organization and external circumstances. Yet these changes have been linked in continuity by the perdurance and reproduction of basic social bonds within the upper-class household and its extensions.

Towards an Anthropology of Power

The roles of both elite and family that have become apparent in Barcelona set new demands for anthropological studies as a whole. The study of elites has emerged from this work, as in other ethnographies used for comparison, as a feasible and significant theme for anthropological research. To understand power in any society, the anthropologist can, and must, be able to speak to those who wield it as much as those oppressed by it. His work, in turn, may complement and refine the more philosophical models of power that anthropologists are seeking in the modern world (Wolf 1969;1982).

The family has emerged here as a key unit in comprehending and explaining the multiple, often mystified, roles of power groups. As such, it is a bridge to studies of differential roles of the family as agent in other classes, whether through the structure in the life of the poor and its relations to shared cultural models or through the development of interaction patterns in middle-class suburbs. The family also provides a vehicle for cross-cultural comparisons of elites, which should be enriched as more material becomes available.

Both foci move beyond documentation of particular cases or completion of social analyses. To deal with the Good Families is to ask who controls, who owns, who acts, in a way very different from either studies of the dominated or studies of abstract systems. This may lead to a different sense of action and agency that demands exploration in future comparative work, in both elite ethnographies and counterbalanced studies of social organization and ideology.

After working among the elite of rural Catalonia two decades ago, Edward Hansen noted that the "rich and powerful"

> appear to exemplify all the things that anthropologists have been vainly seeking in . . . diffuse modern classes. . . . this class is forged of strategic marriages, complex inheritances, instrumental friendships, cliques and factions—in fine, the very stuff of anthropological inquiry. . . . The fact that these organizational principles are being used to control the rest of humanity ought to be of singular moment to anthropologists. (MS:11)

In 1981 Abner Cohen again called for detailed analyses of elites as the basis of comparative theory (1981:237). The social history of power in Barcelona, exemplified in the rise and fall of the Good Families, has profound implications for general questions of structure, process, and agency in human society. These, in turn, reaffirm and extend the demand for further ethnography on modern capitalist elites and wider comparative theories of family and power arising therefrom.

GENEALOGIES AND NOTES
ON THE GÜELLS AND SELECTED
ELITE FAMILIES

Figure 40
The Güell Family

The First Generation

Family	Family Enterprise	Other Companies	Political, Social, & Cultural Roles
JUAN GÜELL FERRER B. Torredembara, on the coast south of Barcelona, 1800. D. Barcelona, 23 November 1872. Family established as craftsmen in the village since the 16th century. Father, PABLO GÜELL ROIG, was an unsuccessful merchant in Santo Domingo, who died in Torredembara in 1837. M. Francisca Bacigalupi Dulcet (1845). She died in 1847, of the aftereffects of childbirth. One son, Eusebio. The Bacigalupis were a merchant-banker family of Italian origin, of modest success. M. Camila Bacigalupi Dulcet (1850). His wife/sister-in-law died in 1853. One daughter, Josefina.	Güell went to Santo Domingo with his father as a child but was sent back to Barcelona to study as a pilot. As an adolescent he went to Cuba, where he rose from clerk to merchant. On his return to Spain he passed through the industrial nations—the United States, England, Belgium, and France—to study their factories. In 1835 he founded Güell, Ramis and Co. in the Barcelona suburb of Sants. By 1840 this plant had a total steam capacity of 80 horsepower, with 114 looms for smooth cloth and 165 for velvets. As of 1855 Güell held 1,355,000 pesetas ($261,515) of the total capital of the company: 2,025,000 pesetas ($390,825). (Carreras 1980:62-64.) The manager of the plant, Sol Padris, was killed in the general strike of 1855. Before his death the firm became Parellada, Flaquer and Co.	Partner in La Barcelonesa, which later merged with another foundry to form La Maquinistra Terrestre y Marítima, 1855-. Partner Canal d'Urgell. Dir. Bank of Barcelona, 1845-1849. Dir. Caixa d'Estalvis i Mont de Pietat de Barcelona (Barcelona Savings and Loan), 1847-1850.	Alderman of Barcelona. National deputy and then senator, 1862-? Founder of the Institut Industrial de Catalunya, 1842, and the Círculo Mercantil of Madrid. Güell was one of the leaders of Catalan protectionism and an influential figure with the central government. Owned a box in the Liceu from its foundation. His portrait hangs in the Gallery of Illustrious Catalans, and a public monument was built to him. His speeches and economic works were widely published.

The First Generation, cont.

Valuation of the Property of JUAN GUELL FERRER

	pesetas	U.S. dollars
Cash	1,012.95	$195.50
Moveable goods	10,000.00	1,930.00
Land and buildings (includes homes and factory sites)	5,268,221.86	1,016,766.82
Bonds (national)	180,862.50	34,906.37
Bonds (international)	1,021,181.59	197,088.05
Securities	4,347.98	838.98
Various debtors	84,851.74	16,376.24
Accounts payable	685,019.72	132,208.67
TOTAL	7,255,498.34	1,400,310.63

Plus 300,000 pesetas ($57,900) in marriage settlement on EUSEBIO GUELL BACIGALUPI.
Active credits 79,097 pesetas ($15,265.71); passive credits 400,532 ($77,302).

Property Alloted to EUSEBIO GUELL BACIGALUPI

	pesetas	U.S. dollars
Marriage settlement	300,000	$57,900
Moveable goods	10,000	1,930
House at Rambla Capuchino, 30; bought by JUAN GUELL in 1862	560,000	108,080
House on Calle Codols	396,360	76,498
House and estate with wine cellar, in Santa Coloma de Cervelló		
Mine, piece of land in St. Boi and various *censos* (pensions)	354,673	68,462
Factory building in Vilasar	210,287	40,587
Share in Parellada, Flaquer and Co. in Sants (the family firm)	1,350,000	260,000
Box 20, First Floor, Gran Teatre del Liceu, purchased 1843	50,000	9,650
French government bonds	177,616	34,280
TOTAL	3,408,936	$657,387

SOURCE: AHPB: Marti Sagrista 1877, 5 April.
NOTE: Güell's estate was divided between his two children, with one-third to his daughter Josefina (d. 1874?), and two-thirds to his elder son and heir, Eusebio. This later share must be presented in more detail since it would constitute the basis of the Güell patrimony in the next generation.

Family	Family Enterprise	Other Companies	Political, Social, & Cultural Roles
EUSEBIO GUELL BACIGALUPI B. Barcelona, 1846. 1st Count Güell, 9 July 1908. D. Barcelona, 9 July 1918. M. Isabel López Bru (1871), daughter of the shipping magnate and financier Antonio López y López, 1st Marquis Comillas, Grandee of Spain. She inherited part of the fortune directly (1/3?) and more with the death–without succession of her brother Claudio López Bru, 2d Marquis Comillas (1927). Ten children.	The textile firm continued. In 1889 Parellada, Flaquer and Co. became Parellada and Co. (RM 18:1193). Eusebio Güell had 2/3 of the capital. His other partners included Esteban Gatell, Mariano Parellada, María C. de Moragas de Quintana (for her late husband), and Claudio López Bru, who ceded the 250,000 pesetas he held from his mother to Eusebio Güell. About this time the factory was moved to a *colonia* in Santa Coloma, outside Barcelona.	LOPEZ GROUP: Dir. Hispano-Colonial Bank, 1876-1918? Dir. Tobacos de Filipinas, 1881-1899. Dir. Trasatlántica, 1882-1918. Dir./pres. ASLAND, 1901-1918? Dir. Caminos de Hierro del Norte de España (RR). Dir./founder FFCC Alcantarilla a Lorca, 1901-? (RR). Dir. Barcelona Savings and Loan, 1877-1883. Dir./founder Banco Vitalicio de Capitalización y de Ahorro, 1913-? (bank). Dir. La Prevision (insurance). Founder Cía. Alumbrado por Acetilino (gas lights).	Alderman of Barcelona, 1875. Provincial deputy, 1875. National senator for life. Member of the Lliga. Pres. Centre Català. Pres. Jocs Florals (Floral Games) of Barcelona, 1900. Member of Fine Arts. Portrait in the Gallery of Illustrious Catalans, 1953. Monument in the Colonia Güell. Gentlemen of the Royal Chamber.
JOSEFINA GUELL BACIGALUPI B. Barcelona, 1853? D. Barcelona, 1874? M. José Ferrer-Vidal Soler, 1st Marquis Ferrer-Vidal (pontifical), son of the president, Foment.	In 1895 it became Güell, Parellada and Co., with a capital of 2,237,825 pesetas ($431,898). Güell still owned 67 percent. He subsequently divided this with his sons as they matured: 100,000 pesetas to Claudio in 1904 and 50,000 to Santiago in 1905. In 1909 the company became a limited partnership, Güell and Co. Isabel López Bru and Consuela Jover were silent partners.	Various smaller companies, partnerships rather than corporations, also appear in the RM: S.E. de Molineria y Panificación, 1899-? (Milling); A. Tramullas, S en C, 1901-?; S. Anglada, S en C (oils); Mundo Serrahima?; M. Folguera, 1902-?	

Family	Family Enterprise	Other Companies	Political, Social, & Cultural Roles
JUAN ANTONIO GUELL LOPEZ B. Comillas, 1874, 2d Count Güell, 3d Marquis Comillas, Count de San Pedro de Ruiseñada (rehabilitated 1916). D. Mallorca, 1955. M. Virginia de Churruca Dotres (1904), sister of Count Churruca. M. Josefina Ferrer-Vidal Parellada, granddaughter of his paternal aunt (1950).	Did not seem to be active in Colonia Güell? President of three firms developing family land as housing sites: San Pedro Martir, 1918-1927; Urbanización Güell, 1920-1932; and Urbanizadora Barcelonesa, 1925-?	LOPEZ GROUP: Dir. Hispano-Colonial Bank, pres., 1929-1930. Dir. Tobacos de Filipinas. Dir. Trasatlántica, 1908-1925; pres., 1925-1939. Dir./pres. ASLAND. Dir. Banco López Bru, 1922; pres., 1925-? Dir. Crédito Ibero-Americano, 1906-1915. Dir. Hotel Ritz de Barcelona, 1917-. Dir. Banco Vitalicio de España. Dir. Gran Metropolitano de Barcelona (subway). ? Minas del Rif (mines in Spanish Morocco). Partner Puigdollers, Bertrán, Verdaguer and Co.: "Iberian-American Judicial Center," 1903-1915 (Lliga).	Monarchist leader in Catalonia. Deputy. Royal Commissioner of Tourism. Mayor of Barcelona, 1930-1931. Catalanist of the Lliga, exiled after the Civil War to Mallorca. Box at Liceu and member Círculo. Pres. Royal Academy of Fine Arts of Sant Jordi. Corps of Catalan Nobility; Gentlemen of the Chamber of H. M. Alfonso XIII. Cross of Carlos III; Cross of Military Merit of Maria Cristina; Légion d'Honneur (France); Papal Chamberlain.

Name & Biography	Role in Family Firm	Business & Civic Positions	Honors & Memberships
CLAUDIO GUELL LOPEZ B. ? 1st Viscount Güell, 2 July 1911. D. 1918, unmarried.	Associate and manager in Güell and Co., which became Colonia Güell, S.A. in 1921. Also involved in the land companies.	Partner, V. Gatell, S en C, 1916-1918 (textiles). Partner, S. Anglada S en C, 1915-1916 (oils).	
SANTIAGO GUELL LOPEZ B. Barcelona? 1st Baron Güell, 2 July 1911. D. Garraf (Barcelona), 2 August 1954. M. María Mercedes Ricart Roger, daughter of the 3d Marquis de Santa Isabel, ennobled financiers. One daughter, Adela, who married Pedro de Ibarra y Mac-Mahon, son of the Marquis Mac-Mahon.	Entered Güell and Co. in 1905. After incorporation in 1921 became president of Colonia Güell, S.A. until it closed in 1943. Also involved in land projects.	Pres. Campfaso, S.A. 1920-1952. Dir. ASLAND (López group). Dir. Aceros San Martín (steel). Dir. Coop. de Fluido Eléctrico, 1921-? Dir. Soc. Carreras de Caballos de Barcelona (race track). Partner, V. Gatell S en C (textiles), 1916-. Partner, Güell, Bastos, Bertrán Bros S. Col, 1913-1920; Bastos and Co., 1920-1940; Dir. Bastos, S.A., 1940-(textiles).	Pres. Spanish Olympic Committee. Royal Equestrian Circle. Liceu, Círculo del Liceu. Cross of Merit of Pius IX.
EUSEBIO GUELL LOPEZ B. Barcelona, 31 December 1877. 2d Viscount Güell. D. Barcelona, 3 July 1955. M. María Consolación Jover de Vidal (1901), 2d Marchioness Gélida, heiress of a family of bankers and shippers.	Dir. Colonia Güell, S.A. His wife also inherited a familial interest in the company through the Jover-Moragas line. Also involved in land projects.	Dir. Hotel Ritz de Barcelona, 1917-. ? Cía Gral de Tranvías (trams). Founder Cía Com Minera de Porman, S.A., 1917-(mines). Partner, M. Folguera S en C.	Consul-general of the Austro-Hungarian Empire in Barcelona. Pres. Royal Artistic Circle of Sant Lluc. V. pres. "Conferencia Club." Hon. pres. Golf Club of Pedralbes. Member of Hispanic Society of America. Cross of Isabel the Catholic; Majordomo of the Week for H. M. Alfonso XIII. Author of books in science, memoirs.

Family	Family Enterprise	Other Companies	Political, Social, & Cultural Roles
ISABEL GUELL LOPEZ	All the sisters shared some limited rights to the family land projects, although actual administration remained with their brothers and husbands.		
M. Carlos de Sentmenat de Sentmenat, 9th Marquis Castelldosrius, 2d Baron Orís, 26th Baron Santa Pau, Grandee.			
MARIA LUISA GUELL			Painter and pianist.
D. unmarried.			
MARIA CRISTINA GUELL			
M. José Bertrán Musitu, minister of justice, president of the Lliga.			
FRANCISCA GUELL			
M. Francisco de P. de Moixó de Sentmenat, son of the Marquis de Sant Mori.			
JOSEFINA GUELL			
D. at 21.			
MARIA MERCEDES GUELL LOPEZ			
D. 1954.			

Kinship and Company in Land Development

The members of the Güell family participated in several close corporations dedicated to the urban development of family estates. These companies included San Pedro Martir, S.A.; Urbanizadoro Barcelonesa, S.A.; and Urbanización Güell, S.A. The organization of the last, founded in 1920 and dissolved in 1932, is typical (RM 133:13,670). The original capital of 1,250,000 pesetas ($241,250) was divided among seven siblings:

JUAN ANTONIO GUELL LOPEZ	27.5 percent	($55,459)
SANTIAGO GUELL LOPEZ	20 percent	($48,250)
MA LUISA GUELL LOPEZ	10.5 percent	($25,331)
ISABEL GUELL LOPEZ	10.5 percent	"
MA CRISTINA GUELL LOPEZ	10.5 percent	"
FRANCISCA GUELL LOPEZ	10.5 percent	"
MERCEDES GUELL LOPEZ	10.5 percent	"

JUAN ANTONIO GUELL LOPEZ became president. Carlos de Sentmenat de Sentmenat, Marquis Castelldosrius and husband to ISABEL GUELL LOPEZ, became vice-president. While all five sisters were *owners*, indicating a different evaluation of the family and land as opposed to the *casa industrial*, women were nonetheless excluded from exercising authority. The directorate was composed exclusively of their brothers and husbands. It is also interesting that the firstborn, Juan Antonio, had by far the largest share. I cannot explain the absence of the other two siblings, who appear in other family land projects.

The Fourth Generation

Line of the Count Güell: Madrid

Family	Family Enterprise	Other Companies	Political, Social, & Cultural Roles
JUAN CLAUDIO GUELL CHURRUCA	Colonia Güell, S.A., closed in 1943; sold to the Bertrand family in 1972.	LOPEZ GROUP:	Decorated soldier with Franco in the Civil War.
B. Barcelona, 13 April 1905. Count San Pedro de Ruiseñada, 1928. D. Tours (France), 1958.		Dir. Hispano-Colonial Bank (absorbed by Banco Central, 1943). Dir. Tabacos de Filipinas, 1925-1939.	V. pres. Provincial Delegation of Barcelona.
M. María de las Angustias de Martós y de Zabalburu (1928), daughter of 4th Count de Heredia-Spinola (Grandees), Marquis de Iturbieta y de Casa-Tilly, and Count Tilly.		Dir. Trasatlántica, 1928-1943; pres. 1943-1958. Pres. Sociedad Hullera.	Fellow of the Royal Academy of Art of Saint George (Barcelona). Chief of staff to the Queen Mother Victoria-Eugenia.
		Pres./founder, Banco Atlántico, 1946-1958.	Gentleman of the Chamber of Alfonso XIII; Cross of Naval Merit; Cross of Saint Gregory the Great. Knight of Malta.
		Pres. Cía Petrolifera Ibérica, S.A. Pres. Cía Exportadora Española. Pres. Astilleros Corcho Hijas (shipbuilding). Pres. Industrial Agro-Pecuarios (livestock). Pres. Transportes Inter-continentales, S.A. Pres. Ultramar Express.	
		V. pres. Banco Vitalicio.	
		Dir. Viajes Marsans. Dir. Equibajes Expreso (travel and luggage).	

Line of the Viscount: Barcelona

Family	Family Enterprise	Other Companies	Political, Social, & Cultural Roles
EUSEBIO GUELL JOVER B. Barcelona, 1904. 3d Viscount Güell, 3d Marquis Gélida. M. Luisa de Sentmenat Güell, daughter of the 9th Marquis de Castelldosríus and first cousin.	Pres. Colonia Güell, S.A.	V. pres. ASLAND. Dir. Barcelona Savings and Loan 1954-1974. Dir. Cía de Previsión y Socorro. Dir. Cía Gral de Asfaltos y Portland. Dir. Inversiones Vasco-Canarias. Dir. Industrial Minero-Astur.	Pres. Amigos de Gaudí. Pres. Amigos de los Museos. Pres. Royal Artistic Circle of Sant Lluc. Member of Royal Academy of Fine Arts. V. pres. Polo Club. Box at Liceu, Circulo.
ROSA GUELL JOVER			

The Fifth Generation

Line of the Count Güell: Madrid

Family	Family Enterprise	Other Companies	Political, Social, & Cultural Roles
ALFONSO GUELL MARTOS 4th Marquis Comillas, Count San Pedro de Ruiseñada. M. María de los Reyes Merry del Val y de Melgarejo (1954), daughter 9th Count Valle de San Juan.		LOPEZ GROUP: Pres. Trasatlántica. Dir. Tabacos de Filipinas. Dir. ASLAND. Dir. Sociedad Hullera. Pres. Naviero Asón (ships). Pres. Cía Industrial Minas-Astur. V. pres. Transportes Intercontinentales Dir. Banco Atlántico. Dir. Banco Central. Dir. Hoteles Unidos. Dir. Corcho Hijos. Dir. Saltos de Nansa.	
JUAN GUELL MARTOS, 3d Count Güell.			
MARIA PILAR GUELL MARTOS M. J. Luis de Carranza de Villalonga, Count de Montagud Alto.			

Line of the Viscount: Barcelona

Family	Family Enterprise	Other Companies	Political, Social, & Cultural Roles
CARLOS GUELL DE SENTMENAT		Pres. ASLAND.	Deputy from Barcelona, 1976-1978.
M. María Mercedes López Satrústegui.		V. pres. Contax, S.A.	Mayoral candidate for Center-Right Catalanist party linked to UCD.
		Dir. Barcelona Savings and Loan.	Alderman and lieutanant mayor, 1978-.
			Círculo de Economistas.
CLAUDIO GUELL DE SENTMENAT			
M. María Isabel López Satrústegui.			
EUSEBIO GUELL SENTMENAT			
M. María Carmen Malet Tracy.			
FELIX GUELL DE SENTMEAT			
Unmarried.			
MARIA LUISA GUELL DE SENTMENAT			
M. Juan José Moixó de Montoliu.			
JUAN GUELL DE SENTMENAT			
M. Isabel Ampuero Urruella.			

Figure 41

The Early Genealogy of the Villavecchia Family

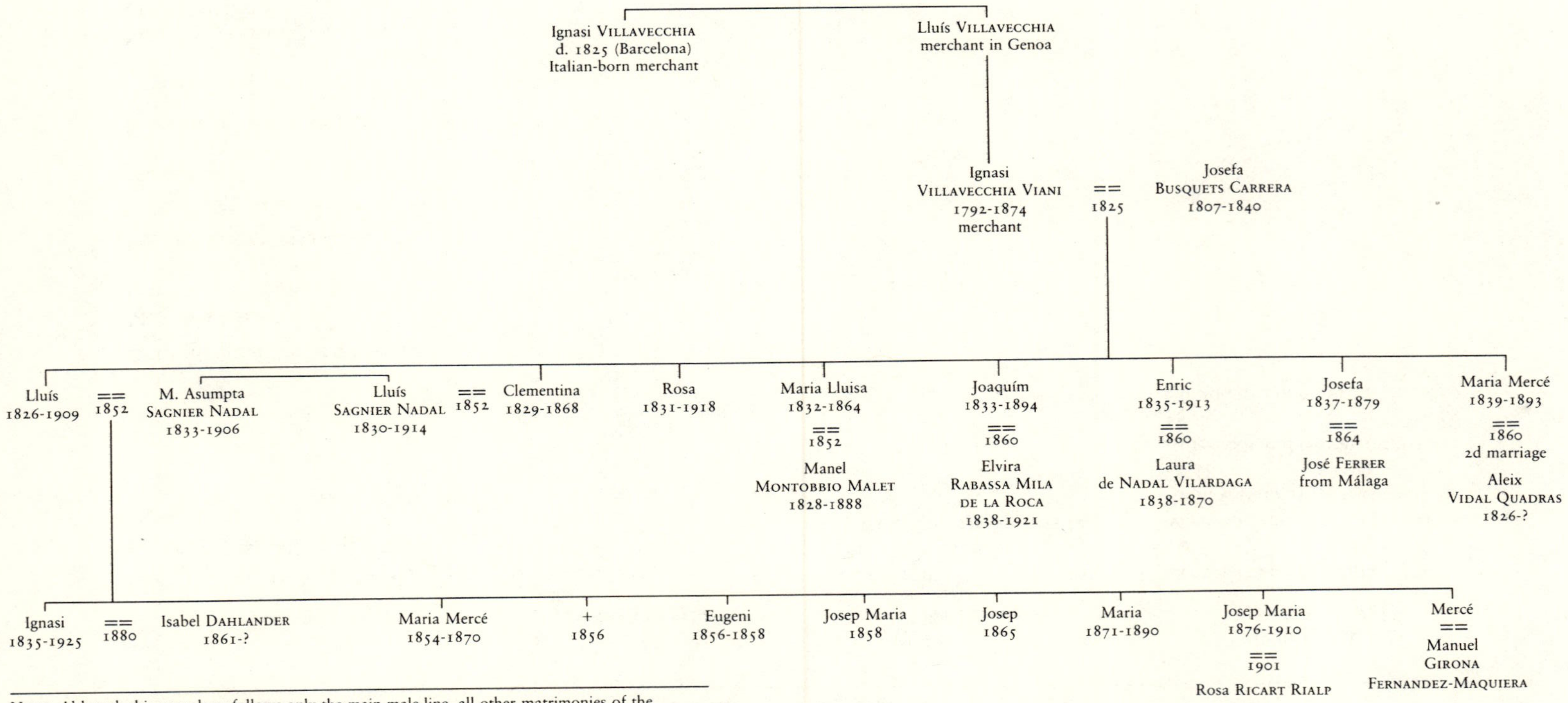

NOTE: Although this genealogy follows only the main male line, all other matrimonies of the VILLAVECCHIA BUSQUETS generation produced offspring whose marriages expanded the social capital of the family.

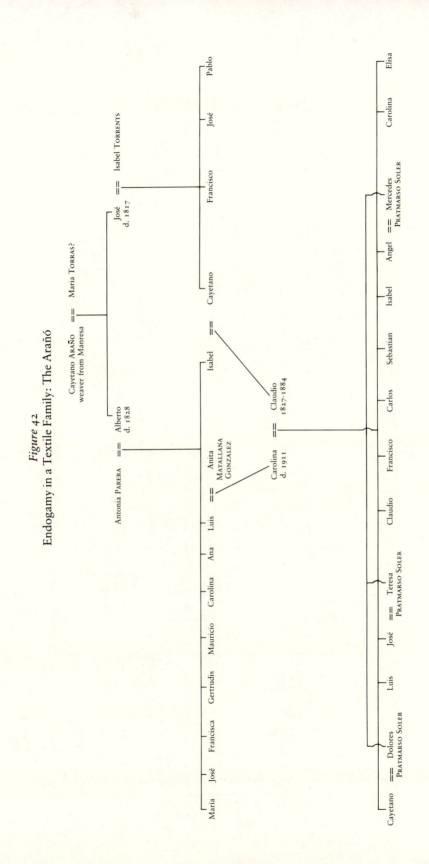

Figure 42
Endogamy in a Textile Family: The Arañó

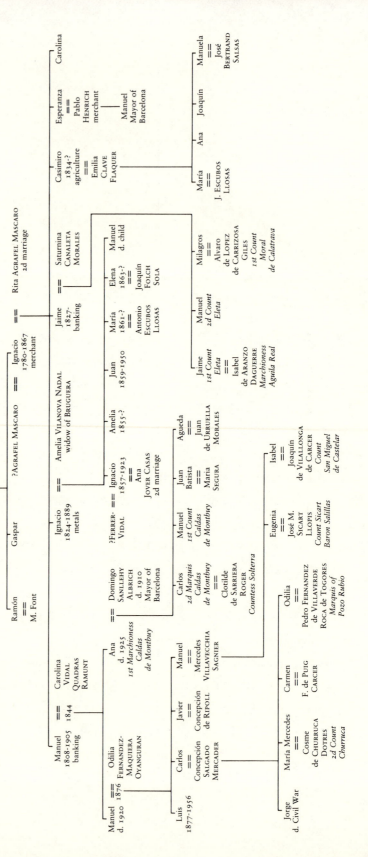

Figure 43
Genealogy of the Girona Family

BIBLIOGRAPHY

A Note on the Sources

While much of this study is based on traditional anthropological resources, such as interviews and participant observation (as discussed in
Chapter I), other critical sources are less familiar and should be reviewed by readers and future researchers. Sources that might normally
be considered secondary, such as historiography and literature, have
often been analyzed for their primary consciousness as products of a
particular period or group. At other times the literary sources have also
provided a means of illustrating real occurrences without violating
family privacy. In each case I have sought to put the text and my usage
of it in a clear analytic framework.

Archival sources have also been of tremendous value, both in basic
historical reconstruction and as a counterpoint to oral history. The following is an annotated list of the primary archives with which I
worked.

Arxiu Històric de Protocols de Barcelona (AHPB). A collection of notarial documents that includes all legal documents of family and business drawn up in Barcelona since the Renaissance. I have consulted
these for wills, marriage contracts, property sales, business agreements,
and similar documents. These are cited in the text by the archive, no-
tary, and year, with occasional reference to the first folio of a document
if relevant, e.g., AHPB: Llobet 1825. There is a one-hundred-year closure on this archive; hence, no documents after 1880 have been consulted.

Registre Mercantil de Barcelona (RM). *The Mercantile Register*, inaugurated in 1881, lists all companies founded in Barcelona to the present day, their partners and/or pirmary incorporators, and any changes
in capitalization or format. With the kind permission of the head of the
registry I surveyed roughly 250 volumes from initiation to the 1930s.
These are of particular interest in elite participation in companies and
in the use of familiar ties in economic life. Documents are cited by date
and inscription number. Fragmentary volumes of an earlier register for
the 1840s are kept in the *Arxiu de la Corona de Arago* (ACA).

Arxiu/Institute Municipal d'Història de Barcelona contains an in-
valuable collection of historical works, biographies, and more ephem-
eral publications. It also houses a useful collection of all newspapers
and periodicals published in modern Barcelona, which are cited here by
name and date.

Other archives consulted less frequently include the *Biblioteca de*

Catalunya (information on the Junta de Comerç, ennoblement of *ciutadans honrats*, and works of fiction), the *Ateneu Barcelonès* (information on the Ateneu; literary works), and *Arxiu de la Catedral de Barcelona* (marriage information). Few individual, family, or company archives proved to be complete enough to merit extended investigation, although specific documents are cited from such sources.

All of these archives and libraries remain rich fields for future investigation. This has often been the exclusive province of historians, Catalans, and others, whose findings have often guided my own analysis. Systematic anthropological investigation of sources such as the Notarial Archives, however, could even further expand our sense of family and change in Catalonia over a long period. Such work is important not only for Catalan studies but also in generating improved theories and models for other areas.

A. M. 1887. *Breve noticia de la edificante vida y santa muerte del Hermano Erasmo Janer.* Barcelona: Hormiga de Oro.

Abad, Camilo M. 1928. *El seminario pontificio de Comillas: historia de su fundación y primeros años (1881-1925).* Madrid: Tipografía Católica de Alberto Fontana.

Aguilar Canosa, Santiago. 1976. *La sociedad anónima familiar o cerrada: su problemática en la pequeña y mediana empresa.* Barcelona: Banco Mas-Sardà.

Agustí, Ignacio. 1969. *Mariona Rebull.* Volume 1 of *La ceniza fue árbol.* Barcelona: Destino. First published 1945.

Alba, Victor. 1978. *Transition in Spain: From Franco to Democracy.* New Brunswick, N.J.: Transaction.

Alegre, Jacinto. 1926. *Un modelo de caridad: Doña Dorotea de Chopitea, Viuda de Serra.* Barcelona: Litúrgica Española.

Aliberch, R. 1952. *Eusebio Bertrand Serra: capitán de industria, economista, político, deportista.* Barcelona: Privately printed.

Alier i Aixala, Roger. 1979. *L'òpera.* Barcelona: DOPESA.

Alonso López, Ampelio; Atienza, Julio de, and Cadenas Vicent, Vicente, eds. 1977. *Elenco de grandezas y títulos nobiliaros españoles.* Madrid: Hidalguía.

Alvarez-Puga, Eduardo. No date. *Matesa: mas allá del escándalo.* Barcelona: DOPESA.

Amelang, James. 1986. *Honored Citizens of Barcelona: Patrician Culture and Class Relations, 1490-1714.* Princeton, N.J.: Princeton University Press.

Amades, Joan. 1947. *Auques comentades.* Barcelona: Dalmau.

Amsden, Jon. 1972. *Collective Bargaining and Class Conflict in Spain.* London: L.S.E. Research Monograph.

Aracil, Lluís V. 1982. *Papers de sociolingüística*. Barcelona: La Magrana.

Aribau, Bonaventura Carles. 1979. *La pàtria*. In J. M. Castellet and J. Molas, editors, *Antologia general de la poesia catalana Barcelona*, 62:139-140. First published 1833.

Ariès, Philippe. 1962. *Centuries of Childhood: A Social History of Family Life*. New York: Random House, Vintage Books.

──── . 1975. *Essais sur l'histoire de la mort en Occident du Moyen-Age à nos jours*. Paris: Du Seuil.

──── . 1977. *L'homme devant la mort*. Paris: Du Seuil.

Artís, A., ed. 1950. *Primer centenario de la Sociedad del Gran Teatro del Liceo*. Barcelona: Privately printed.

Azcárate Ristori, Isabel. 1968. *La enseñanza primaria en Barcelona: la educación de la mujer*. In *Cuadernos de arquitectura e historia de la ciudad: estudios dedicados a Durán Sanpere a 80 años*, 2:177-192. Barcelona.

Badia Margarit, Antoni M. 1969. *La llengua dels barcelonins: resultats d'una enquesta sociològica-lingüística*. Barcelona: 62.

Bahamonde Magro, A., and Toro Mérida, J. 1978. *Burguesia, especulación y cuestión social en el Madrid del siglo XIX*. Madrid: Siglo XXI de España.

Balcells, Albert. 1974. *Cataluña contemporánea I (1900-1939)*. Madrid: Siglo XXI de España.

──── . 1977. *Cataluña contemporánea II (siglo XIX)*. Madrid: Siglo XXI de España.

Baltzell, E. Digby. 1964. *The Protestant Establishment: Aristocracy and Caste in America*. New York: Random House.

──── . 1979. *Puritan Boston and Quaker Philadelphia*. New York: Free Press.

Banco Hispano-Colonial. 1943. *Historia del Banco Hispano-Colonial*. Barcelona: Privately printed.

Barcelona. Exposición Universal de 1888. 1888. *Catálogo oficial, especial de España*. Barcelona: Narciso Ramírez.

Barcelona. Negociado de padrón, estadística e impuestos. 1903–. *Anuario estadístico de Barcelona*.

Barcelona y sus exposiciones. 1929. Barcelona: Supplement to *Las Noticias*.

Bard, Rachel. 1982. *Navarra: The Durable Kingdom*. Reno: University of Nevada Press.

Batllori, Miguel. 1979. *A través de la història i la cultura*. Montserrat: Abbey of Montserrat.

Benguerel Llobet, Xavier. 1955. *El testament*. Barcelona: Club Editors.

Berkner, Lutz. 1972. "The Stem-Family and the Development Cycle of the Peasant Household: An Eighteenth-Century Austrian Example." *American Historical Review* 77:398-418.

Bertrán, Marcos José. 1931. *El Gran Teatro del Liceo de Barcelona, 1837-1930*. Barcelona: Instituto Gráfico Oliva de Vilanova.

Birmingham, Stephen. 1973. *Real Lace: America's Irish Rich*. New York: Harper and Row.

Bofarull i Brocà, Antonio de. 1878. *Barcelona: su pasado, su presente, y su porvenir*. Barcelona.

Bofill Matas, Jaume. 1979. *Prat de la Riba i la cultura catalana*. Edited by J. Cassasas Ymbert. Barcelona: 62. First published 1910.

Bohigas, Oriol. 1973. "Los cementerios como catálogo de arquitectura." *CAU (Construcción, Arquitectura, Urbanismo)* 17:56-65.

Bottomore, T. B. 1964. *Elites and Society*. New York: Basic Books.

Bourdieu, Pierre. 1976. "Marriage Strategies as Strategies of Social Reproduction." In R. Forster and O. Ranum, editors, *Family and Society*, pp. 117-144. Baltimore: The Johns Hopkins University Press.

———. 1977. *Outline of a Theory of Practice*. Cambridge: At the University Press.

———. 1979. *La distinction: critique du jugement sociale*. Paris: Minuit.

———, and Passeron, Claude. 1976. *The Inheritors: French Students and Their Relation to Culture*. Chicago: University of Chicago Press.

Boyd, Caroline. 1979. *Praetorian Politics in Liberal Spain*. Chapel Hill: University of North Carolina Press.

Breton, Françoise, and Barruti, Lorea. 1978. *La família i el parentiu*. Barcelona: DOPESA.

Bru, Francisco. 1857. *Fortunas improvisadas*. Madrid: T. Fortunet.

———. 1885. *La verdadera vida de Antonio López y López, por su cuñado*. Barcelona: Leodagario Obradors.

Bruno, G. M. 1914. *Historia de España*. Madrid: Atocha.

Bulbena Reig, Glòria. 1976. *Barcelona: trossos de vida i records de l'ahir*. Barcelona: Pòrtic.

Cabana Vancells, Francesc. 1965. *La Banca a Catalunya: apunts per a una història*. Barcelona: 62.

———. 1972. *Bancs i banquers a Catalunya (capítols per a una història)*. Barcelona: 62.

———. 1978. *Història del Banc de Barcelona, 1844-1920*. Barcelona: 62.

Caja de Ahorros y Monte de Piedad de Barcelona. 1944. *Centenario de la Caja de Ahorros y Monte de Piedad de Barcelona*. Barcelona.

———. 1977. *Memoria*. Barcelona.

Calders, Pere. 1984. "Amb l'ajut de l'informàtica." In *De teves a meves*, pp. 15-23. Barcelona: Laia.

Calvet Pascual, Agustí (Gaziel). 1958. *Tots els camins diuen a Roma: història d'un destí (1893-1914)*. Barcelona: Pòrtic.

———. 1971. *Història de la Vanguardia, 1884-1936*. Paris: Catalanes de Paris.

Campo Vidal, Manuel. 1980. "Cataluña: un suburbio industrial de Europa y del INI." *Triunfo* 198 (15 March): 20-24.

Candel, Francesc. 1964. *Els altres catalans*. Barcelona: 62.

Capmany Farrés, Aurelio. 1943. *El Café del Liceo, 1837-1937: El teatro y sus bailes de máscaras*. Barcelona: Dalmau.

Capmany Farrés, Maria Aurelia. 1969. *La Dona a Catalunya: consciència i situació*. Barcelona: 62.

Capmany i de Montpalau, Antoni de. 1779-1792. *Memorias históricas sobre la marina, comercio, y artes de la ciudad de Barcelona*. Madrid.

Carreras Candi, Francisco. 1913. *Geografia general de Catalunya*. 6 vols. Barcelona: Alberto Martín. Final volume published 1918.

Carreras Verdaguer, Carles. 1974. *Hostafrancs: un barri de Barcelona*. Barcelona: Selecta.

———. 1980. *Sants: anàlisi del proces de producció de l'espai urbà de Barcelona*. Barcelona: Serpa.

Cartilla Moderna de urbanidad. 1928. Barcelona.

Casals, Muriel, and Sans, Carme. 1972. "El negoci—trist—de la industria textil cotonera." In Francese Artal et al., editors, *Economia crítica: una perspectiva catalana*, pp. 29-48. Barcelona: 62.

Castillo, Alberto del. 1955. *La Maquinista Terrestre y Marítima, personaje histórico, 1855-1955*. Barcelona: Privately printed.

Cataldo, B. F. 1953. "Limited Liability with One-Man Companies and Subsidiary Corporations." *Law and Contemporary Problems* 18, no. 4: 437-504.

Cerdá, Ildefonso. 1968-1971. *Teoría general de la urbanización y aplicación de sus principios y doctrinas a la reforma de Barcelona*. 3 vols. Barcelona: Instituto de Estudios Fiscales. First published 1867.

Cien años del Liceo: libro commemorativo de su primer centenario, 1847-1947. 1948. Barcelona: Londres.

Cil, Joaquín; de Letamendi, José; Domenech, R.; and Arrau, J. 1858. *Informe dado a la instancia de la Illustre Junta Administrativa del cementerio general de Barcelona*. Barcelona: Tomas Gorchs.

Claramunt, Salvador. 1978. "Prosperitat del mon urbà entre el 1200 i el 1350." In J. Salrach, editor, *Història Salvat de Catalunya*, 3:87-100. Barcelona: Salvat.

Claret Serra, Andreu. 1973. "Los cincuenta catalanes." *Cambio 16* 71:13-17.

Climent, Josep. 1775. *Plática que en conformitat de lo que disposa lo pontificat Romà, feu lo Illustríssim Senyor Bisbe de Barcelona en lo dia 13 de mars de est any 1775 antes de comensar en la bendicció del cementiri que de ordre y a costas de Sa Illustríssima ha constuhit, comu a totes les parroquies de esta cituat.* Barcelona.

Cohen, Abner. 1981. *The Politics of Elite Culture: Explorations in the Dramaturgy of Power in a Modern African Society.* Berkeley: University of California Press.

Colección de los epitafios mas notables que existen en el cementerio de Barcelona, seguida de un catálogo de las personas mas distinguidas cuyos restos yacen en los nichos del mismo cementerio a comprender hasta 31 diciembre de 1841. 1842. Barcelona: A. Bosch.

Collier, Peter, and Horowitz, David. 1977. *The Rockefellers: An American Dynasty.* New York: New American Library, Signet Classics.

Colomer, Josep M.; Ainaud, J., and de Riquer, Borja. 1978. *Els anys del franquisme.* Barcelona: DOPESA.

Colonia Güell y fabrica de panas y veludillos de Güell y Cia, S. en C. Breve reseña histórica escrita con motivo de la visita hecha a dicha colonia por los señores congresistas de la semana social. 1910. Barcelona: Henrich.

Compañía Trasatlántica. 1950. *Centenario de la Compañía Trasatlántica.* Barcelona: Velez.

Compilació de dret civil especial de Catalunya. 1982. Barcelona: Generalitat de Catalunya, Departament de Justícia.

Connell, R. W. 1977. *Ruling Class, Ruling Culture: Studies of Conflict, Power, and Hegemony in Australian Life.* Cambridge: At the University Press.

Cossió, Francisco de. 1952. *Cien años de vida sobre el mar: la Compañía Trasatlántica.* Madrid: Vicente Roca.

Curet, Francesc. 1935. *Teatres particulars a Barcelona en el segle XVIIIè.* Barcelona: Institució de Teatre.

———. 1952. *Visions barcelonines, 1760-1860: miralles enllà.* Barcelona: Dalmau Jover.

Darrow, Margaret H. 1979. "French Noblewomen and the New Domesticity, 1750-1850." *Signs* 5, no 2:41-67.

Davidoff, Leonore. 1973. *The Best Circles: Women and Society in Victorian England.* Totowa, N.J.: Rowman and Littlefield.

Delgado, Jaime. 1944. *El hidalgo español.* Madrid: Cisneros.

Dent, Edward. 1978. "Introduction." In Alfred Loewenberg, *Annals of*

Opera, 1597-1940, pp. xvii-xxv. Totowa, N.J.: Rowman and Littlefield.

DiGiacomo, Susan. 1984. "The Politics of Identity: Nationalism in Catalonia." Ph.D. dissertation, University of Massachusetts.

Dirección General de los Registros y del Notariado. Anuario. Volumes consulted: 1918-1978.

Dodd, E. Merrick. 1948. "The Evolution of Limited Liability in American Industry: Massachusetts." *Harvard Law Review* 61:1,351-1,379.

Domhoff, G. William. 1967. *Who Rules America?* Englewood Cliffs, N.J.: Prentice-Hall.

————. 1970. *The Higher Circles.* New York: Random House.

————. 1974. *The Bohemian Grove and Other Retreats: A Study in Ruling-Class Cohesiveness.* New York: Harper & Row.

————. 1978. *The Powers That Be: Processes of Ruling-Class Domination in America.* New York: Random House.

Domingo, Andreu. 1985. "Els discurs eclesiàstics sobre la mort: els sermons funeraris." *L'Avenç* 78 (January): 72-75.

Dumont, Jean-Paul. 1978. *The Headman and I.* Austin: University of Texas Press.

Duocastella, R. 1975. "El mapa religioso de España." In Almerich et al. editors, *Cambio social y religión en España*, pp. 129-162. Barcelona: Fontanella.

Dwyer, Kevin. 1982. *Moroccan Dialogues: Anthropology in Question.* Baltimore: The Johns Hopkins University Press.

Elliott, J. H. 1963. *The Revolt of the Catalans: A Study in the Decline of Spain (1598-1640).* Cambridge: At the University Press.

Espíritu y fuerza de la industria textil catalana. 1945. Barcelona.

D'Esplugues, Miquel. 1921. *El primer Comte de Güell: notes psicològiques i assaig sobre el sentit aristocràtic a Catalunya.* Barcelona: Nicolau Porcell.

Evocación del excelentísimo señor D. Luis Ferrer-Vidal y Soler (Barcelona 1861-1936), presidente fundador de la Caja de Pensiones para le Vejez y de Ahorros de Cataluña y Baleares. 1961. Barcelona: A. Nuñez.

Fabra Fontanills, Camilo de. 1889. *Código o deberes de buena sociedad.* Barcelona.

Fabre, J., and Huertas Claveria, J. M. 1976. *Els barris que foren independents.* Vol. 3 of *Tots els barris de Barcelona.* Barcelona: 62.

————. 1977. *L'Eixample i la Barcelona Vella.* Vol. 5 of *Tots els barris de Barcelona.* Barcelona: 62.

Fàbregas Surroca, Xavier. 1975. *Les formes de diversió en la societat catalana romàntica.* Barcelona: Curial.

Fàbregas Surroca, Xavier. 1979. *Iconologia de l'espectacle*. Barcelona: 62.

Falcón, Lidia. 1973. *Mujer y sociedad*. Barcelona: Fontanella.

Falguera, Félix Ma. 1862. *Formulario completo de notaria. Arreglada a la ley hipotecaria y a la enjuiciamiento civil, revisada y aprobada por la academia de notarios de este territorio con un apéndice sobre la ley del notariado y otro sobre la ley hipotecaria*. 2d. ed. Barcelona: Tomas Gorchs.

————. 1889. *Conferencias de derecho catalán dadas en el Ateneo Barcelonès en 1870 y 1880*. Barcelona: Juan Llordachs.

Faus Condomines, Josep. 1908. *Els capítols matrimonials a la comarca de Guissona. Conferencies dades a l'Academia de Jurisprudencia i Llegislació de Barcelona*. Barcelona: J. Jepus.

Fernández de Pinedo, Emiliano. 1974. *Crecimiento económico y transformaciones sociales del País Vasco 1100/1850*. Madrid: Siglo XXI.

Figueras, J. M. 1979. *L'empresa catalana front la nostre integració a la C.E.E. Conferencia del president de la Cambra Oficial de Comerç, Industrial, i Navegació de Barcelona*. Barcelona: Cambra Oficial de Comerç.

Fitzgerald, Frances. 1979. *America Revised*. Boston: Little, Brown.

Flores, Antonio. 1968. *La sociedad española de 1850*. Madrid: Alianza. First published in 1850.

Fluvià Escorsa, Armand de. 1967. "La casa de Sentmenat. Línea de los M. de Castelldosríus, Grandes de España." *Hidalguía* 15:353-376.

————. 1970. "Una familia catalana de industriales y mecenas ennoblecidas: los Güell." *Hidalguía* 18:433-442.

Fomento de la Producción. 1980. "Los 2,500 españoles mas ricos." Vol. 26, no. 9,792, pp. 8-35.

Fontana, Josep. 1963. *Bonaventura Carles Aribau i la industria cotonera catalana*. Barcelona: Dalmau.

Font Rius, José M. 1969. "Las fuentes históricas de la 'compilación.'" *Revista Jurídica Catalana* 59, no. 2: 399-406.

Font Sagué, N. 1899. *Història de Catalunya*. Barcelona: Ediciones Catalanes.

Formación Política: lecciones para las Flechas. No date. Madrid: Sección Feminína de F.E.T. y de las J.O.N.S.

Forster, Robert. 1960. *The Nobility of Toulouse in the Eighteenth Century: A Social and Economic Study*. Baltimore: The Johns Hopkins University Press.

————. 1981. *Merchants, Landlords, and Magistrates: The Depont*

Family in Eighteenth-Century France. Baltimore: The Johns Hopkins University Press.

Foucault, Michel. 1965. *Madness and Civilization: A History of Insanity in the Age of Reason*. New York: Pantheon Books.

————. 1972. *The Archeology of Knowledge*. New York: Pantheon.

————. 1977. *Discipline and Punish: The Birth of the Prison*. New York: Random House, Vintage Books.

Fraser, Ronald. 1979. *Blood of Spain: An Oral History of the Spanish Civil War*. New York: Pantheon Books.

Freedman, Charles E. 1979. *Joint-Stock Enterprises in France, 1807-1867: From Privileged Company to Modern Corporation*. Chapel Hill: University of North Carolina Press.

de la Fuente Pertegaz, P. 1921. *Los heredimientos capitulares en Cataluña: memoria premiada por la Real Academia de Ciencias Morales y Politicas*. Madrid: Jaime Rates.

Fuster Ortells, Joan. 1979. *Literatura catalana contemporània*. Barcelona: Curial.

Gal, Susan. 1979. *Language Shift: Social Determinants of Language Change in Bilingual Austria*. New York: Academic Press.

Galí Coll, Alexandre. 1953. *Rafel d'Amat i de Cortada, Baró de Maldà. L'escriptor. L'ambient*. Barcelona: Aedos.

García Cárcel, Ricardo. 1985. "Morir a la Barcelona del Barroc." *L'Avenç* 78 (January): 58-59.

García Delgado, José Luis. 1975. *Orígenes y desarrollo del capitalismo en España: notas críticas*. Madrid: Cuadernos para el Dialogo.

García Parreño, Joaquín. 1873. *El dinero y la nobleza*. Barcelona: Espasa Hermanos Salvat.

García Venero, Maximiliano. 1944. *Historia del nacionalismo catalán*. Madrid: Nacional.

Garrigues, Joaquín, and Uría, Rodrigo. 1953. *Comentario a la ley de Sociedades Anónimas*. Madrid: Samaran.

Geertz, Clifford. 1973. *The Interpretation of Cultures*. New York: Basic Books.

Gibernau, J. A. 1976. *El mercado común y sus efectos sobre el sector industrial de Cataluña*. Barcelona: Banco Mas-Sardà.

Giddens, Anthony. 1974. "Elites in the British Class Structure." In P. Stanworth and A. Giddens, editors, *Elites and Power in British Society*, pp. 1-21. Cambridge: At the University Press.

Gilbert, Dennis. 1981. "Cognatic Descent Groups in Upper Class Lima." *American Ethnologist* 8, no. 4: 739-757.

Gilmore, David. 1980. *The People of the Plain: Class and Community in Lower Andalusia*. New York: Columbia University Press.

Ginzburg, Carlo. 1980. *The Cheese and the Worms: The Cosmos of a*

Sixteenth-Century Miller. Baltimore: The Johns Hopkins University Press.

Giral, Eugeni. 1972. "Un capítol de la història dels Empresaris Catalans de Posguerra: el 'Círculo de Economia.' " In Francesc Artal et al., editors, *Economia crítica: una perspectiva catalana*, pp. 89-114. Barcelona: 62.

Giralt, Emili; Balcells, Alberti; and Termes Ardevol, Josep. 1978. *Els moviments socials a Catalunya, País Valencià, i les Illes: cronologia 1800-1939.* Barcelona: La Magrana.

Goblot, Edmond. 1967. *La barrière et le niveau.* Paris: Presses Universitaires de la France. First published 1925.

Gómez de la Serna, P., and Reus García, José. 1869. *Código de comercio arreglado a la reforma decretada el 6 de diciembre de 1868, anotado y concordado, precedido de una introducción histórica comparada, seguido de las leyes y disposiciones posteriores a su publicación, que lo reforman y completan y de las leyes especiales de enjuiciamiento en los negocios y causas de comercio y de un repertorio de la legislación mercantil por los autores de la revista general de legislación.* Madrid: C. Bailly-Baillière.

González Casanova, J. A. 1976. "Pròleg." In A. Ribas, *La ciutat cremada*, pp. 4-9. Barcelona: Laia.

Goode, William J. 1963. *World Revolution and Family Patterns.* New York: Free Press.

Gower, L.C.B. 1953. "The English Private Company." *Law and Contemporary Problems* 18, no. 4: 535-545.

Goytisolo, Juan. 1966. *Señas de identidad.* Mexico: Joaquín Martiz.

Graell, Guillermo. 1911. *Historia del Fomento de Trabajo Nacional.* Barcelona: Viuda de Luis Tasso.

Gramsci, Antonio. 1957. *The Modern Prince and Other Writings.* New York: International Publishers.

Gual Villalbí, Pedro. 1923. *Memorias de un industrial de nuestro tiempo.* Barcelona: Sociedad General de Publicaciones.

———. 1953. *Biografía de Eusebio Güell Bacigalupi, primer Conde Güell.* Barcelona: Galería de Catalanes Ilustres.

Güell Ferrer, Juan. 1866. *Preocupaciones sobre la balanza de comercio y remedios de la crisis monetaria.* Barcelona: Narciso Ramírez.

———. 1871. *Rebelión cubana.* Barcelona: Narciso Ramírez.

———. 1880. *Escritos económicos.* Barcelona: Gráfica Barcelonesa.

Güell López, Eusebio. 1947. *De Alfonso XII a Tutankhamen: perspectivas de la vida.* Barcelona: J. Porter.

Güell López, Juan Antonio. 1928. *Apuntes y recuerdos.* Barcelona: Privately printed.

———. 1932. *Apuntes y recuerdos.* Barcelona: Mimeographed.

Guiotto, Luigi. 1979. *La fabbrica totale: paternalismo industriale e città sociali in Italia*. Milano: Giangiacomo Fletrinelli.

Hall, Peter D. 1977. "Family Structure and Economic Organization in Massachusets Merchants, 1700-1850." In T. Hareven, editor, *Family and Kin in Urban Communities, 1700-1930*, pp. 38-61. New York: New Viewpoints.

———. 1982. *The Organization of American Culture, 1700-1900: Private Institutions, Elites, and the Origins of American Nationality*. New York: New York University Press.

Hannerz, Ulf. 1969. *Soulside: Inquiries into Ghetto Culture and Community*. New York: Columbia University Press.

Hansen, Edward C. 1974. "The Transformation of Family Structure in Rural Catalonia: An Essay on the Demise of a Regional Tradition." *NORD MYTT* 2:130-142.

———. 1976. "Economic Internationalism and the Expansion of State Power: A Discussion of Two Major Problems in the Ethnography of Spain." In J. Aceves, E. Hansen, and G. Levitas, editors, *Economic Transformation and Steady State Values: Essay in the Ethnography of Spain*, pp. 77-81. Flushing, N.Y.: Queens College Publications in Anthropology, no. 2.

———. 1977. *Rural Catalonia under the Franco Regime: The Fate of Regional Culture since the Spanish Civil War*. Cambridge: At the University Press.

———. MS. "Transnational Corporations and Anthropology: A Review of R. J. Barnet and R. E. Mueller, *Global Reach: the Power of Multinational Corporations*."

———, and Parrish, Timothy. 1983. "Elites versus the State? Towards an Anthropological Contribution to the Study of Hegemonic Power in Capitalist Society." In G. Marcus, editor, *Elites: Ethnographic Issues*. pp. 257-278, Santa Fe: School of American Research.

Hareven, Tamara K. 1978. *Amoskeag: Life and Work in an American Factory Town*. New York: Pantheon Books.

———. 1982. *Family Time and Industrial Time: The Relationship between Family and Work in a New England Industrial Community*. Cambridge: At the University Press.

———, ed. 1977. *Family and Kin in Urban Communities, 1700-1930*. New York: New Viewpoints.

Harrison, J. B. 1978. *An Economic History of Modern Spain*. New York: Holmes and Meier.

———. 1978a. "El món de la gran industria i el fracàs del nacionalisme català de dreta (1901-1923)." *Recerques: Historia, Economia, Cultura* 8:83-97.

Heráldica: Guía de Sociedad. Originally edited by Abderram Muley (pseudonym). Later volumes edited by E. González Vera. Various years consulted: 1945-1978. Madrid.

Herr, Richard. 1958. *The Eighteenth-Century Revolution in Spain*. Princeton, N.J.: Princeton University Press.

Holley, John C. 1981. "The Two Family Economies of Industrialism: Factory Workers in Western Scotland." *Journal of Family History* 6, no. 1: 57-69.

Hunter, Floyd. 1953. *Community Power Structures*. Chapel Hill: University of North Carolina Press.

———. 1980. *Community Power Succession*. Chapel Hill: University of North Carolina Press.

Iglésies, J. 1968. *Els conflictes del canal d'Urgell*. Barcelona: Dalmau.

Imbert, Erasme de. 1952. *Erasmo de Gònima, 1746-1821: apuntes para una biografía y estudio de su época*. Barcelona: Horta.

Izard, Miguel. 1973. *Industrialización y obrerismo: las tres clases de Vapor, 1869-1913*. Barcelona: Ariel.

———. 1974. "Dependencia y colonialismo: la Compañía General de Tabacos de Filipinas." *Moneda y Crédito* 130:47-89.

———. 1979. *Manufactureros, industriales, y revolucionarios*. Barcelona: Crítica.

Jackson, Gabriel. 1965. *The Republic and the Civil War, 1931-1939*. Princeton, N.J.: Princeton University Press.

Jameson, Fredric. 1981. *The Political Unconscious: Narrative as a Socially Symbolic Act*. Ithaca, N.Y.: Cornell University Press.

Janik, Allan, and Toulmin, Stephen. 1973. *Wittgenstein's Vienna*. New York: Simon & Schuster.

Jardí, Enric. 1978. *Mil famílies catalanes*. Barcelona: DOPESA.

Jiménez, Losantos, J. 1979. *Lo que queda de España*. Barcelona: Ajoblanco.

Jiménez Lozano, José. 1978. *Los cementerios civiles y la heterodoxia española*. Barcelona: Taurus.

Joaquinet, Aurelio. 1955. *Alfonso Sala Argemí, Conde de Egara*. Madrid: Espasa-Calpe.

Jones, Norman L. 1976. "The Catalan Question since the Civil War." In P. Preston, editor, *Spain in Crisis: The Evolution and Decline of the Franco Regime*, pp. 234-267. Hassocks, Sussex, Eng.: The Harvester Press.

Joyce, Patrick. 1980. *Work, Society, and Politics: The Culture of the Factory in Later Victorian England*. New Brunswick, N.J.: Rutgers University Press.

Jutglar, Antoni. 1972. *Història crítica de la burgesia a Catalunya*. Barcelona: DOPESA.

Kahane, Harry, and Kahane, Renee. 1979. "Decline and Survival of

Western European Prestige Languages." *Language* 55, no. 1:183-198.

Keller, Suzanne. 1963. *Beyond the Ruling Class*. New York: Random House.

Kelso, Ruth. 1929. "The Doctrine of the English Gentleman in the Sixteenth Century with a Bibliographical List of Treatises on the Gentleman and Related Subjects Published in Europe to 1625." *University of Illinois Studies in Language and Literature* 14:1-2. Champaign: University of Illinois Press.

Kenny, Michael. 1962. *A Spanish Tapestry: Town and Country in Castile*. Bloomington: Indiana University Press.

Kern, Robert W. 1974. *Liberals, Reformers, and Caciques in Restoration Spain, 1875-1909*. Albuquerque: University of New Mexico Press.

————, and Dolkart, Ronald, eds. 1973. *The Caciques: Oligarchical Politics and the System of Caciquismo in the Luso-Hispanic World*. Albuquerque: University of New Mexico Press.

Kessler, Harry. 1930. *Walter Rathenau: His Life and Works*. New York: Harcourt Brace.

Kolodin, Irving. 1966. *The Metropolitan Opera, 1883-1966: A Candid History*. New York: Alfred A. Knopf.

Kotz, David. 1978. *Bank Control of Large Corporations in the United States*. Berkeley: University of California Press.

Kramer, Robert. 1953. "Introduction." *Law and Contemporary Problems* 18, no. 4:433-434.

Kuznesof, Elizabeth. 1980. "An Analysis of Household Composition and Headship as Related to Changes in Mode of Production, 1765-1836." *Comparative Studies in Society and History* 22:78-108.

Labov, William. 1972. *Sociolinguistic Patterns*. Philadelphia: University of Pennsylvania Press.

Landes, David. 1965. "Japan and Europe: Contrasts in Industrialization." In W. Lockwood, editor, *The State and Economic Enterprise in Japan: Essays in the Political Economy of Growth*, pp. 93-182. Princeton, N.J.: Princeton University Press.

————. 1969. "The Old Bank and the New: The Financial Revolution of the Nineteenth Century." In F. Crouzet, W. H. Chaloner, and W. M. Stern, editors, *Essays on European Economic History*, pp. 112-127. London: Edward Arnold.

————. 1976. "Religion and Enterprise: The Case of the French Textile Industry." In Edward C. Carter et al., editors, *Enterprise and Entrepreneurship in Nineteenth- and Twentieth-Century France*, pp. 47-86. Baltimore: The Johns Hopkins University Press.

Laslett, Peter. 1972. "Characteristics of the Western Family Considered over Time." *Journal of Family History* 2, no. 2: 89-116.

———. 1978. "The Stem-Family Hypothesis and Its Privileged Position." In K. Wachter, J. Hammel, and P. Laslett, editors, *Statistical Studies of Historical Social Structure*, pp. 89-112. New York: Academic Press.

Lautman, Françoise. 1976. "Differences or Changes in Family Organization." In R. Forster and O. Ranum, editors, *Family and Society*, pp. 251-260. Baltimore: The Johns Hopkins University Press.

Le Play, Frédéric. 1866. *La Réforme sociale en France: déduite de l'observation comparée de peuples européens*. Paris: E. Dentu.

———. 1871. *L'organisation de la famille selon le vrai modèle signalé par l'histoire de toutes les races et tous les temps*. Paris: Tequi Bibliothèque de l'Oeuvre Saint Michel.

Lewis, Oscar. 1959. *Five Families: Mexican Case Studies in the Culture of Poverty*. New York: Basic Books.

———. 1961. *The Children of Sanchez: Autobiography of a Mexican Family*. New York: Random House.

Linz, Juan J., and de Miguel, Amando. 1966. "Within-Nation Differences and Comparisons: The Eight Spains." In R. L. Merritt and S. Rokkan, editors, *Comparing Nations: The Use of Quantitative Data in Cross-National Research*, pp. 267-319. New Haven, Conn.: Yale University Press.

Linz, Juan J., and Stepan, Alfred. 1978. *The Breakdown of Democratic Regimes*. Baltimore: The Johns Hopkins University Press.

Llor, Miquel. 1958. *Un camí de Damasc*. Barcelona: Selecta.

Llorens, Montserrat. 1958. "Biografies." In Jaume Vicens Vives, *Industrials i polítics del segle XIX*, pp. 305-432. Barcelona: Vicens-Vives.

Loewenberg, Alfred. 1978. *Annals of Opera, 1597-1940*. Totowa, N.J.: Rowman and Littlefield.

Lomnitz, Larissa, and Pérez Lizaur, M. 1978. "History of a Mexican Urban Family," *Journal of Family History* 3, no. 4:392-409.

Lukacs, John. 1985. *Historical Consciousness or the Remembered Past*. New York: Schocken Books. First published 1968.

Lundberg, Ferdinand. 1937. *America's Sixty Families*. New York: Vanguard Press.

———. 1968. *The Rich and the Super-Rich*. New York: Lyle Stuart.

McClachen, James. 1970. *American Boarding Schools: A Historical Study*. New York: Charles Scribner's Sons.

McKey, William Francis. 1976. *Bilinguisme et contacte des langues*. Paris: Editions Hinncksieck.

Malefakis, Edward. 1970. *Agrarian Reforms and Peasant Revolutions in Spain*. New Haven, Conn.: Yale University Press.

Manjarrés y de Bofarull, José. 1854. *Guía de señoritas en el gran mundo*. Barcelona: Tomas Gorchs.

Maragall, Joan. 1929. *Obres completes*. 2 vols. Paris: Barna.

Marcus, George. 1980. "Law in the Development of Dynastic Families among American Business Elites: The Domestication of Capital and the Capitalization of Family." *Law and Society Review* 14, no. 4: 859-903

———. 1983. " 'Elite' as Concept, Theory, and Research Tradition." In G. Marcus, editor, *Elites: Ethnographic Issues*, pp. 7-28. Santa Fe: School of American Research.

———. MS. *Spending: The Hunts, Silver, and Dynastic Families in America*.

Marfany, Joan Lluís. 1978. *Aspectes del modernisme*. Barcelona: Curial.

———. 1978a. "El modernisme literari." In J. Salrach, editor, *Història Salvat de Catalunya*, 5:269-280. Barcelona: Salvat.

Marion, John Francis. 1977. *Famous and Curious Cemeteries: A Pictorial, Historical, and Anecdotal View of American and European Cemeteries and the Famous and Infamous People Who Are Buried There*. New York: Crown.

Martínez Gil, José. 1962. "El Impuesto como causa de desuso de las capitulaciones matrimoniales." *Revista Jurídica Catalana* 61:346-350.

Martínez Ruiz, J. [Azorín]. 1961. *La generación del 98*. Edited by Angel Cruz Rueda. Salamanca: Anaya.

Marx, Karl. 1972. "Theses on Feuerbach." In Robert Turner, editor, *The Marx-Engels Reader*, pp. 107-109. New York: W. W. Norton. First published 1888.

Maspons Anglasell, Francesc. 1907. *Nostre dret familiar segons els autors clássichs y les sentencies del antic suprem tribunal de Catalunya*. Barcelona: Alvar Verdaguer.

———. 1935. *Le llei de la família catalana*. Barcelona: Barcino.

———. 1938. *El règim successori català*. Barcelona: Barcino.

Masriera Colomer, Arturo. 1924. *Los buenos barceloneses: hombres, costumbres, y anécdotas de la Barcelona ochocentista (1850-1870)*. Barcelona: Políglota.

———. 1926. *Oliendo a brea: hombres, naves, hechos, y cosas de mar de la Cataluña ochocentista*. Barcelona: Políglota.

———. 1930. *Barcelona isabelina y revolucionaria: episodios, anécdotas, recuerdos, y documentos*. Barcelona: Políglota.

Matheu, Roser. 1972. *Quatre dones catalanes*. Barcelona: Fundació Salvador Casajuana.

Mayer, Arno. 1981. *The Persistence of the Old Regime: Europe to the Great War*. New York: Pantheon Books.

Mendoza, Eduardo. 1979. *El misterio de la cripta embrujada*. Barcelona: Seix Barral.

Mendoza Guinea, J. M. 1954. *Formación del Espíritu Nacional*. Madrid.

Milà, José Luis. 1978. "Interview." *Por Favor* 4:197.

Milà de la Roca, José Nicasio. 1844. *Los misterios de Barcelona*. Barcelona.

Mills, C. Wright. 1956. *The Power Elite*. Oxford: Oxford University Press.

Molas, Isidre. 1972. *Lliga Catalana*. 2 vols. Barcelona: 62.

Molas Ribalta, Pere. 1975. *Economia i societat al segle XVIII*. Barcelona: La Paraula Viva.

———. 1977. *Comerç i estructura social a Catalunya i València als segles XVII i XVIII*. Barcelona: Curial.

Monserdà i Vidal de Macià, Dolors. 1900. *La familia Asparó: novela de costums del nostre temps*. Barcelona: La Renaixensa.

———. 1906. *La Quitèria*. Barcelona: Illustració Catalana.

———. 1907. *El feminisme a Catalunya*. Barcelona: F. Puig.

———. 1908. *Del món*. Barcelona: L'Avenç.

———. 1909. *Estudi feminista: orientacions per la dona catalana*. Barcelona: Lluis Gili.

———. 1916. *Tasques socials: recull d'articles, notes rurals, i conferenciaes per Dolors Monserdà i Vidal de Macià, amb una carta-pròleg del Pare Ignasi Casanovas*. Barcelona: Miquel Parera.

———. 1917. *Maria Glòria: novel.la de costums barcelonins*. Barcelona: Llib. Parera.

———. 1920. *Buscant una ánima: novel.la de costums barcelonins*. Barcelona: Políglota.

———. 1929. *La Montserrat*. Barcelona: La Renaixensa. First published 1893.

———. 1972. *La fabricanta: novel.la de costums barcelonines (1860-1875)*. Barcelona: Selecta. First published 1904.

Morales Roca, Francisco. 1976. "Privilegios nobiliarios del Principado de Cataluña: Dinastía de Borbon, 1700-1838." *Hidalguía* 23:81-96, 241-272, 613-623, 725-740.

Moret Prendergast, and Silvela, Luis. 1863. *La familia foral y la familia castellana*. Madrid: Señora Viuda e Hijos de José Cuesta.

Moreu Lacrus, P. 1921. *Noticia biográfica de D. Manuel de Pascual y de Bofarull, M. de Pascual*. Barcelona.

Moreu Rey, Enric. 1967. "Una dinastia industrial: els Rosal de Berga."
    In *Homenaje a Jaime Vicens Vives*, 2:447-257. Barcelona.
Mosca, Gaetano. 1939. *The Ruling Class*. Edited by A. Livingston.
    New York: McGraw-Hill.
Moya, Carlos. 1975. *El poder económico en España*. Madrid: Tucar.
Moya-Angeler, J. 1978. "La saga de los Muntadas-Prim: Quien es
    quien en la familia." *Destino* 2,106:13-15.
———. 1978a. "Muere el Liceo?" *Destino* 2,109:21-23.
Muñoz, Juan. 1969. *El poder de la banca en España*. Madrid: XYZ.
———; Roldán, Santiago; and Serrano, Angel. 1978. *La internaliza-
    ción del capital en España, 1959-1978*. Madrid: EDICUSA.
Muñoz Espinalt, Carles. 1966. *Un mercat per al Senyor Esteve*. Barce-
    lona: Edicions d'Aportació Catalana.
Muntadas Rovira, Vicente. 1950. *Sobre participación de los trabaja-
    dores en los beneficios de las empresas: opinión de un patrón ca-
    tólico*. Barcelona: Ariel.
Myers, Gustavus. 1936. *History of Great American Fortunes*. New
    York: Random House. First published 1909-1911.
Nadal, Joaquim de. 1975. *Catalunya i el Mercat Comú*. Barcelona:
    Proa.
Nadal, Jordi. 1971. *La población española: siglos XVI a XX*. Barce-
    lona: Ariel.
———. 1973. *El fracaso de la revolución industrial en España*. Barce-
    lona: Ariel.
———. 1973a. "Spain, 1830-1914." In C. Cipolla, editor, *The Fon-
    tana Economic History of Europe: The Emergence of Industrial
    Societies*, pt. 2, pp. 532-627. London: Collier.
———, and Giralt, Emili. 1963. "Barcelona en 1717-1718: un modelo
    de sociedad pre-industrial." In *Homenatge a Ramón Carande*,
    2:277-306. Madrid.
Nadal Ferrer, Joaquín M. de. 1942. *Aquella Barcelona*. Barcelona:
    Dalmau.
———. 1943. *Mi calle de "Fernando": visión sentimental un poco
    meditiva, de una institución barcelonesa*. Barcelona: Dalmau.
———. 1946a. *Cromos de la vida vuitcentista: memòries d'un barce-
    loní*. Barcelona: Dalmau.
———. 1946. *Recuerdos y chismes de la Barcelona ochocentista*. Bar-
    celona: Dalmau.
———. 1950. "La proyección social del teatro del Liceo." In A. Artís,
    editor, *Primer centenario de la sociedad del Gran Teatro del Li-
    ceo*, pp. 133-135. Barcelona.
———. 1952. *Memòries d'un estudiant barceloní*. Barcelona: Dalmau.

Nadal Ferrer, Joaquín M. de. 1965. *Memòries: vuitanta anys de since-ritats i silencis*. Barcelona: Selecta.

Ngô Bá Thanh. 1963. *La sociedad anónima familiar ante la ley español de 1951*. Barcelona: Hispano Europa.

Nonell Mas, Jaime. 1892. *Vida ejemplar de la excelentísima señora Da Dorotea de Chopitea, Vda. de Serra*. Barcelona-Sarriá: Tipografía y Librería Salesianas.

Una oligarquía político financiero: la situación bancaria en Barcelona. 1921. Madrid: Arces.

Oliver, Miguel S. 1974. *La literatura del desastre*. Introduction and notes by Gregori Mir. Barcelona: Peninsular.

Oller, Narcís. 1948. *Obres completes*. Barcelona: Selecta. Works published at the turn of the century.

Ostrander, Susan. 1984. *Women of the Upper Class*. Philadelphia, Pa.: Temple University Press.

Pabón, Jesús. 1952-1969. *Cambó*. 3 vols. Barcelona: Alpha.

Paniker, Salvador. 1966. *Conversaciones en Cataluña*. Barcelona: Kairos.

Pareto, Vilfredo. 1950. *The Ruling Class in Italy before 1900*. Edited by Giuseppe Prezzolini. New York: S. F. Vanni.

———. 1980. *Compendium of General Sociology*. Abridged in Italian with approval of the author by Giulio Fari from Pareto's *Trattato di Sociologia Generale*. English text edited and collated by Elizabeth Abbott. Minneapolis: University of Minnesota Press.

Parpal Brua, J. A., and Lladó, J. M. 1970. *Ferran Valls Taberner, un polític per a la cultura catalana*. Barcelona: Ariel.

Petonnet, Colette. 1982. "L'observation flottante: l'exemple d'un cimitière parisien." *L'Homme* 22, no. 4:37-47.

Pi Arimón, Andrés A. 1854. *Barcelona; antigua y moderna ó descripción é historia de esta ciudad desde su fundación hasta nuestros días*. Barcelona: Imprenta y Librería Politécnica de T. Gorchs.

Pinilla de las Heras, E. 1967. *L'empresari català*. Barcelona: 62.

Piñol Agulló, José. 1956. *Del esplendor a la decadencia en los contratos matrimoniales en Cataluña*. Barcelona: J. Sabater.

Pin Soler, Josep. 1980. *La família dels Garriga*. Barcelona: 62. First published in 1887.

Pi Sunyer, José M. 1958. *Gaudí y la familia Güell*. Barcelona.

———. 1960. "La compilación del derecho civil especial de Cataluña como logro romántico de los abogados catalanes." *Revista Jurídica Catalana* 59:419-426.

Pi Sunyer, Oriol. 1971. *The Limits of Integration: Ethnicity and Nationalism in Modern Europe*. Research Reports No. 9. Amherst: University of Massachusetts Press.

————. 1974. Elites and Noncorporate Groups in the European Mediterranean: A Reconsideration of the Catalan Case. *Comparative Studies in Society and History* 16, no. 1: 117-131.

Pla, Josep. 1942. *Rusiñol y su tiempo*. Barcelona: Barna.

————. 1945. *Un señor de Barcelona*. Barcelona: Destino.

————. 1956. *Obres completes*. Barcelona: Selecta.

Pons Gurí, Josep. 1976. "Josep Xifré Casas i els seus." *Vida Parroquial* (Arenys). January-May.

Post, Emily. 1922. *Etiquette*. New York: Funk and Wagnalls.

Pourret, Pedro Andrés. 1796. *Noticia histórica de la familia Salvador de la ciudad de Barcelona*. Barcelona. Revised Edition 1844.

Prat de la Riba Sarrà, Enric. 1898. *Ley jurídica de la industria*. Barcelona: Penella Bosch.

————. 1978. *La nacionalitat catalana*. Barcelona: 62. First published 1905.

Press, Irwin. 1980. *The City as Context: Urbanism and Behavioral Constraints in Seville*. Urbana: University of Illinois Press.

Preston, Paul, ed. 1976. *Spain in Crisis: The Evolution and Decline of the Franco Regime*. Hassocks, Sussex, Eng.: The Harvester Press.

Prewitt, Kenneth, and Stone, Alan. 1973. *The Ruling Elites: Elite Theory, Power, and American Democracy*. New York: Harper & Row.

Price, Richard, and Price, Sally. 1966. "Stratification and Courtship in an Andalusian Village." *Man* 1, no. 4: 526-533.

Puig Alfonso, Francisco. 1907. *Biografía de José Ferrer-Vidal*. Barcelona: Mariano Galvé.

————. 1943. *Recuerdos de un setentón*. Barcelona: Dalmau.

Puig Brutau, José. 1958. "Algunas consideraciones sobre la llamada sociedad anónima familiar." *Revista Jurídica Catalana* 57:567-576.

————. 1960. "El testamento del empresario." *Revista de Derecho Privado* 44:845-858.

Quijano, G. 1785. *Vicios de las tertulias*. Barcelona: Piferrer.

Raventós Domenech, Jaume. 1928. *Memories d'un cabaler*. Vilafranca.

Rebagliato, Joan. 1978a. "Evolució demográfica i dinámica social al segle XIX." In J. Salrach, editor, *Història Salvat de Catalunya*, 5:3-17. Barcelona: Salvat.

————. 1978b. "L'evolució demográfica entre el 1900 i el 1940." In J. Salrach, editor, *Història Salvat de Catalunya*, 6:3-13.

————. 1978c. "L'evolució demográfica entre el 1940 i el 1975." In J. Salrach, editor, *Història Salvat de Catalunya*, 6:249-262.

Regatill, J. 1948. *Un marqués modelo: el siervo de dios Claudio López Bru, II Marqués de Comillas*. Barcelona.

Reglamento interior de la Iltre Junta Administrativa del cementerio general de esta ciudad. 1877. Barcelona: Narciso Ramírez.

Reglas de la buena crianza civil i cristiana. 1767. Barcelona: Successive editions issued by various publishers without change until 1833.

Ribas Massana, Albert. 1978. *L'economia de Catalunya sota el franquisme (1939-1953)*. Barcelona: 62.

Riera, Guilera, Carme. 1981. *Els cementiris de Barcelona (una aproximació)*. Photography by Colita. Barcelona: EDAASA.

Riquer, Borja de. 1976. *Lliga regionalista: la burgesia catalana i el nacionalisme (1898-1904)*. Barcelona: 62.

Robert Surís, Agustín. 1904. *A las clases directoras de Barcelona*. Barcelona: A. López Robert.

Robinson, Michael. 1972. *Naples and Neapolitan Opera*. Oxford: Clarendon Press.

Roca, Encarna. 1977. *¿Qui és català?* Barcelona: DOPESA.

Romero Maura, Joaquín. 1974. *La rosa de fuego: republicanos i anarquistas. La política de los obreros barceloneses entre el desastre colonial y la semana trágica, 1899-1909*. Barcelona: Grijalbo.

Rosaldo, Renato. 1980. *Ilongot Headhunting 1883-1974: A Study in Society and History*. Stanford, Ca.: Stanford University Press.

Roselló Garcia, J. L., and Roselló Garcia, Maria D., eds. 1962-. *Directorio de consejeros i directores (DICODI)*. Madrid: DICODI.

Rosenthal, Harold. 1958. *Two Centuries of Opera at Covent Garden*. London: Putnam.

Rovira Virgili, Antoni. 1912-1914. *Història dels moviments nacionalistes*. Barcelona: Societat Catalana d'Edicions.

Rubirola, Miquel. 1972. "La dimensió de les grans empreses a Catalunya." In Francesc Artal et al., editors, *Economia crítica: una perspectiva catalana*, pp. 49-88. Barcelona: 62.

Ruiz, Juan, and Muncunill, María A. 1904? *Virtud y patria*. Barcelona.

Rungta, Radhe Shyan. 1970. *The Rise of Business Corporations in India, 1851-1900*. Cambridge: At the University Press.

Rusiñol, Santiago. 1968. *L'auca del Senyor Esteve. L'Alegria que passa. "Gente bien."* Barcelona: Selecta.

Rusiñol Denis, Maria. 1950. *Santiago Rusiñol vist per la seva filla*. Barcelona: Aedos.

S. A. [Sebastian Auger?]. 1978. "Ha muerto un señor!" *Mundo Diario*. November 20.

Sagarra de Castellarnau, Josep Maria de. 1954. *Memòries*. Barcelona: Selecta.

———. 1977. *Vida privada*. Barcelona: Aymá. First published 1932.

Sagrado Corazón, Colegio del. 1912. *Catálogo de los antiguos alumnos del Colegio del Sagrado Corazón*. Barcelona.

Sahlins, Marshal. 1981. *Historical Metaphors and Mythical Realities: Structure in the Early History of the Sandwich Islands Kingdom*. Ann Arbor: University of Michigan Press.

Salisachs, Mercedes. 1975. *La gangrena*. Barcelona: Planeta.

Sallarés, José. 1895. *José Ferrer-Vidal y su tiempo*. Barcelona: Fomento Nacional de Trabajo.

Salvador, Joan. 1972. "Viatge d'Espanya i Portugal (1716-1717)." Edited by Ramon Folch Guillèn.

Sánchez-Albornoz, Nicolás. 1977. *España hace un siglo: una economía dual*. Madrid: Alianza.

San Pedro, Ramón de. 1952. *Don Evaristo Arnús y de Ferrer, banquero barceloneś. Notas biográficas y bosquejo del ambiente bursatil y financiero de su época*. Barcelona: Banco Atlántico.

———. 1953. *Don Gaspar de Remisa y Miarons, Marqués de Remisa*. Barcelona: Banco Atlántico.

———. 1954. *Don José Xifré Casas: Industrial, naviero, comerciante, banquero, y benefactor. Historia de un indiano catalán (1777-1856)*. Madrid: Banco Atlántico.

Sanpere Miquel, Salvador. 1879. "Biografía (de F. Martorell Peña)." In *Apuntes arqueológicos de Francisco Martorell Peña. Barcelona*.

Schneider, Jane; Schneider, Peter; and Hansen, Edward. 1972. "Modernization and Development: The Role of Regional Elites and Non-Corporate Groups in the European Mediterranean." *Comparative Studies in Society and History* 14:328-350.

Schorske, Carl. 1980. *Fin-de-siècle Vienna*. New York: Random House.

Smith, Hedrick. 1977. *The Russians*. New York: Ballantine.

Socolow, Susan M. 1979. *The Merchants of Buenos Aires, 1778-1810*. Cambridge: At the University Press.

Solà, Maria Angels. 1977. "L'elit barcelonina a mitjan segle XIX." 2 vols. Ph.D. dissertation, Universitat de Barcelona.

———. 1981. "Tres notes entorn les actituds i valors de l'alta burgesia barcelonina a mitjan segle XIX." *Quaderns de l'Institut Catala d'Antropologia* 3-4:101-128.

Solà-Morales, Ignasi. 1976. "L'Exposició Internacional de Barcelona (1914-1929) com a instrument de política urbana." *Recerques* 6:137-148.

Soldevila Zubiburu, Carles [Myself]. 1927. *La dona ben educada*. Barcelona: Barcino.

———. 1954. *Del llum de gas al llum elèctric: memòries d'infància i joventut*. Barcelona: Aedos.

Soldevila Zubiburu, Ferran. 1936. *Les dones en la nostra història*. Barcelona: Conferència Club.

Soler, Maria, and Espinos, Josefa. 1824. *Enseñanza de niñas a cargo de María Soler y Josefa Espinos con assistencia de las maestras necesarias en Barcelona*. Barcelona: Miguel y Tomas Gaspar.

———. 1827. *Enseñanza de niñas con real aprobación a cargo de Doña María Soler y Doña Josefa Espinos con asistencia de las maestras necesarias*. Barcelona.

Soler Humbert, J. [Serafí Pitarra]. 1855. *Liceístas y Cruzados*. Barcelona.

Solé-Tura, José. 1974. *Catalanismo y revolución burguesa*. Madrid: EDICUSA.

Stack, Carol. 1974. *All Our Kin: Strategies for Survival in a Black Community*. New York: Harper and Row.

Stone, Lawrence. 1965 *The Crisis of Aristocracy, 1558-1641*. Oxford: Clarendon.

———. 1977. *The Family, Sex, and Marriage in England, 1500-1800*. London: Weidenfeld and Nicolson.

———. 1981. *The Past and the Present*. London: Routledge & Kegan Paul.

Story, Ronald. 1980. *The Forging of an Aristocracy: Harvard and the Boston Upper Classes*. Middletown, Conn.: Wesleyan University Press.

Strubell Trueta, Miguel. 1981. *Llengua i població a Barcelona*. Barcelona: La Magrana.

Suleiman, Ezra. 1971. *Elites in French Society: The Politics of Survival*. Princeton, N.J.: Princeton University Press.

Suriñach Sentiés, Ramon. 1921. *El tresor dels pobres i altres contes de consol, estímul i dignitat per als nois de condició humil*. Barcelona: Ciutat de Barcelona.

Sweezy, Paul. 1953. *The Present as History: Essays and Reviews on Capitalism and Socialism*. New York: Monthly Review Press.

Tamames, Ramon. 1977. *La oligarquía financiera en España*. Barcelona: Planeta.

Tatjer, Mercedes. 1973. *La barceloneta del segle XVIII al plan de la Ribera*. Barcelona: Saturno.

Tavera, José María. 1976. *Gaspar de Remisa*. Barcelona: Fundación Ruiz Mateos.

Terradas Saborit, Ignasi. 1978. "The Industrial Colonies: A Test Case for the Relationship between Politics and Economics in Industrial Capitalism." *Critique of Anthropology* 3, no. 12: 39-57.

———. 1979. *Les colònies industrials: un estudi entorn del cas de l'Ametlla de Merola*. Barcelona: Laia.

———. 1980. "Els origens de la institució d'hereu a Catalunya. Vers una interpretació contextual." *Quaderns de l'Institut Català d'Antropologia* 1:65-99.

Thomas, Hugh. 1961. *The Spanish Civil War*. New York: Harper & Row.

Torelló Borrás, R. 1888. *Necrologia de Don Claudio Arañó y Arañó*. Barcelona: Sucesores de Narciso Ramírez.

Torras Bages, Josep. 1967. *La tradició catalana*. Barcelona: Biblioteca Selecta. First published 1892.

Tortella Casares, Gabriel. 1968. "El principio de responsabilidad limitada y el desarrollo industrial de España, 1829-1868." *Moneda y Crédito* 104:69-84.

———. 1975. *Los orígenes del capitalismo en España: banca, industria, y ferrocarriles en el siglo XIX*. Madrid: Tecnos.

Treillard, Jacques. 1953. "The Close Corporation in French and Continental Law." *Law and Contemporary Problems* 18, no. 4: 546-557.

Trias de Bes, José M. 1960. "Los jurisconsultos catalanes del siglo XIX y la recopilación del derecho civil de Cataluña." *Revista Jurídica Catalana* 59:402-418.

Tuñon de Lara, Manuel. 1967. *Historia y realidad del poder: el poder y las élites en el primer tercio de la España del siglo XX*. Madrid: EDICUSA.

———. 1969. *Introducción a la historia del movimiento obrero*. Barcelona: Nova Terra.

———. 1972. *Estudios sobre el siglo XIX español*. Madrid: Siglo XXI de España.

Ullman, Joan C. 1968. *The Tragic Week: A Study of Anticlericalism in Spain, 1875-1912* Cambridge, Mass.: Harvard University Press.

Universidad de Barcelona. Facultad de Derecho. 1973. *Estudios sobre la legítima catalana*. Barcelona: Durán i Bas.

Uría, Rodrigo, and Menéndez, Aurelio. 1977. *Código de las sociedades mercantiles*. Madrid: Civitas.

Valero de Turnos, J. 1888. *Barcelona tal cual es, por un madrileño (de ninguna academia)*. Barcelona: Sucesores de Narciso Ramírez.

Van Zanten, David. 1977. Architectural Composition at the Ecole des Beaux-Arts from Charles Percier to Charles Garnier. In A. Drexler, editor, *The Architecture of the Ecole des Beaux-Arts*, pp. 111-324. New York: Museum of Modern Art.

Vedruna, Joaquina de. 1969. *Epistolario*. Navarra.

Vicens Vives, Jaume. 1957-1959. *Historia social y económica de España y America*. Barcelona: Teide.

Vicens Vives, Jaume. 1958. *Industrials i polítics del segle XIX*. Barcelona: Vicens Vives.

———, and Nadal Oller, Jordi. 1959. *Manuel de historia económica de España*. Barcelona: Teide.

Vicente Caravantes, José de. 1850. *Código de Comercio estractado con la esposición al pie de cada artículo de los fundamentos de sus disposiciones y con la solución de las principales dificultades que presentan el testo*. Madrid: D. S. Omañá.

Vilar, Pierre. 1962. *La catalogne dans l'Espagne moderne*. 3 vols. S.E.V.P.E.N.

———. 1973. *Assaigs sobre la Catalunya del segle XVIII*. Barcelona: Curial.

Virella Boada, Albert. 1977. *Les clases socials a Vilanova i la Geltrú en el segle XIX*. Barcelona: Dalmau.

Vives de Fabregas, Elias. 1945. *Vida feminina barcelonesa de 1840 a 1920*. Barcelona: Dalmau.

Voltes Bou, Pedro. 1963. *La banca barcelonesa de 1840 a 1920*. Barcelona: Institut Municipal de Història.

———. 1965. *Las Cajas de Ahorro barcelonesas: su pasado, su presente, su porvenir*. Barcelona: Fondo Cultural de la Caja de Ahorro Provincial de Barcelona.

Wais, Francisco. 1974. *Historia de los ferrocarriles españoles*. Madrid: Nacional.

Wallerstein, Immanuel. 1974. *The Modern World System: Capitalist Agriculture and the European World Economy*. New York: Academic Press.

———. 1979. *The Capitalist World Economy*. Cambridge: At the University Press.

Weber, Max. 1946. *From Max Weber: Essays in Sociology*. Translated and edited by H. Gerth and C. Wright Mills. Oxford: Oxford University Press.

———. 1978. *Economy and Society: An Outline of Interpretive Sociology*. Berkeley: University of California Press.

Weinreich, Uriel. 1968. *Languages in Contact: Findings and Problems*. The Hague: Mouton.

Wells, H. G. 1906. *Complete Works*, vol. 26, *The Future in America*. New York: Charles Scribner's Sons.

Wikan, Unni. 1980. *Life among the Poor of Cairo*. London: Tavistock.

Wolf, Eric. 1969. "American Anthropologists and American Society." In D. Hymes, editor, *Reinventing Anthropology*, pp. 251-263. New York: Random House.

———. 1982. *Europe and the People without History*. Berkeley: University of California Press.

Woolard, Kathryn A. In press. *The Politics of Language and Ethnicity in Barcelona.* Stanford, Ca.: Stanford University Press.

Wright, E. O. 1978. *Class, Crisis, and the State.* London: NLB.

Ynfante, Jesus. 1970. *La prodigiosa aventura del Opus Dei. Génesis y desarrollo de la Santa Mafia.* Paris: Ruedo Iberico.

———. 1974. *Los negocios de Porcioles. Las sagradas familias de Barcelona.* Toulouse: Midi-Livre.

INDEX

LIBRARY OF CONGRESS CATALOGING-IN-PUBLICATION DATA

MCDONOGH, GARY W.
GOOD FAMILIES OF BARCELONA.

BIBLIOGRAPHY: P.   INCLUDES INDEX.
1. ELITE (SOCIAL SCIENCES)—SPAIN—BARCELONA—
HISTORY.   2. BARCELONA (SPAIN)—SOCIAL CONDITIONS.
3. KINSHIP—SPAIN—BARCELONA—HISTORY.   4. POWER
(SOCIAL SCIENCES)—HISTORY.   I. TITLE.
HN590.Z9E45 1986   305.5'22'094672   86-5067
ISBN 0-691-09426-8